AF411974

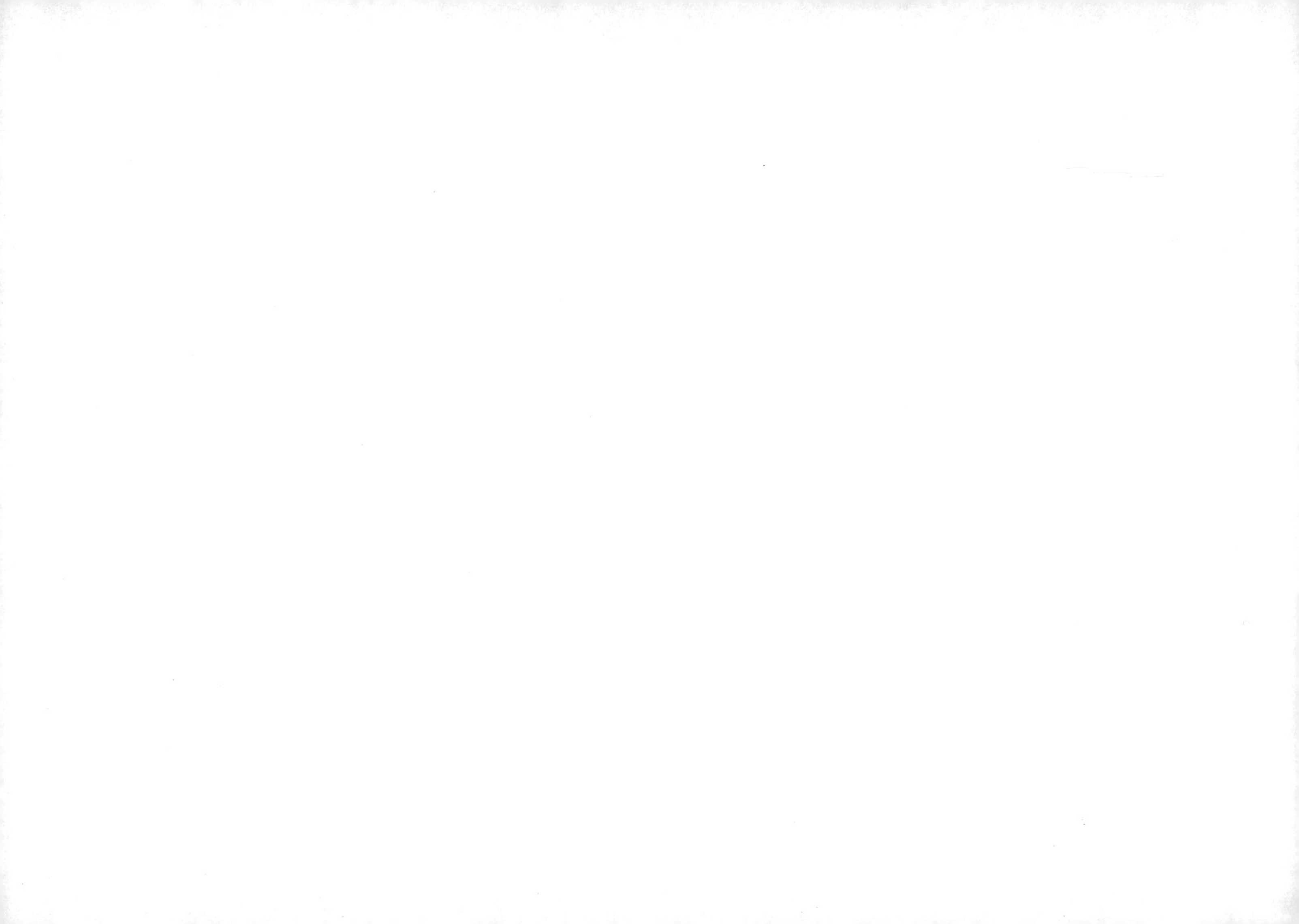

The BrewDogs of Colorado

All the best from our
BrewDogs family.
Brian Bennett
Becky Bennett

Dogs — Beer — Colorado
It doesn't get much better!

To Our BrewDogs

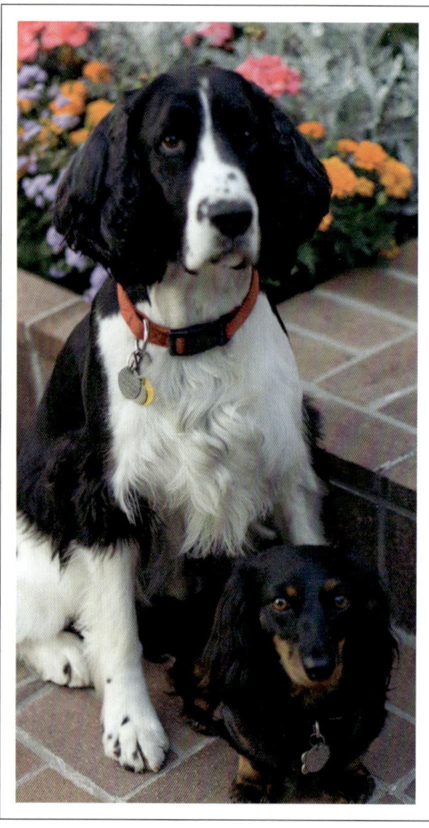

Baxter, 6, English Springer Spaniel

Ozkar (Ozzie), 2, Longhaired Dachshund

The BrewDogs of Colorado

by

Brian Bennett

Becky Bennett

Lauren Olson

Kristen Olson

Woof !))) Media LLC

Thanks and Acknowledgements

We are especially grateful to all of the wonderful people we met as we sometime interrupted busy work schedules for a photo session, in most cases requiring after hours times with their dogs.

A special thanks goes to our friend of many years, Mike Bristol, of the Bristol Brewing Company in Colorado Springs. His encouragement, support (especially through introductions) and enthusiasm for the project have been an immense help. We would also like to thank our friend Laura Long, for her advice and encouragement.

To Larry Hulst, who shared his professional digital photographic knowledge, guiding us through some early rough spots in our creative efforts. Thanks to Jason Yester, Trinity Brewing Company, an enthusiastic supporter; Mark Pannell, Esq., an early consultant and confidante; Elaine Cowles, proofreader, file organizer and reviewer; The Honorable John Hickenlooper, Denver Mayor and Colorado brewpub pioneer; and Wynkoop Brewing Company's Jamie Webb, who was willing to share her knowledge of the brewing community in Northern Colorado.

To Brendan Scott, who went on the road with Kristen and assisted with many of her photo sessions and to Ariel Jantzen, who was a great help to Lauren. Thanks go to Bob Hill, father-in-law, dad and grandfather, for his help with proofreading text.

Finally, to our production team from the Bellandi Group: Gina Tinker-Lewis, our graphic designer, and Laura Ettinger, production coordinator and copy editor, for their calm demeanors in coaching us to a non-violent project completion.

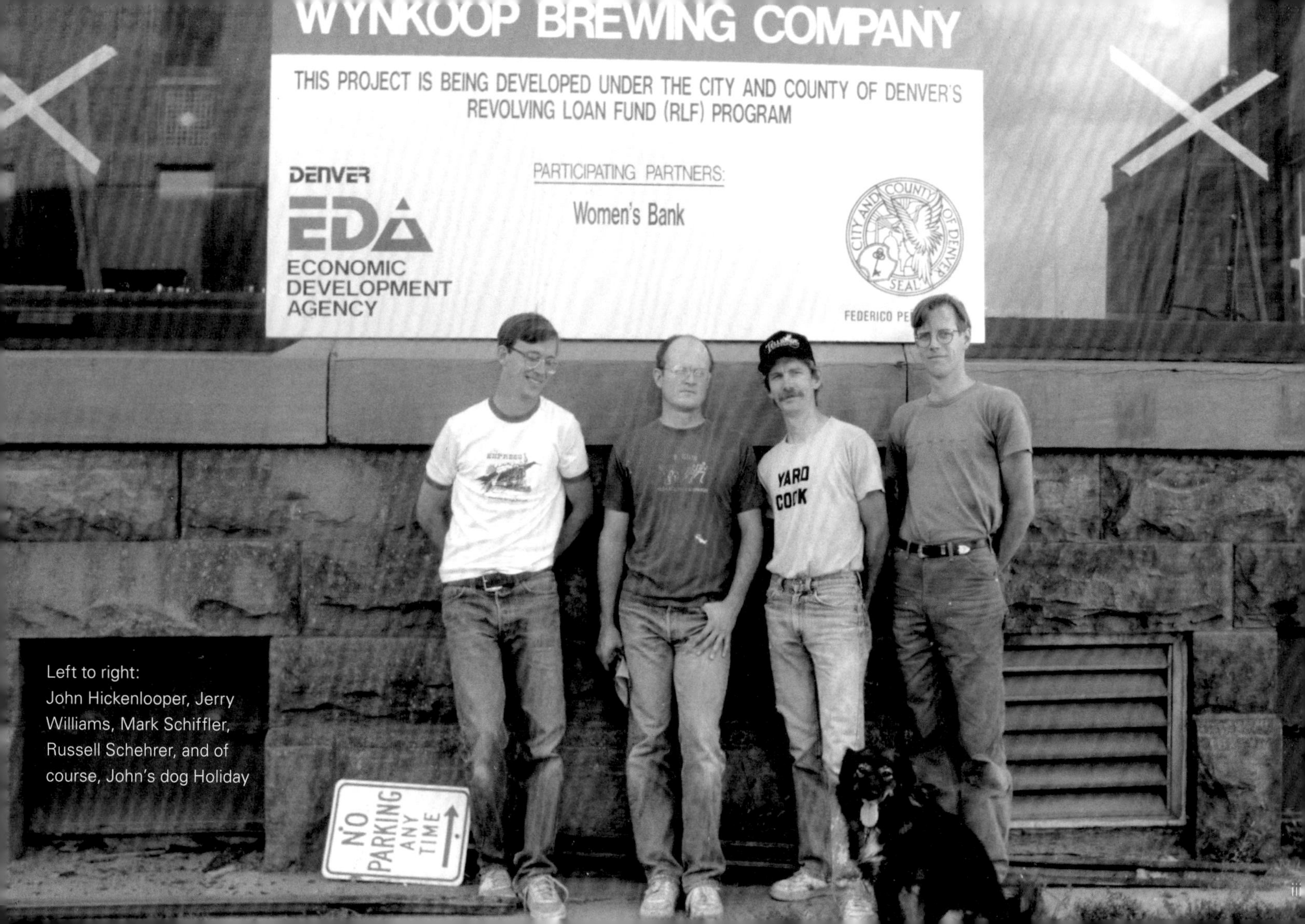

Left to right:
John Hickenlooper, Jerry Williams, Mark Schiffler, Russell Schehrer, and of course, John's dog Holiday

Foreword

As a long-time dog owner and, before becoming Denver's Mayor, a brewery owner, I am well aware of the special bond that exists between a dog and his owner. Everyone in the brewing business knows that the long, sometimes lonely work hours can be shortened by the company of a dog or the expectation of that enthusiastic "welcome home."

I am happy to introduce *The BrewDogs of Colorado*, a photographic tribute to the exceptional place dogs have in the Colorado craft brewing industry – that is, as an established part of the social landscape in communities throughout Colorado. The publishers, a Colorado family, hope that after reading their book you will know more about brewing, great beer, dogs and our beautiful State. Most of all, they hope you smile, laugh and feel good.

Obviously, I am pleased that my friends and former colleagues from the Wynkoop Brewing Company and their dogs are well represented in the book. When my partners and I started Colorado's first brewpub in 1988, we sure never expected to see the 100 breweries and pubs that we have now – not to mention all the dogs!

The authors tell me that more than half of the dogs pictured in *The BrewDogs of Colorado* are rescue dogs, and that several breweries support animal rescue organizations in their communities. That doesn't surprise me because, from my experience, I know that Colorado's brewers always seem to "step up" to do good in their respective communities.

As you settle in with a glass of your favorite brew, I hope you enjoy *The BrewDogs of Colorado*.

Cheers,

John Hickenlooper
Denver Mayor

Contents

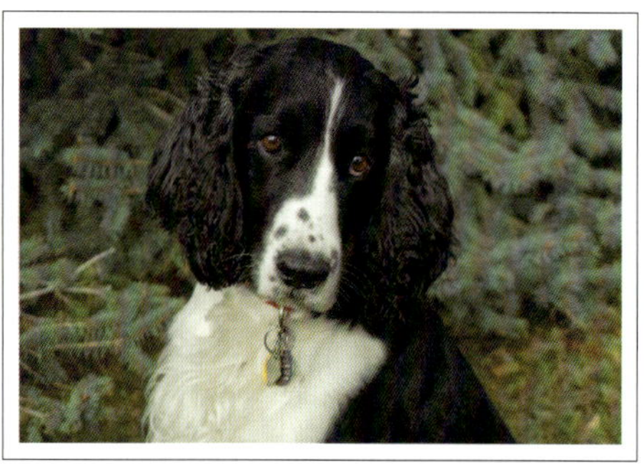

The Brew Fest

On any given weekend it is likely that a brew festival can be found somewhere in Colorado. These events sometimes celebrate the brew and others benefit worthy charitable causes. The public can sample a wide variety of great beers that are also judged by a panel with awards presented.

For most, a beer festival is a great excuse to enjoy a party with great beers.

For the industry, the competition is serious. Medals mean getting noticed, and a reputation for great beer translates to sales.

Held annually in Denver, the Great American Beer Festival, abbreviated as GABF in this book, is the American brewing industry equivalent to the Academy Awards. Started in 1987, medals are given in 78 categories and overall awards for brewing excellence are given as well. In 2009, Dry Dock Brewing Company in Aurora won the Best Small Brewing Company, and the Small Company Best Brewer Award. Lachlan McLean, of the Dry Dock team, and his brewdogs, Barley Bear and Maggie Moo are pictured herein.

In 2009, nearly 500 breweries competed, entering over 3,300 beers to be judged by 132 panelists from 10 countries. Colorado was the top medal winning state in 2009 with 45 medals.

While the GABF is the largest commercial beer competition in the world, the many local community-based festivals in Colorado are more accessible to Coloradans who enjoy sampling great craft brews.

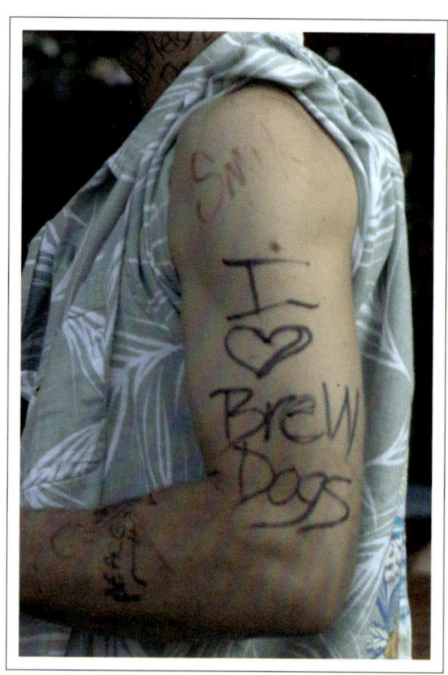

Preface

What the heck is a "brewdog" anyway? Actually, that's a question we asked ourselves. Much akin to the maritime slang for sailors' "sea dogs," we discovered that over the centuries, brewers and brewery workers were sometimes called "brew dogs." In fact, we found the term to be in use in a few places in Colorado, in the same ancient context.

Our team has chosen a more liberal definition: Brewdogs are dogs (canines) that belong to brewers and to anyone associated with a brewery. In many cases, they are truly brewdogs, and you will meet some of them, such as Bear in Estes Park, who escapes from home to go to the brewery. Or Syndy Lu, who went to the brewery every day until her owner Matt passed away in October 2008.

Other Colorado brewdogs that we learned of along the way have passed on, like Avery's Ellie (1992-2002) who is memorialized in Ellie's Brown Ale, or New Belgium's Mighty Arrow, who also has "Mighty Arrow Pale Ale," as her namesake.

To us, the term "brewdog," while fanciful, has some meaning that goes beyond just slang. It also pays respect to the animals and their owners, and their special relationships. The term is also a compliment to the dedication and hard work it takes to produce products that can lay claim to be among the finest beverages in the world. The medals are there to prove it.

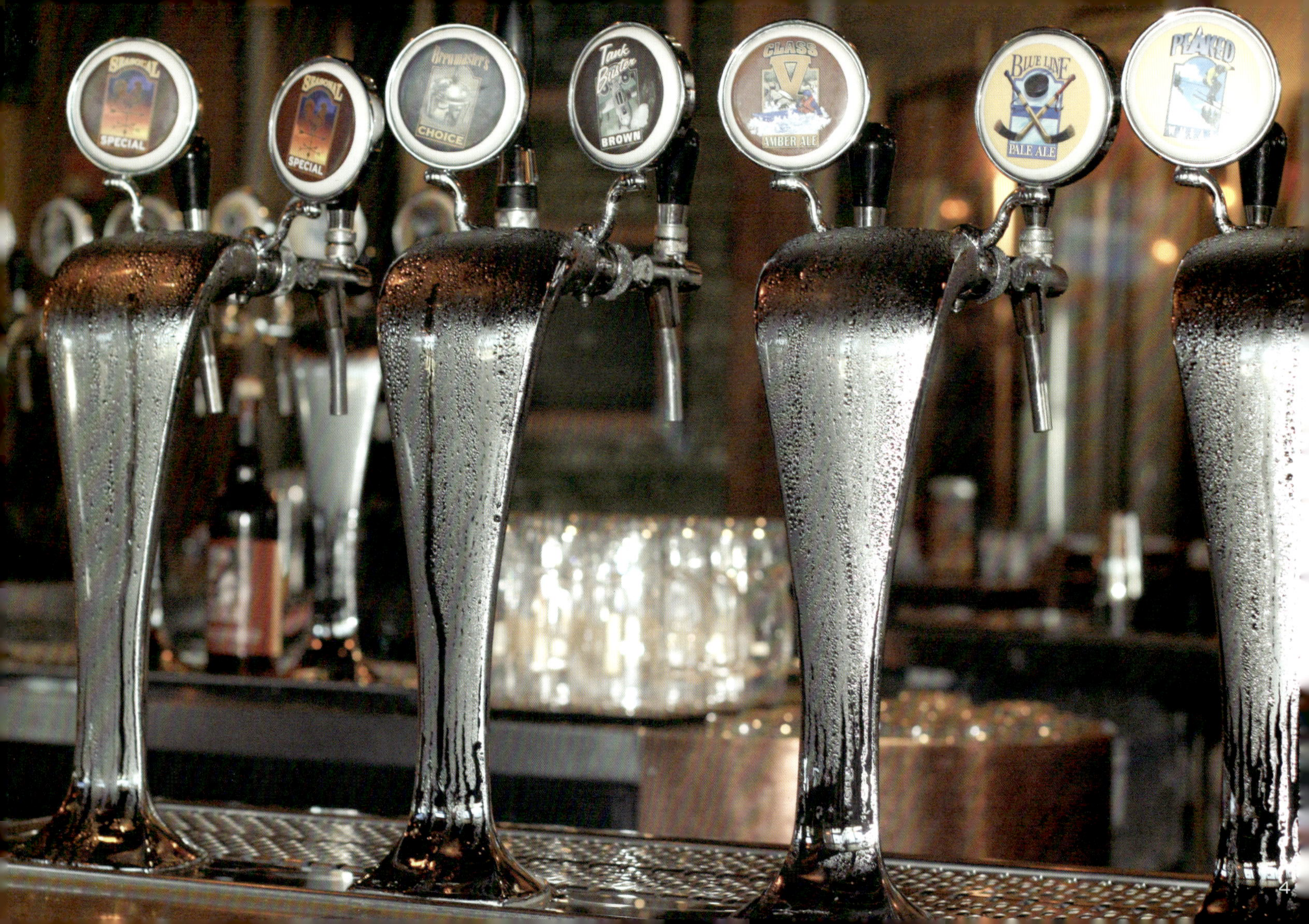

SEASONAL SPECIAL
SEASONAL SPECIAL
BREWMASTER'S CHOICE
Tank Buster BROWN
CLASS V AMBER ALE
BLUE LINE PALE ALE
PEAKED

Introduction

The BrewDogs of Colorado was conceived in the summer of 2009 as a family project. Our entire blended family loves dogs, and all of us have developed an appreciation for the quality, creativity, flavors and fun that the Colorado craft brewing industry represents.

Sisters Lauren and Kristen Olson, along with mom and step-dad Becky and Brian Bennett, all participated in the project. At one time or another, we all were photographers, interviewers, copywriters, helpers and, when the time was right, beer tasters.

Colorado's breweries are scattered all across the state, reminding us of its size and scope. We discovered and rediscovered some hidden treasures in the landscape along the way. Colorado has 54 peaks higher than 14,000 feet in elevation, (The locals know them as fourteeners, and you will encounter the term in this book) and we traveled in the shadow of many of them this summer.

Seventy dogs from 37 of Colorado's craft breweries are pictured, from the smallest (Three Barrel, Del Norte) to the largest (New Belgium, Fort Collins), from the first (Boulder Beer, Boulder) to the newest (Draft House, Boulder). You will also see one of the largest AKC breeds (Irish Wolfhound) and one of the smallest (Chihuahua.)

Over half of the subjects in this book are rescue dogs and they, and their owners, are clearly grateful for the efforts of the animal welfare and rescue organizations in their communities. We urge you to support the animal shelter and rescue organizations in your community.

We also found that of all the brewers we met, only a handful were brewers by education. Indeed, college degrees in the arts were more frequent, which might lead one to appreciate why "craft" brewing is what it is: "Art" and science.

We hope you enjoy meeting some of Colorado's brewdogs and their owners.

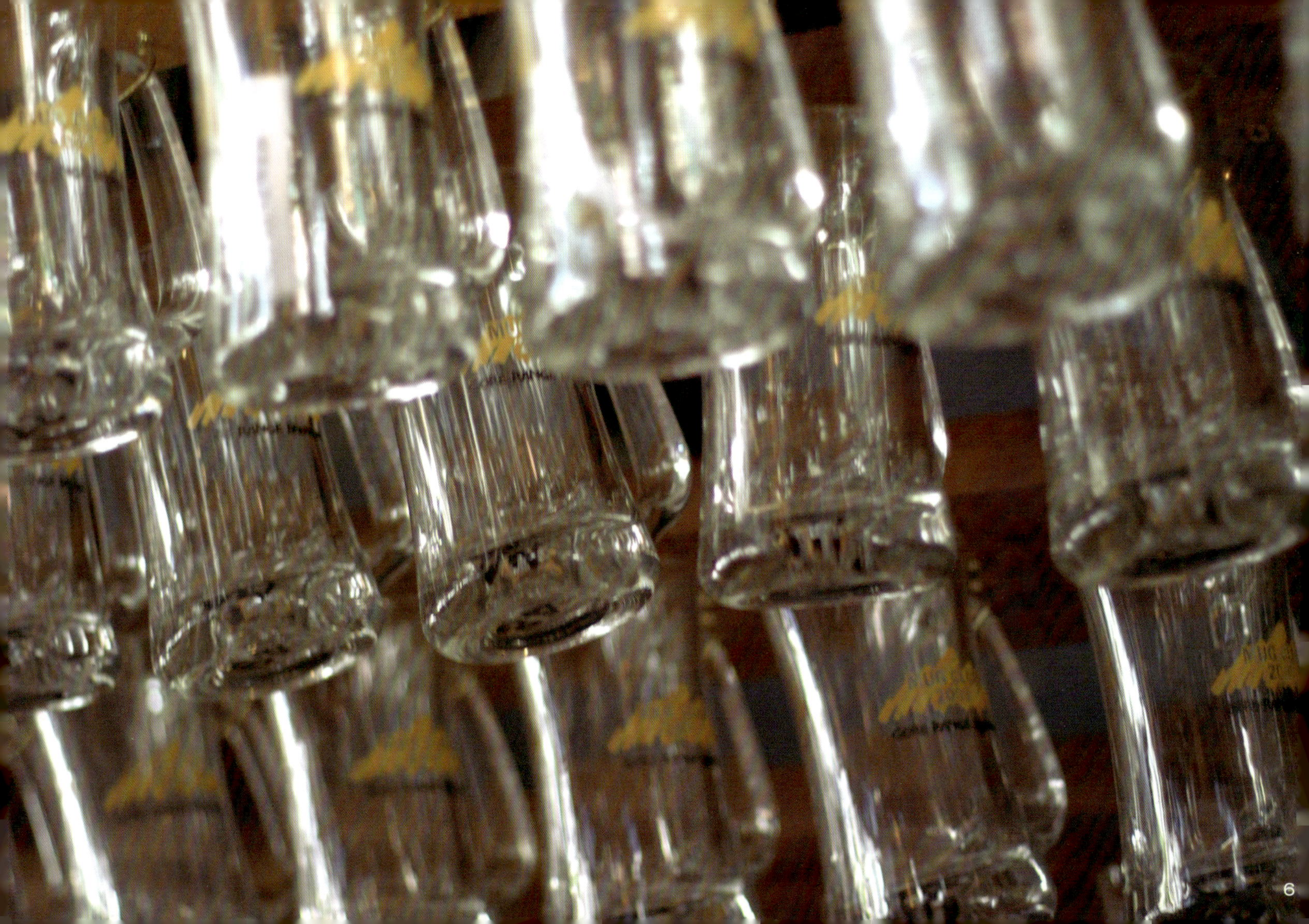

No dogs were harmed or intoxicated
in the production of this book.

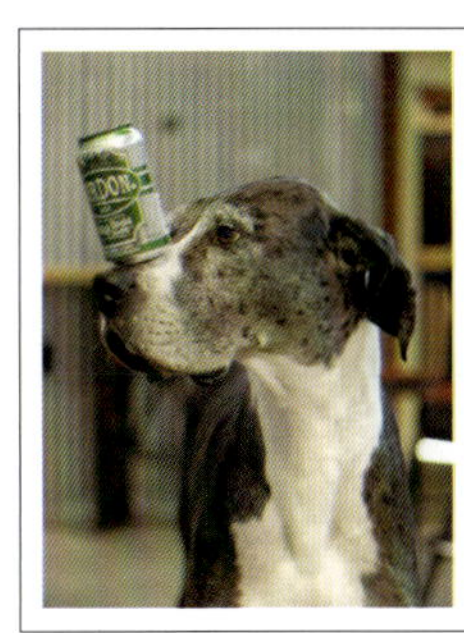

Camden

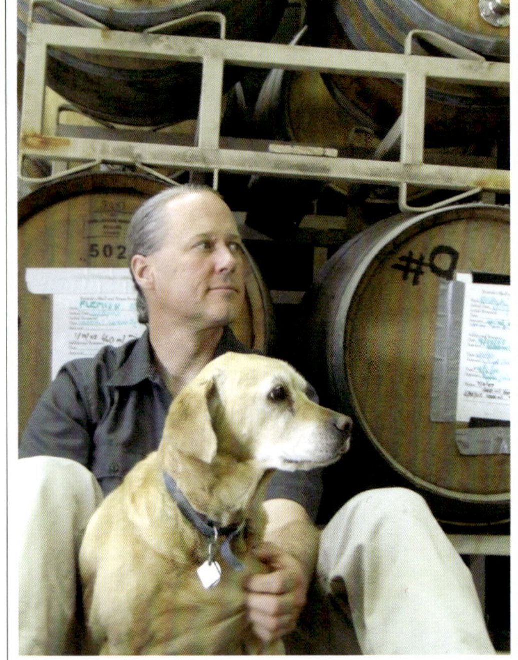

Favorite Toy: Any available bone

Funny Habit: Likes to hide bread or bagels in the fireplace ashes

Naughtiest Deed: Once ate an entire pound of bacon off of the counter

Favorite Beer: Laughing Lab

Founded in 1994

Laughing Lab has won over 10 medals in worldwide beer competitions

In August 2009, Bristol partnered with Colorado State University to offer beer-related Continuing Ed classes

Which came first: Camden or Laughing Lab? Owner Mike Bristol isn't telling Camden. At fifteen years old (that's 105 in dog years) Camden has been gored by a deer, and has twice survived being struck by a car. She still chases deer and barks at bears. Camden was a member of the Bristol family before their three sons were born, and she has trained the Bristol boys to share their dinner with her. At the brewery, the pretzel bowls are Camden-inspired. They are stainless steel dog dishes adorned with Laughing Lab stickers. These days, though, Camden herself doesn't hang out there much anymore. 🐾

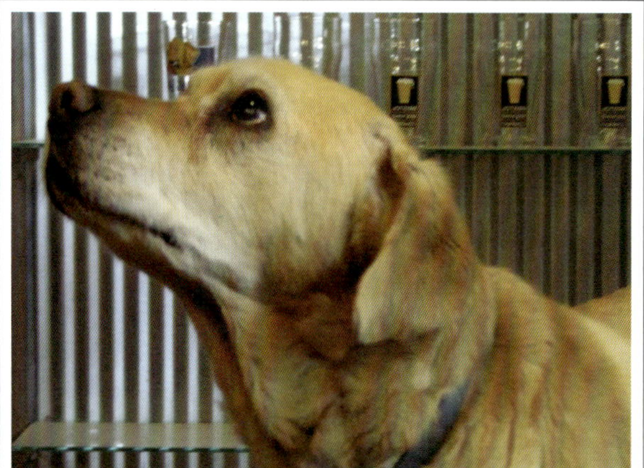

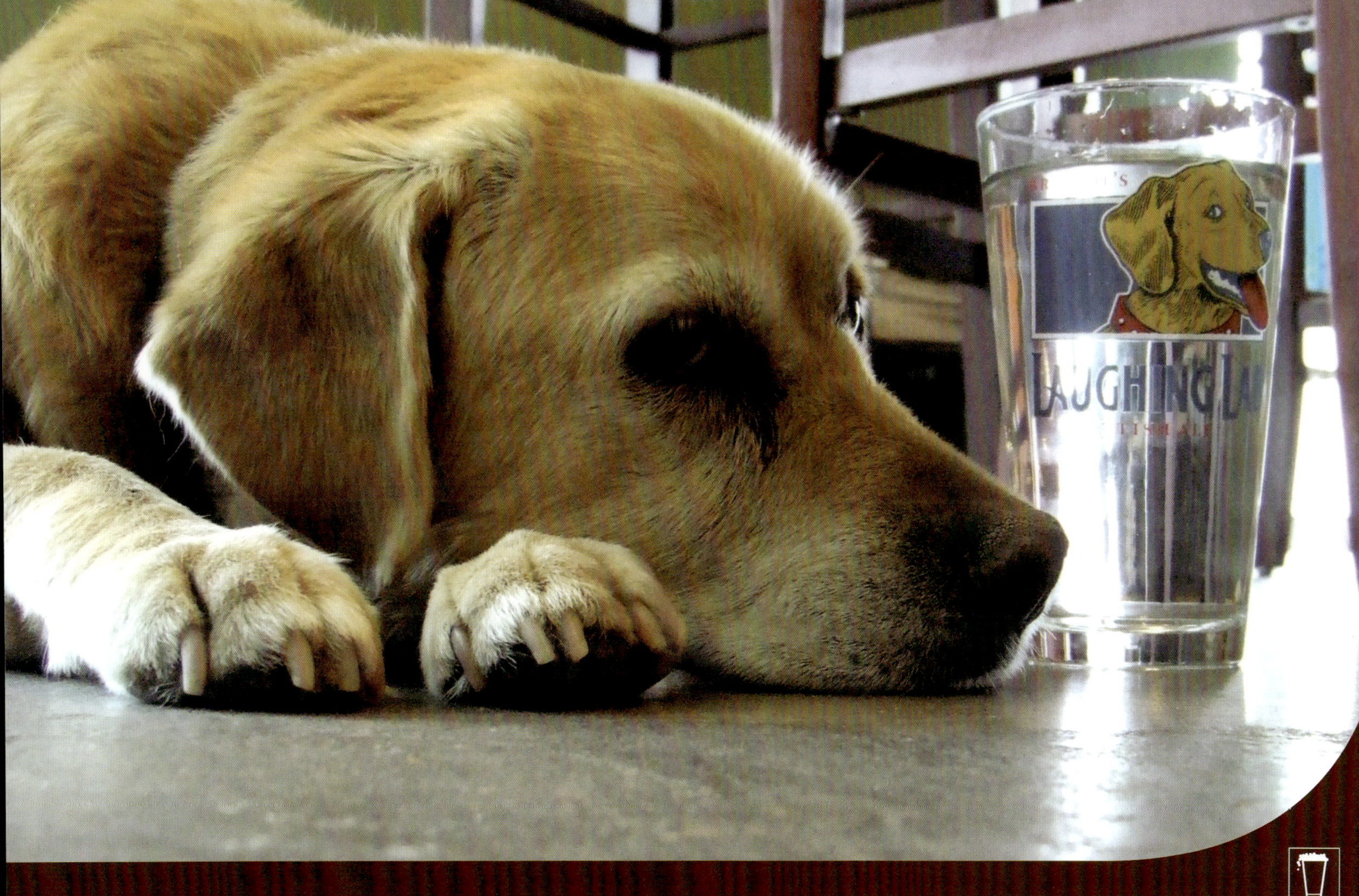

Camden, 15, Yellow Labrador Mix   Owner: Mike Bristol

BRISTOL BREWING COMPANY

Bunny and Marley

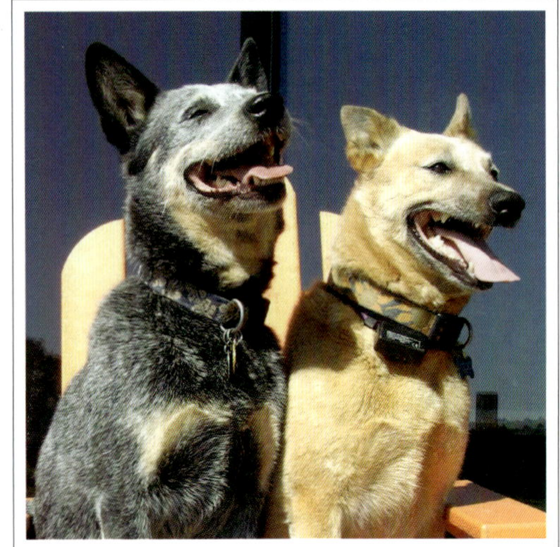

Hangout: Dog park

Accomplice: Each other

Favorite Toy: Cong with peanut butter

Annoying Habit: Jumping

Opened August 2008

Facility built with recycled and reclaimed materials

Gold Medal, Great American Beer Festival, 2009

Able to leap tall buildings in a single bound (well, almost), is what makes these dogs famous, or infamous. Trinity's co-owner/brewmaster Jason Yester says, "With one straight spring into the air, they can be anywhere," whether it's jumping high into his arms to greet him or jumping through screens. Marley has even scaled six-foot fences, going from doggie door to doggie door, eating the neighborhood pet food. 🐾

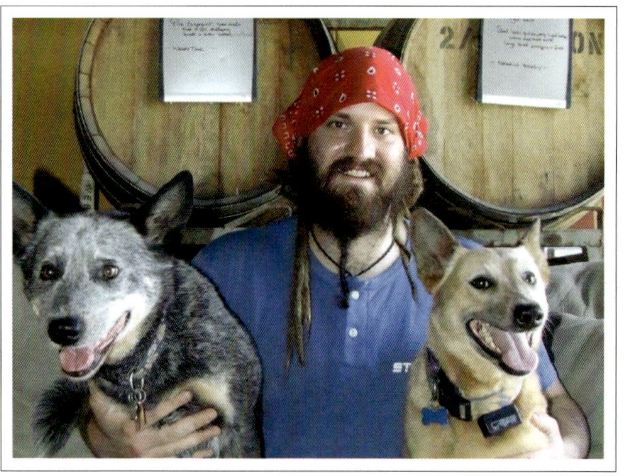

"

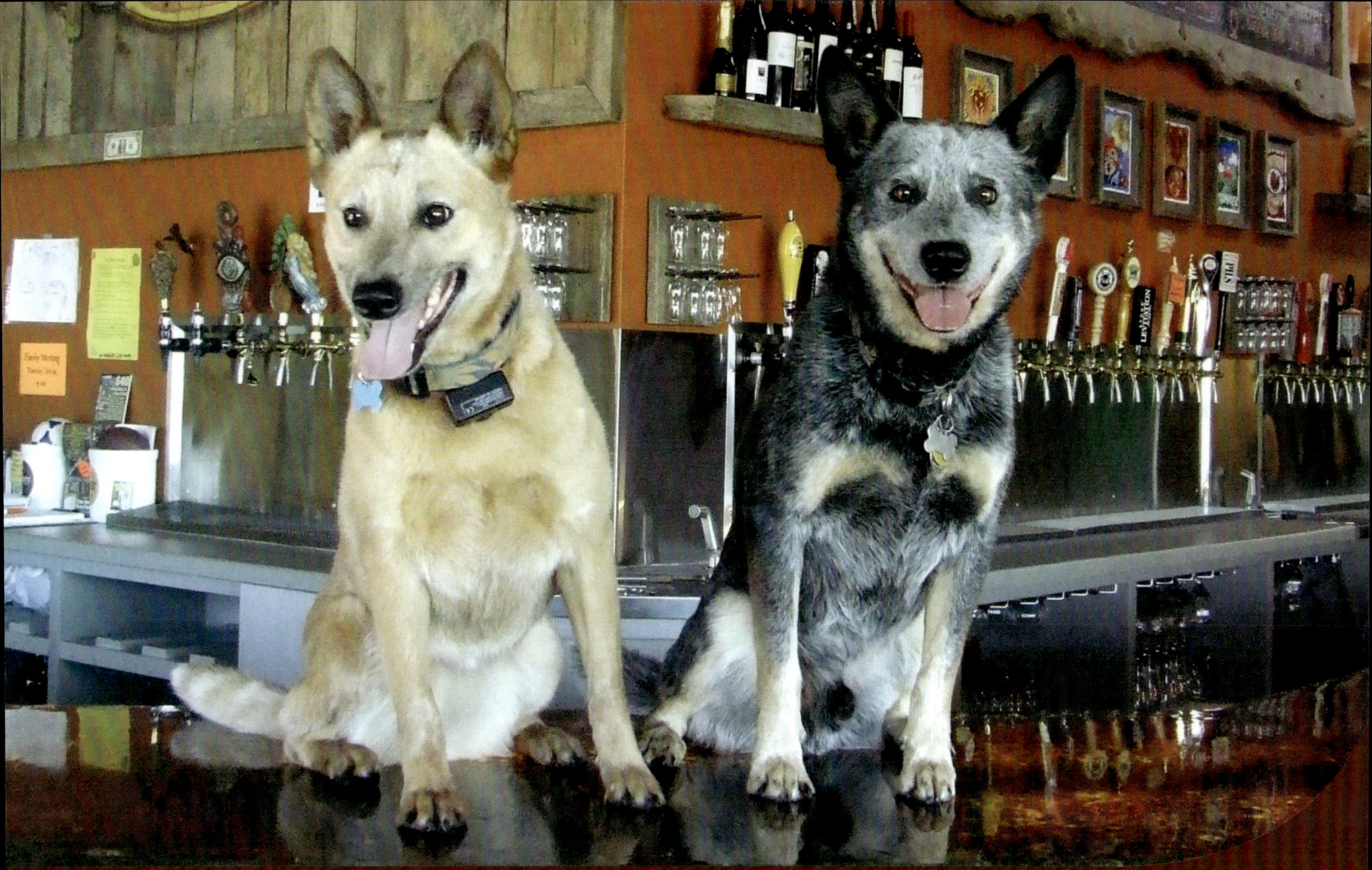

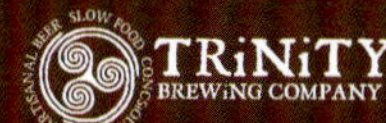

 Bunny, 5 1/2 & Marley, 9, Red Heeler & Blue Heeler   Owner: Jason Yester

Poppy (short for Popeye)

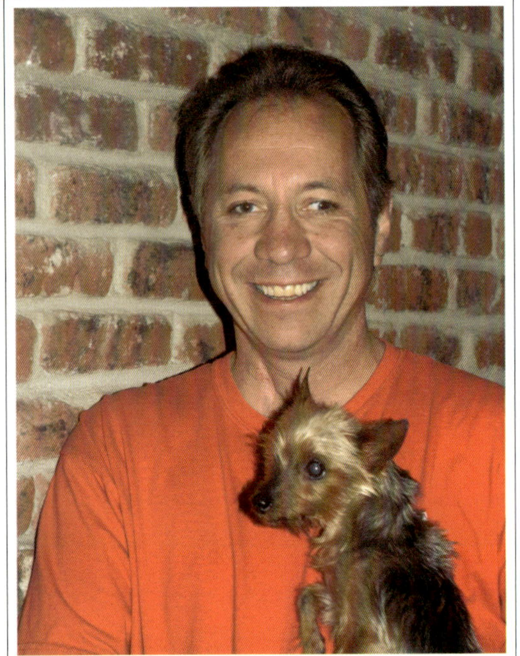

Favorite Pastimes: Chasing squirrels and thinking about chasing them

Most Excellent Adventure: Being rescued in Oklahoma/the airplane ride to Colorado

Favorite Hangout: On the sofa wrapped in an afghan

Favorite Outfit: Glittery green dragon costume

OLD MILL BREWERY AND GRILL
LITTLETON

Brewing since 1994

Designated Historic Landmark

Produces 500 barrels annually

"**S**he's been starved, abused** and has no right eye," the caller said. Brewmaster Greg Shofner recalls, "I knew it was meant to be, since I am sightless in my left eye." When Poppy arrived at Greg's just a short time ago, she was frail and frightened; it took about a week for her to get comfortable. "As Poppy recovers and gains strength, her next years will be her best," says Greg. In addition to being an award-winning brewer, Greg has been a professional magician and fire eater since he was 16 years old. Who knows, Poppy may have a future as Greg's assistant. 🐾

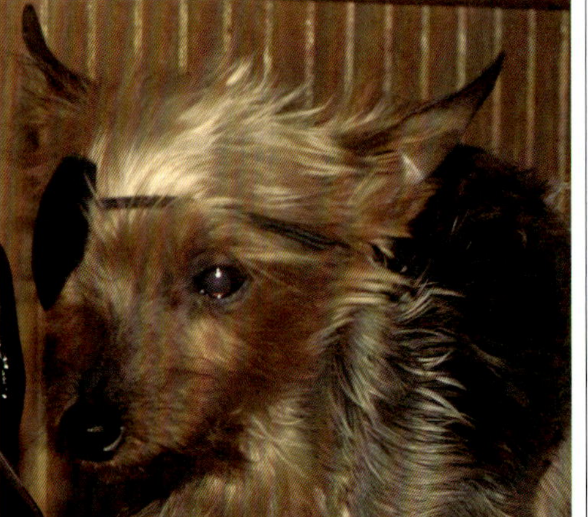

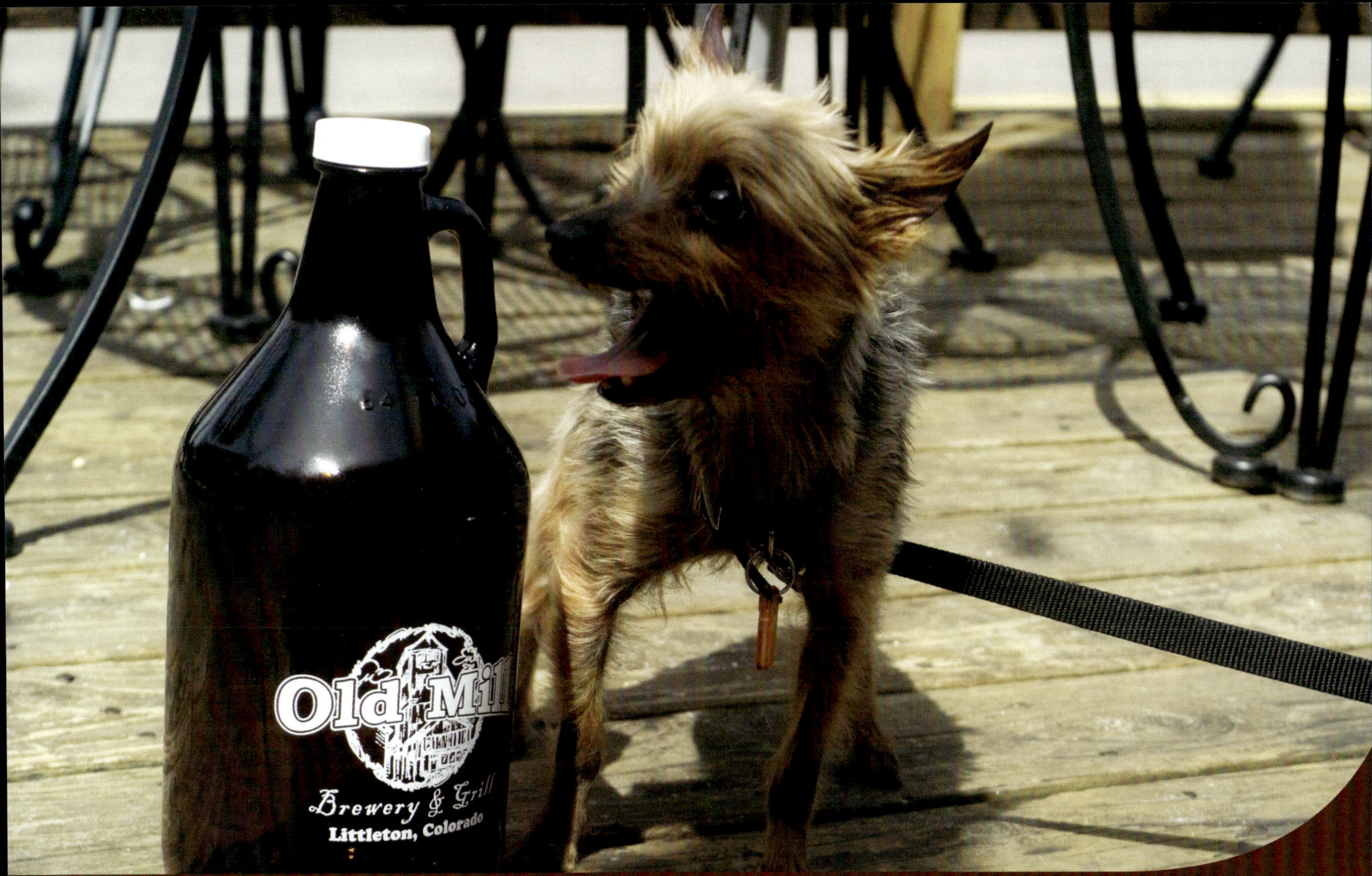

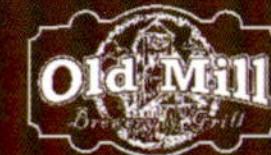

13 Poppy (short for Popeye), 10, Yorkshire Terrier   Owner: Greg Shofner

Jack

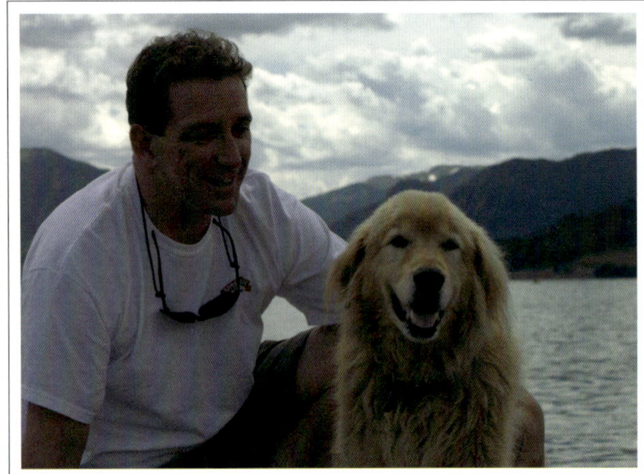

Pet Peeve: The vet and Silverthorne police

Favorite Food: Prime Rib

Best Trick: Catch a treat off of nose

Favorite Toy: Other dogs' toys

Opened in 1997 first as a steakhouse, and then added brewery

Fourth microbrewery in Colorado to start canning its beers

Won 18 medals in last six years

Dog at large! By the time Jack was five years old, he had been arrested 14 times while patrolling the streets by himself. Even with his independent personality, Jack remains very loyal to John, owner of Pug Ryan's Steakhouse and Brewery, and loves to hang out there. While hiking in the Sangre de Cristo mountain range, Jack got separated from the group for six hours. As John and his friends hiked down the mountain, Jack waited dutifully at the Willow Creek trailhead. 🐾

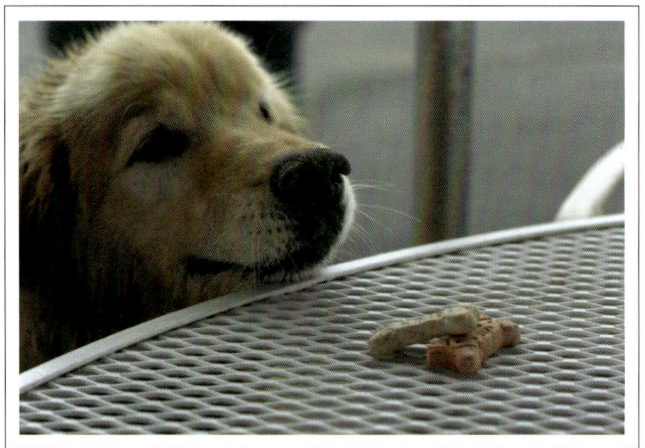

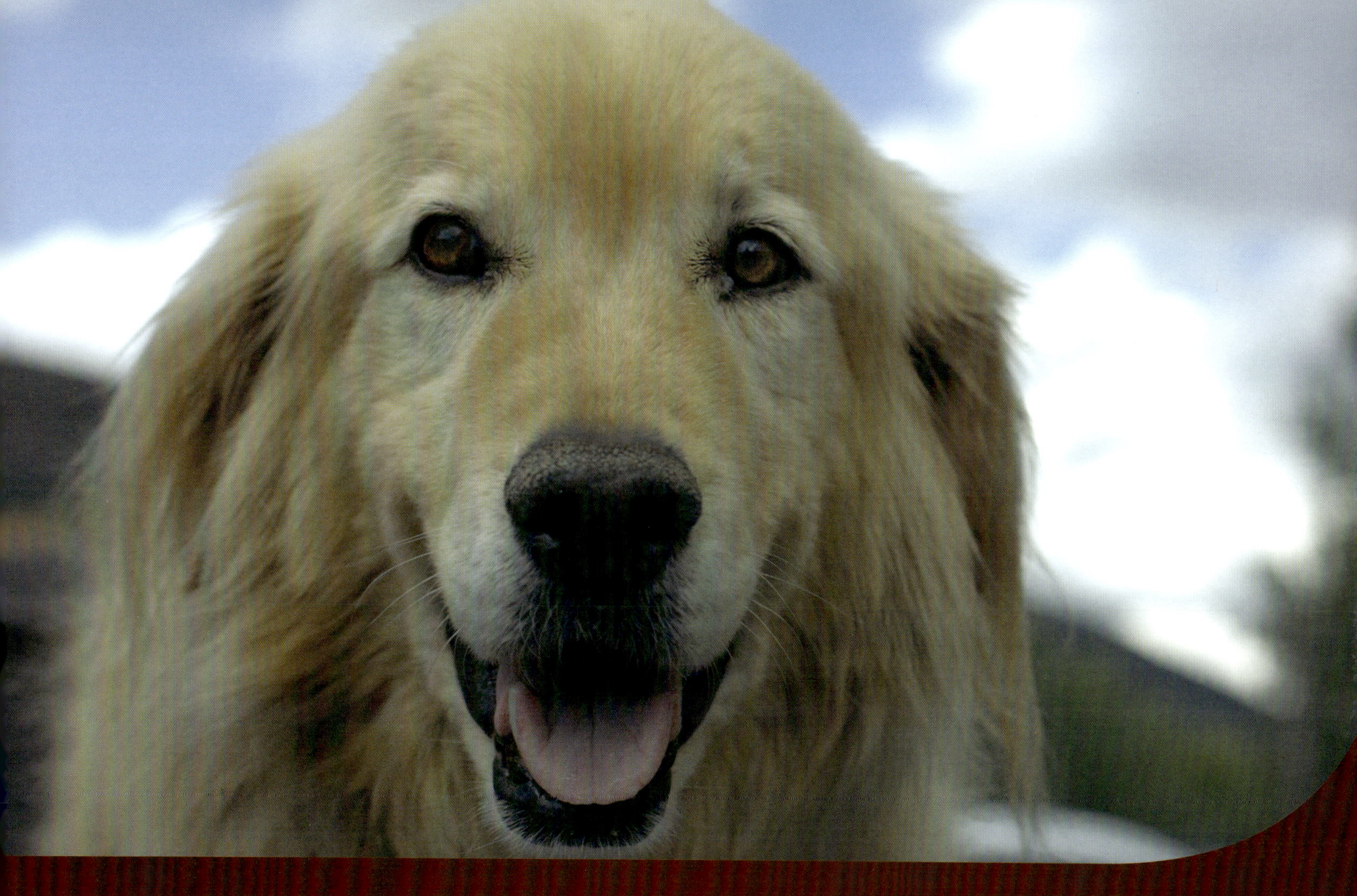

Jack, 11, Golden/Chow/Lab Owner: John Maginity

Pug Ryan's
Steakhouse and Brewery

Dobson and Lola

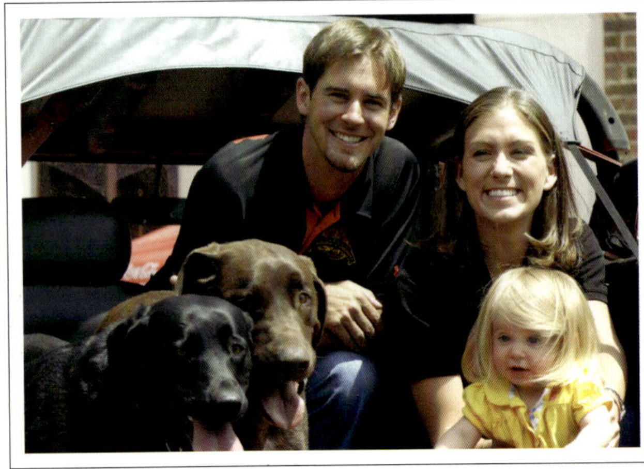

Favorite Hobbies: Hiking/troublemaking/frolicking

Annoying Habits: Dobson: Barks at everything Lola: Close talker

Naughtiest Deed: Lola chases cows and was almost shot by farmer

Personality: Happy-go-lucky, fun-loving

Established in 2006

Began as homebrewers

Garnered awards at state and local beer festivals

Labradors to the core, Dobson and Lola are the ideal brewdogs. If they aren't making trouble or outside enjoying Colorado weather, they are probably thinking about it. Enthusiastic hosts; every greeting is like the first. For brewdogs, they have rather pedestrian tastes: Dobson will eat anything off the counter he can filch; Lola adores ice cream. They love hiking and camping and have surprised owners Scott and Angie Graber by ascending 14,000-foot mountains by themselves. 🐾

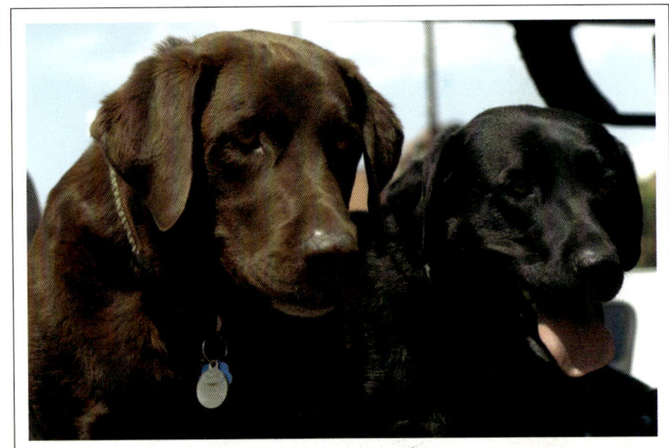

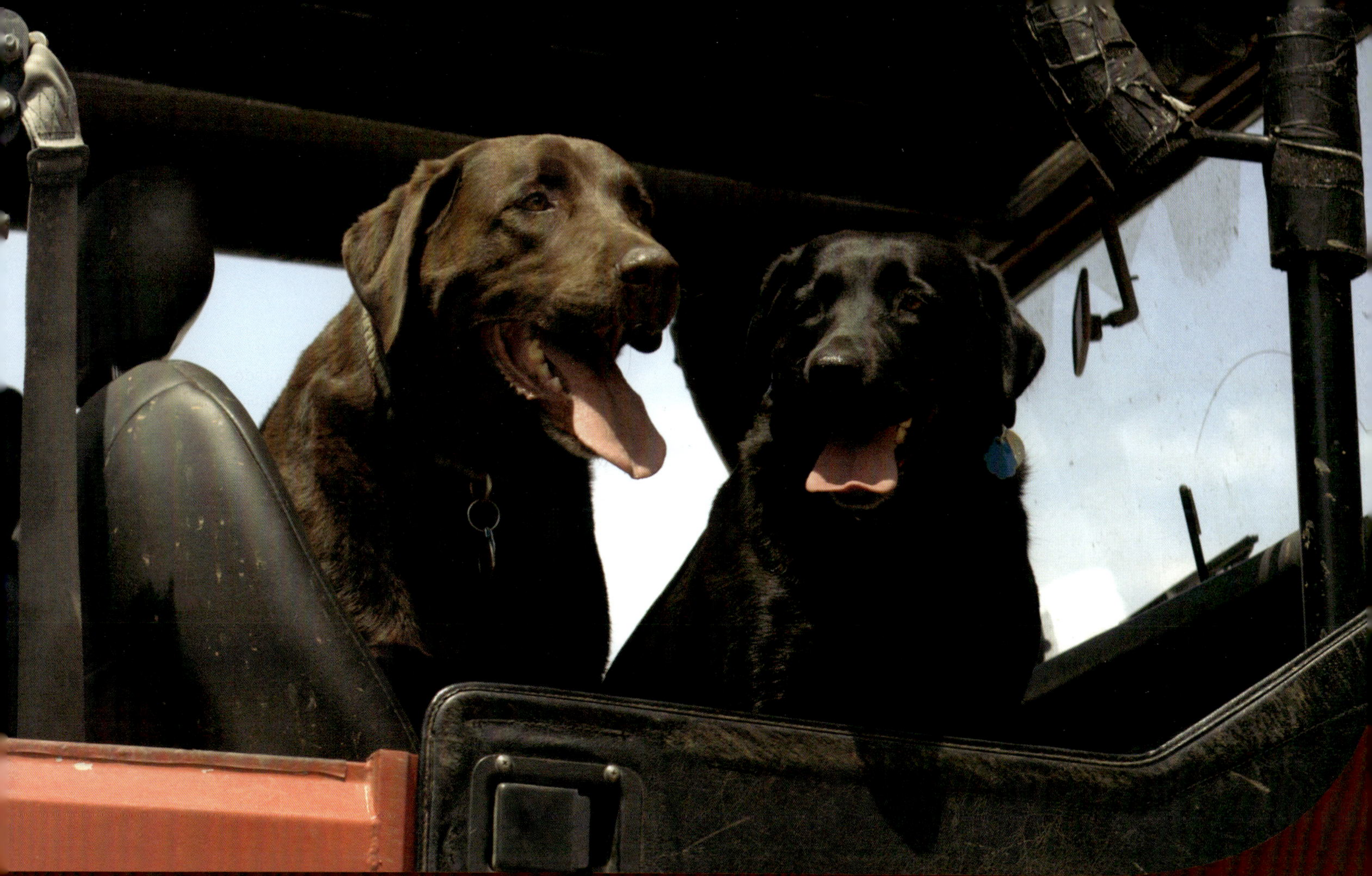

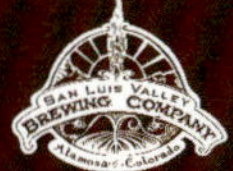

7 Dobson, 6 & Lola, 5, Chocolate Lab & Black Lab   Owners: Scott & Angie Graber

Larry

Opened 1990

Boulder's original brewpub

2008 Silver Medal GABF

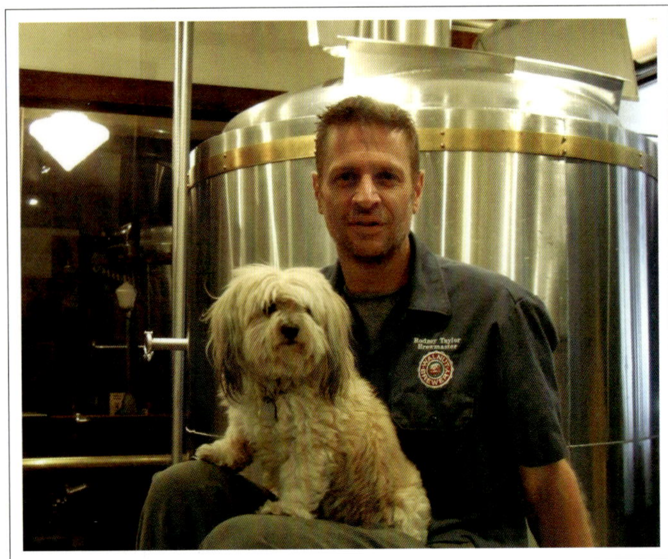

She's a beach dog in the mountains. Larry just loves the sand. She rolls in it, digs in it and runs in it. Brewmaster Rodney says that she escapes through a hole in the fence to visit the kids down the street, who have nicknamed her "Loony." They must have a sandbox. She does get a bit "loony" when she thinks Rodney is heading for the door, thinking it's time for a walk. 🐾

Favorite Treat: "Pup-corn"

Favorite Toy: Stuffed puppy she's had for three years

Pet Peeve: Big dogs, tries to take them on

Funny Habit: Cheese addict

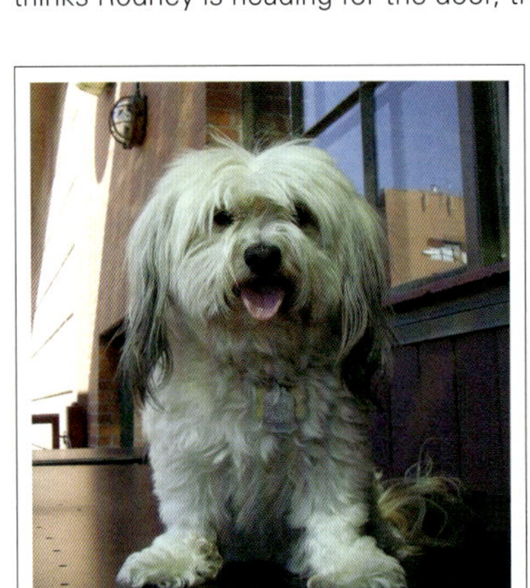

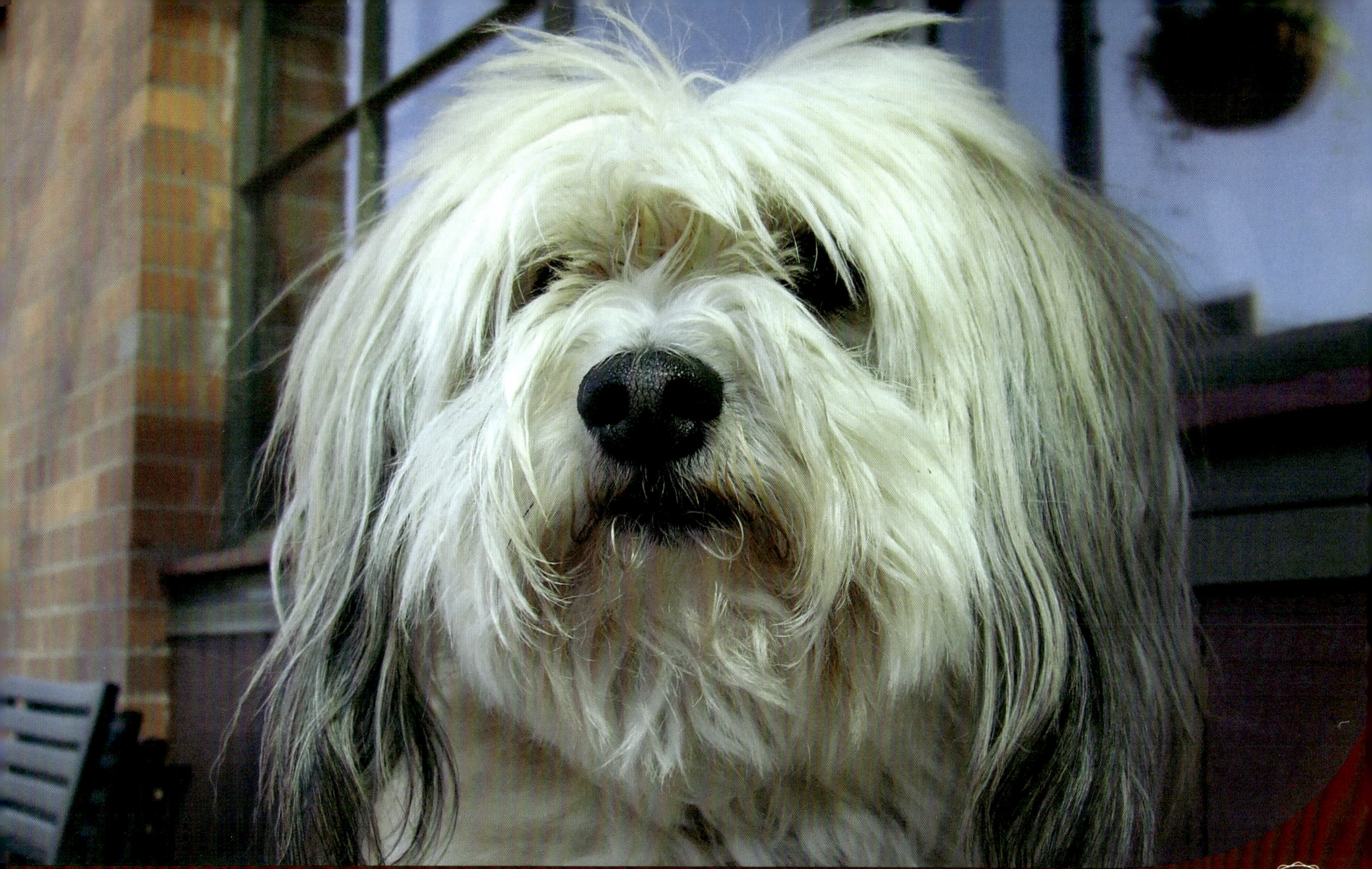

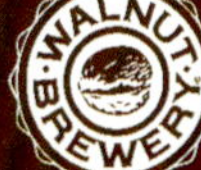

Larry, 8, Shih Tzu Mix   Owner: Rodney Taylor

Syndy Lu

Established 1997

Produces 2,000 barrels per year

Gold Medal 2008, GABF

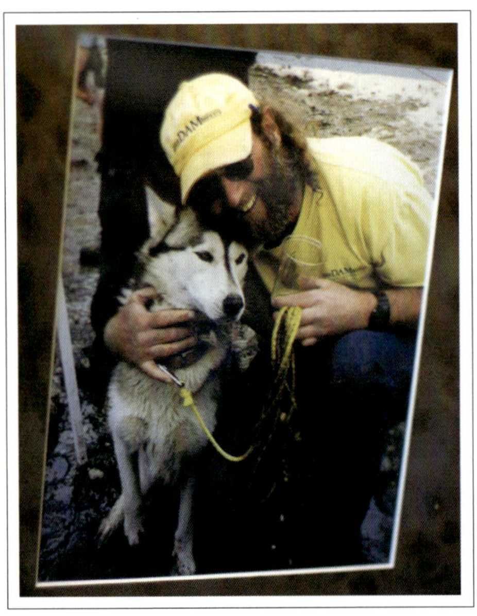

Matt J. Luhr (1962-2008)

Favorite Toy: Elk leg

Naughtiest Deed: Disappearing into the woods for days while on camping trips

Attention Getter: Howls like a wolf

Favorite Pastime: Camping

Until Matt's death, Syndy Lu and brewmaster Matt Luhr were inseparable companions. She came to work with Matt every day and stayed under the picnic table behind the brewery. Matt was lost to a brain aneurysm in October 2008, and although he was nearly 100 miles away from Dillon in a Denver hospital, Syndy Lu began a soulful howl that lasted for 7 ½ hours. It was later learned her vigil began at the moment of Matt's death. Syndy Lu is now lovingly cared for by Rusty Simmons, Matt's fianceé, who comments, "She's not really a breed, but a blood line." This accounts for some of her unusual behavior. "Syndy Lu is not just a dog, but a companion." 🐾

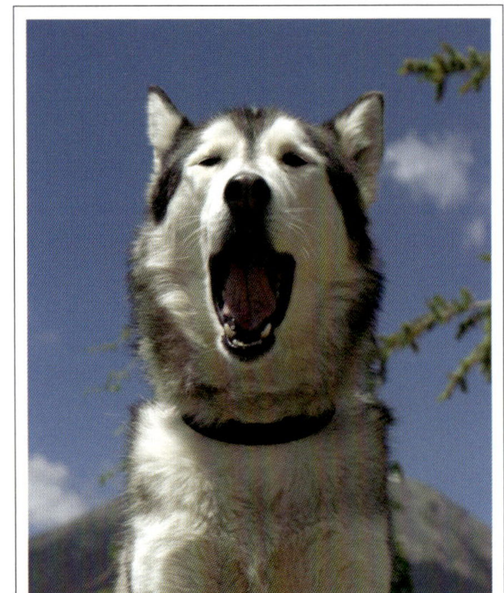

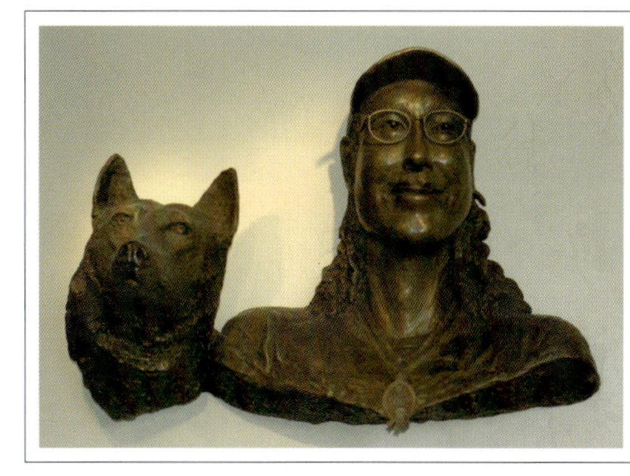

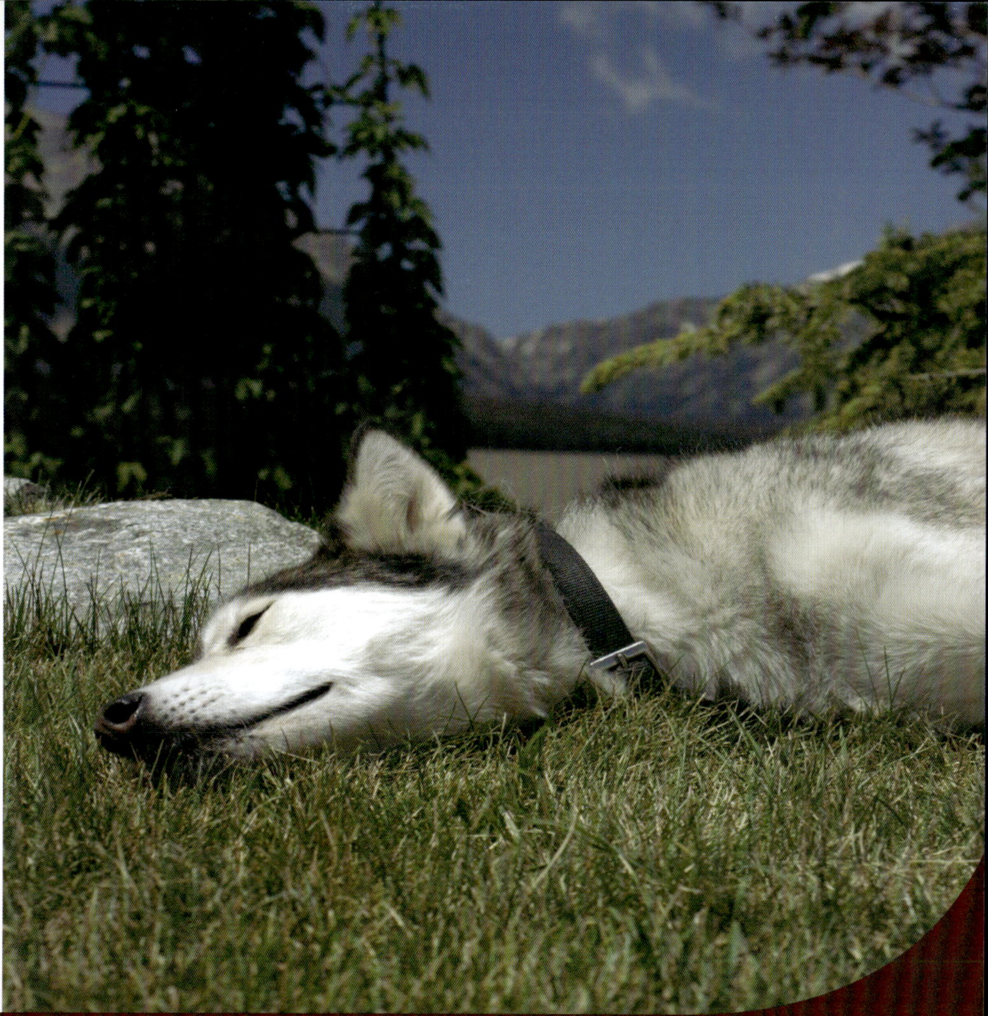

Syndy Lu, 9, Grey Wolf/Alaskan Malamute   Matt J. Luhr (1962-2008)

Chi

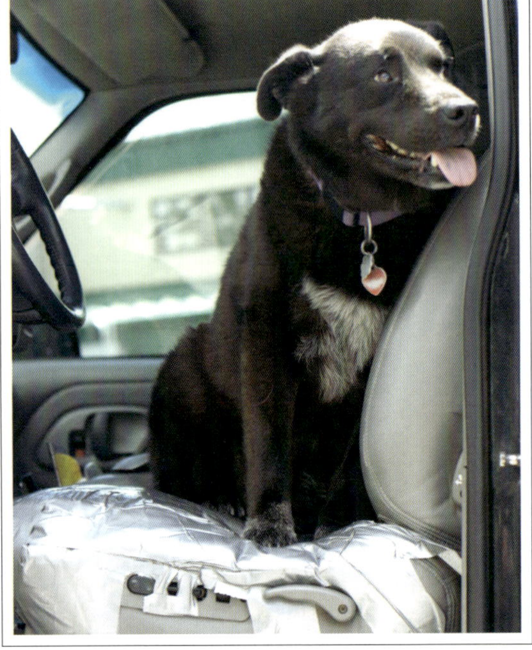

Naughtiest Deed: Destroyed truck seat three times; now held together with duct tape

Favorite Hangout: Green Mountain Reservoir

Best Friend: Syndy Lu

Favorite Toy: Tennis balls: "He thinks they grow on trees"

Established 1997

Double Gold and Double Silver Medals Colorado State Fair 2009

Among largest U.S. brewpubs (31/1,000)

Chi **loves to go to work** every day with brewmaster Cory. "As soon as we get close to the brewery, Chi starts to freak out," Cory explains. Chi's favorite treats are the canine carry-outs, but he doesn't like to eat alone. In fact, if his dish is in another room, he will carry a mouthful of food to eat, bit by bit, in the company of others. Chi has been one happy pup ever since his adoption from the Summit County Animal Shelter.

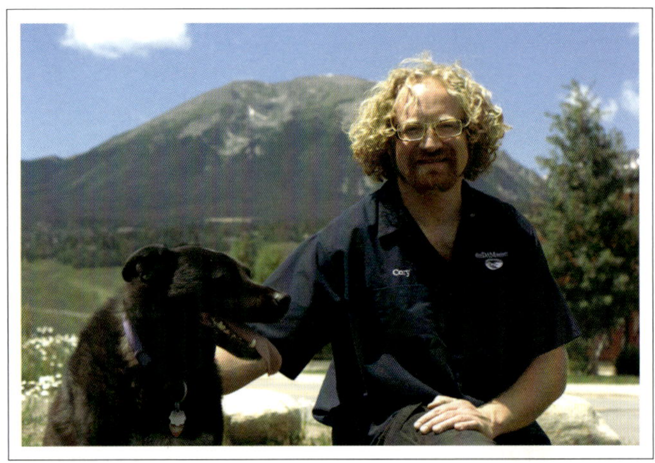

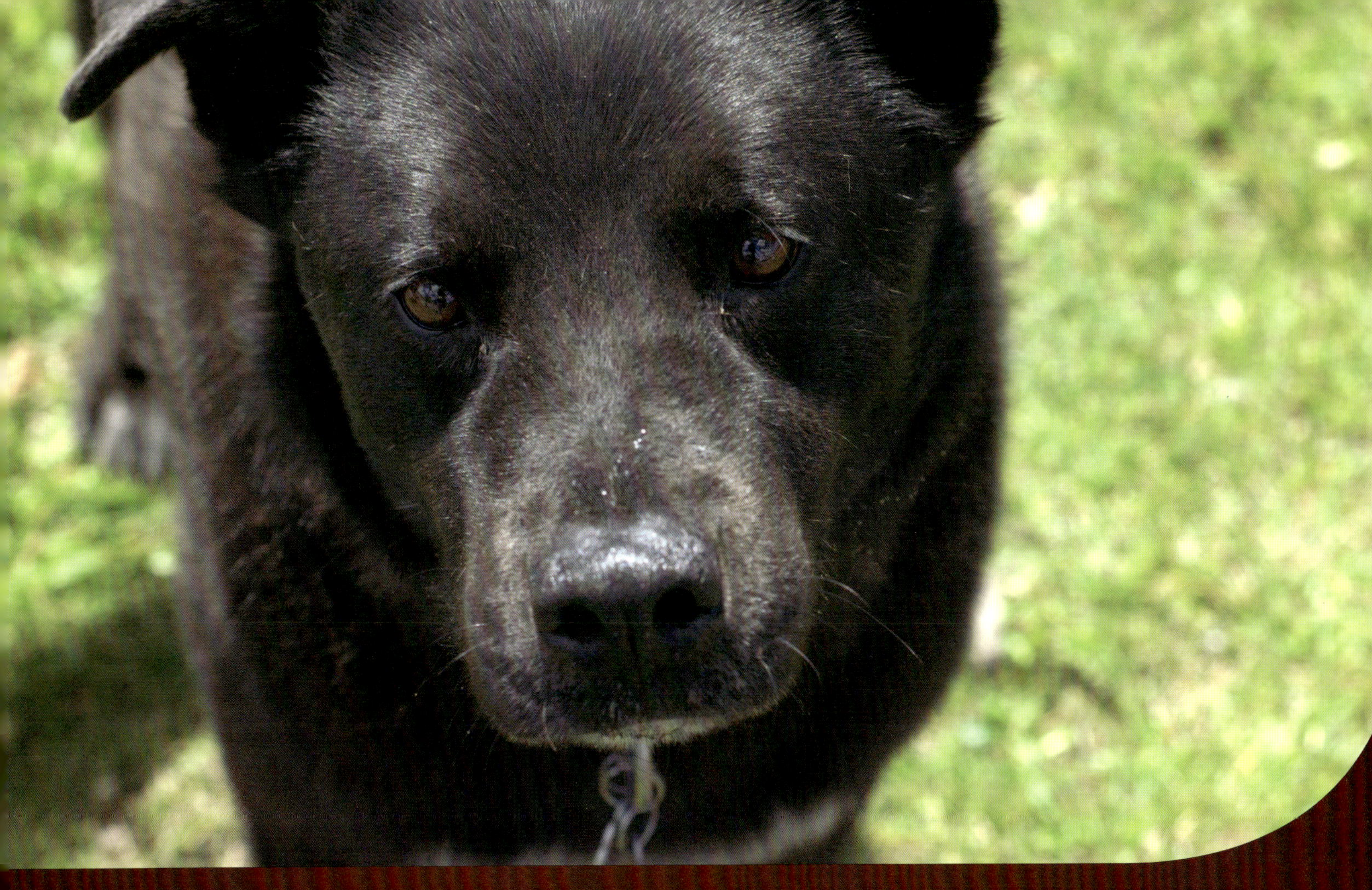

 Chi, 9, Chow/Black Lab   Owner: Cory Forster

Lily

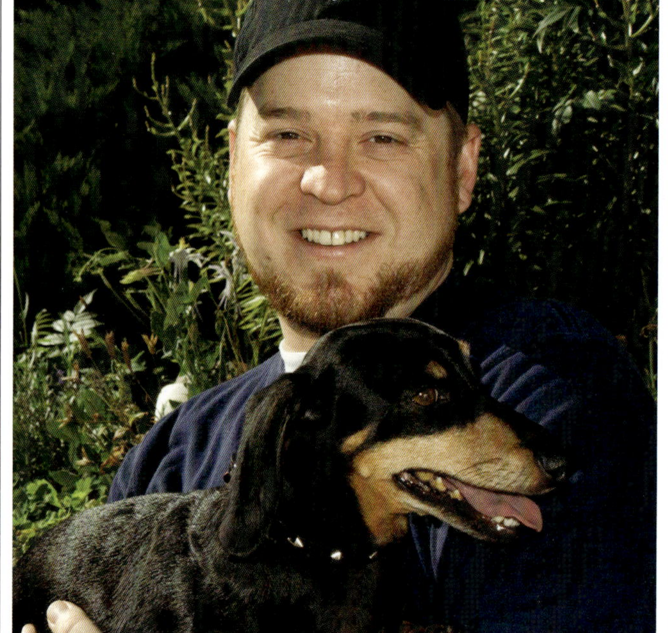

Excellent Adventure: Digging underground tunnels

Best Trick: Stand on back legs and circle for treats-two step

Annoying Habit: Trying to French kiss everyone

Accomplice: Best friend Zeke, German Shorthaired Retriever

PHANTOM CANYON BREWING COMPANY
COLORADO SPRINGS

Established 1993

First downtown Colorado Springs restaurant on the
National Register of Historical Places

Popular downtown billiard hall

She ate a pair of panties…followed by a trip to the ER to have them extracted! That's not her only chewing vice. If she is lucky enough to find socks, she will add them to her menu. "She's a magnificent tunneler," says Tom, manager at Phantom Canyon. She can excavate full passageways under fences. Lily's mischievous streak is balanced by her loving and caring nature. 🐾

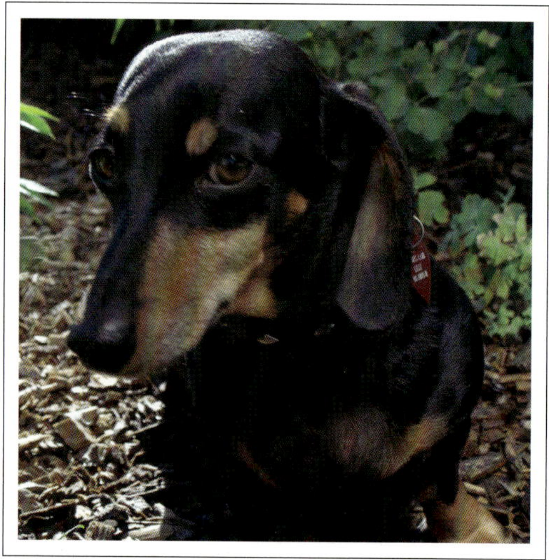

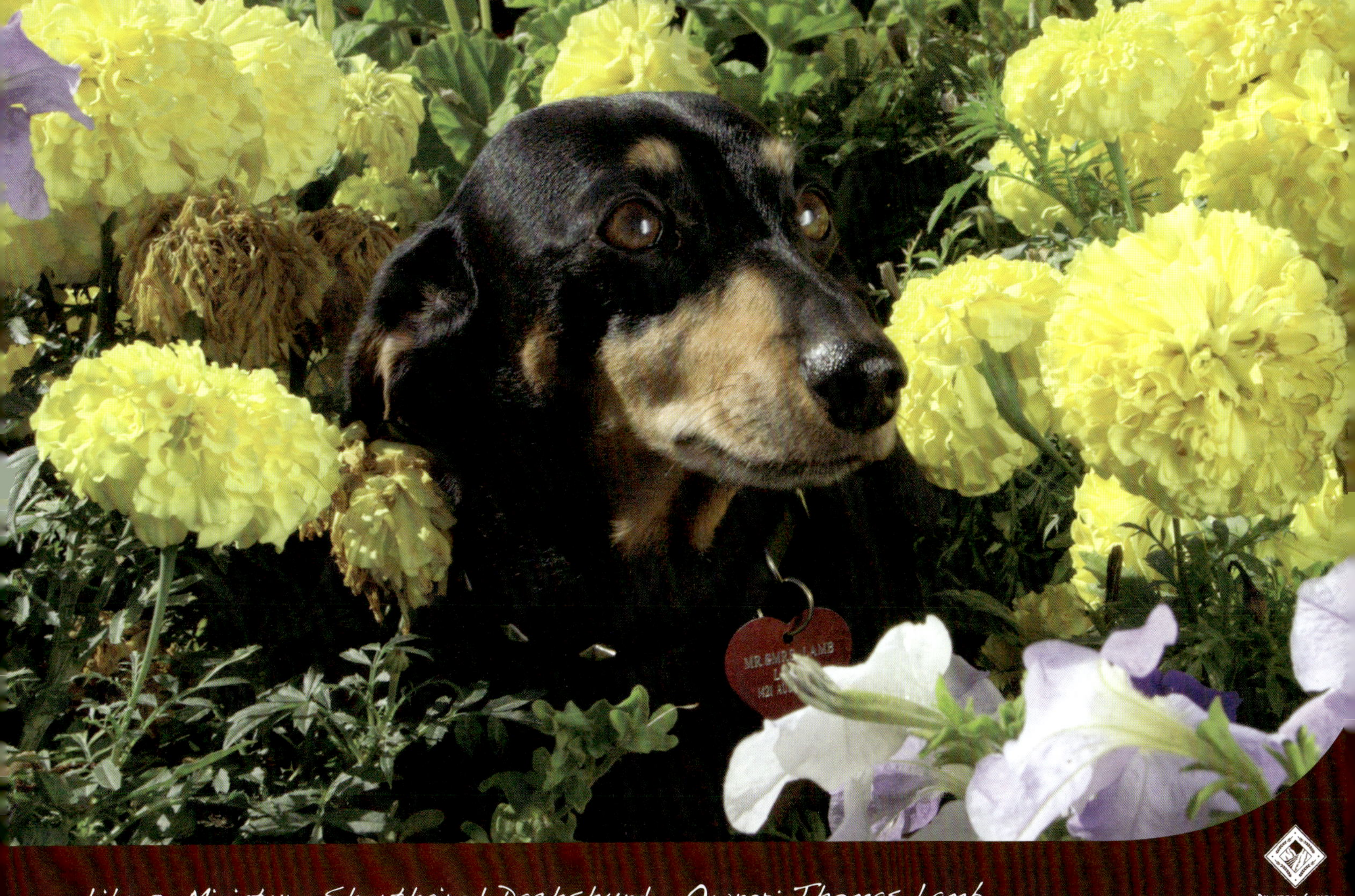

Lily, 8, Miniature Shorthaired Dachshund   Owner: Thomas Lamb

PHANTOM CANYON
BREWING CO

Chumley

Began brewing in 1996

Out of Bounds Stout was a Gold Medal winner at GABF in 1994

Brews over 20 different ales

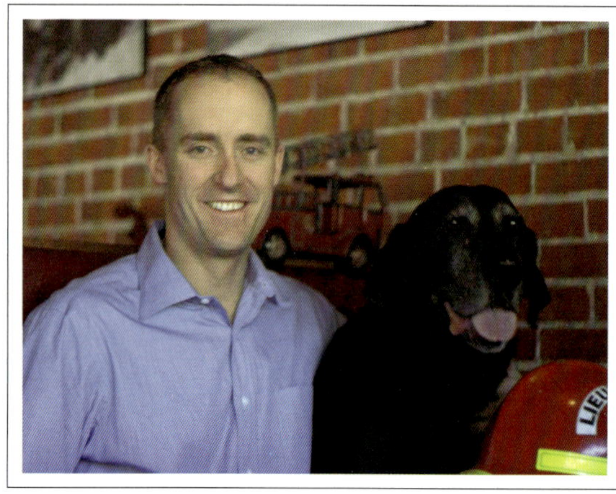

Most Annoying Habit: Pillow thief and bed hog

Favorite Pastime: Jumping and swimming in Boulder Creek

Quirky Behavior: Carries food bowl to carpet to enjoy more comfortable dining

Naughtiest Deed: Stealing the kids' food

Plates of bacon! Chumley probably dreams every night about mounds of his favorite breakfast treat. Ross Hagen, Pumphouse's managing partner, says that, when left to his own devices, Chumley actually opens the refrigerator by himself to expand his gourmet selections. "He's a foodie," says Ross. A chair propped in front of the fridge serves as the first line of defense for now.

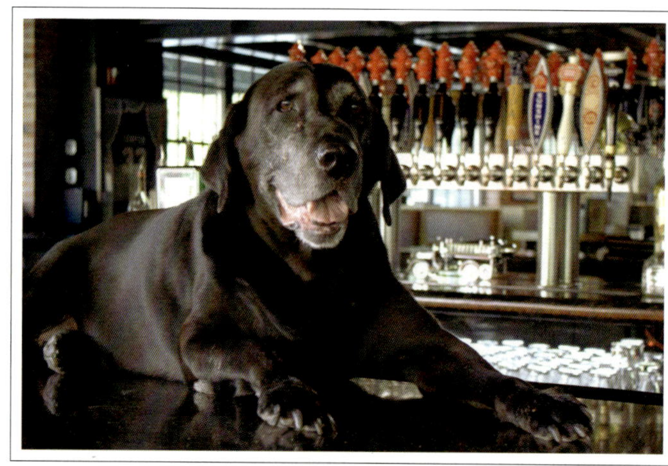

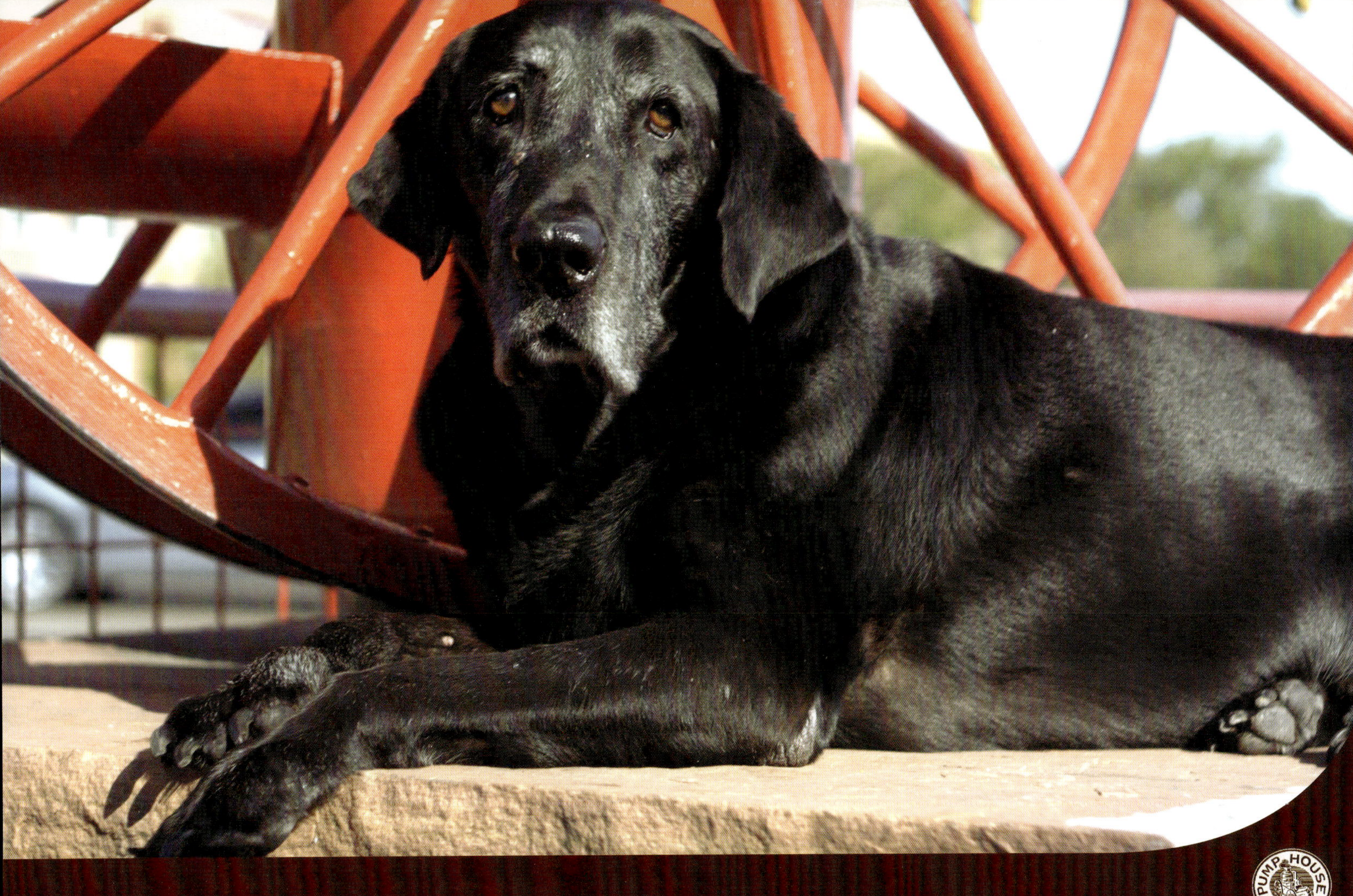

 Chumley, 12, Black Lab   Owner: Ross Hagen

Kahlua

Began in Estes Park 1993, moving from Boulder

The brewery is a green business, recycling glass, cardboard and other materials

Located in the original event center in Estes Park

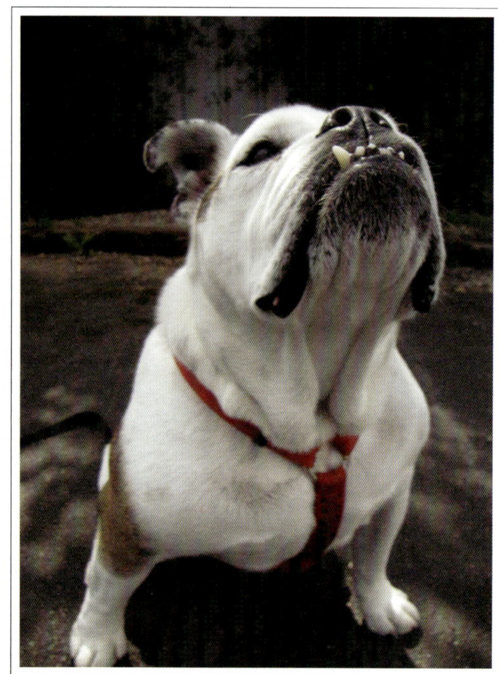

Kahlua is a mountain bulldog. With her short legs, one would never imagine that Kahlua loves to hike in the mountains around Estes Park. On long treks with brewery co-owner Tyler, she used to literally "run up the mountain." Naturally, you would expect a bulldog to fight with other dogs, but Tyler says, "Not so much anymore." Kahlua hangs around the house a lot, loves kids – and they love her – probably because she can find the chocolate and knows how to open a jar. Even at age nine, she still loves to jump into the kids' beds, and play keep-away with their toys.

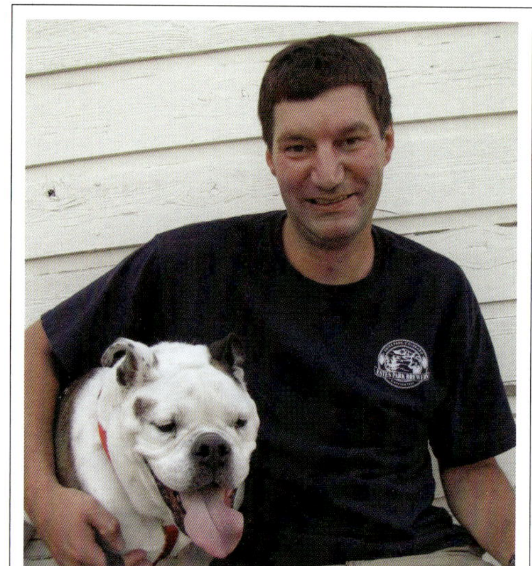

Most Annoying Habit: Bites at the vacuum cleaner

Favorite Toy: Squeaky dinosaur

Naughtiest Deed: Once ate a full tray of chocolate

Most Endearing Trait: Great with kids; allows them to dress her up with bows

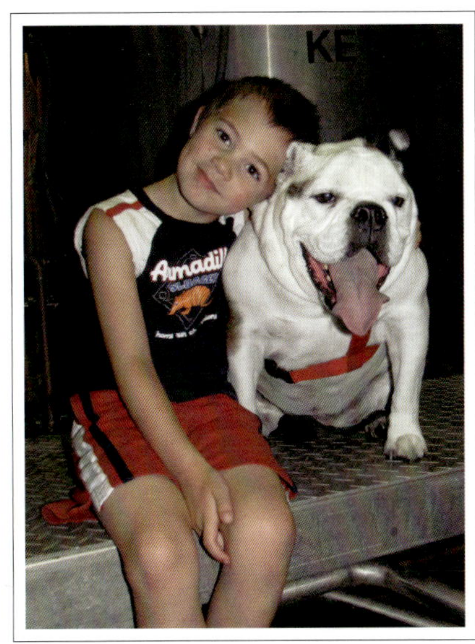

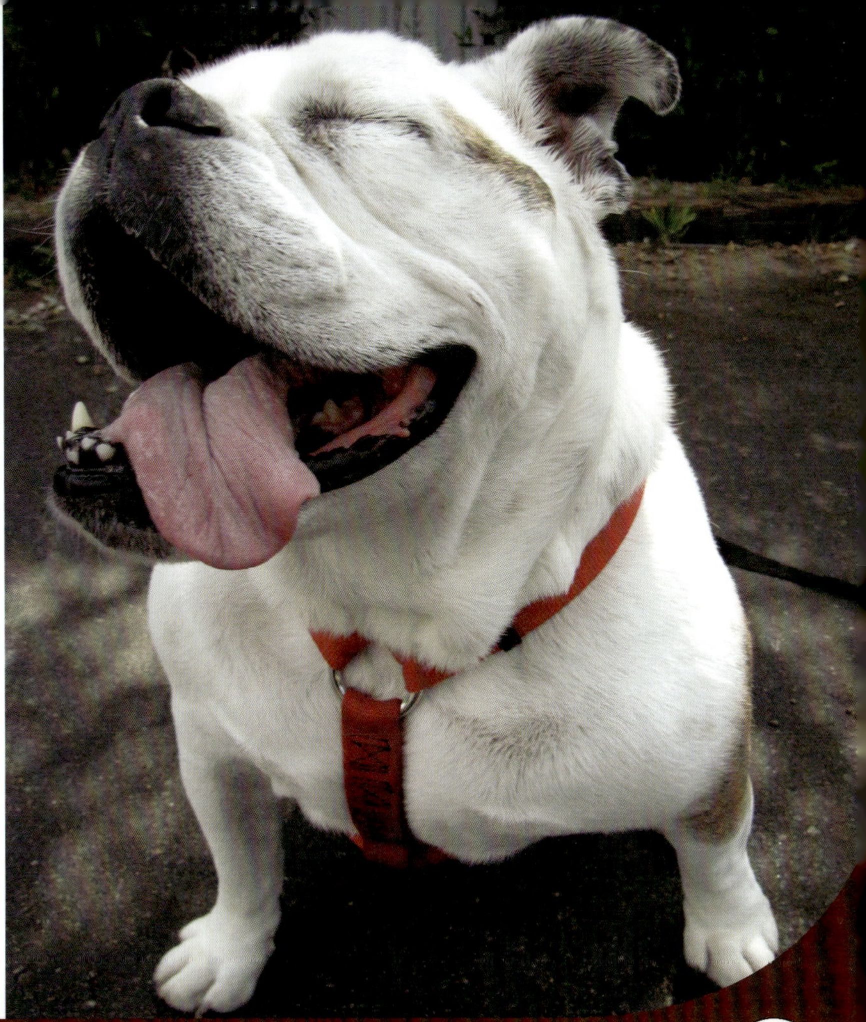

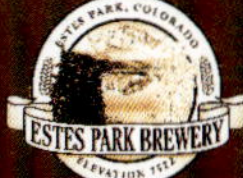

 Kahlua, 9, English Bulldog   Owner: Tyler Lemirande

Pickles and Pickles, Jr.

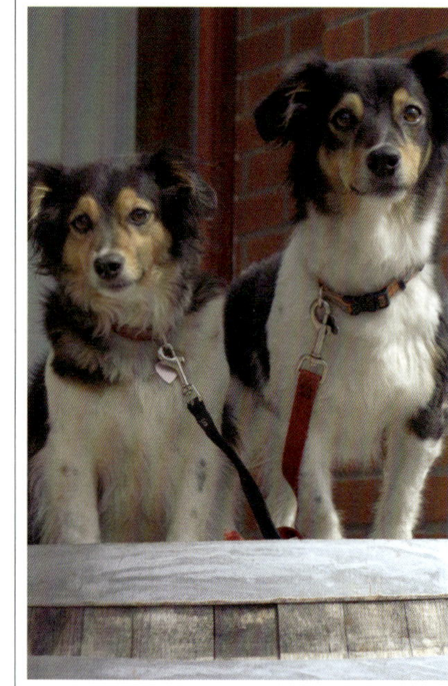

Favorite Toy: Pickles: tennis ball   Pickles, Jr.: Pickle's tennis ball

Best Trick: Pickles: riding a jet ski   Pickles Jr.: riding an ATV

Favorite Pastimes/Hobbies: Pickles, Jr.: likes kitties
Pickles: likes to herd horses

Most Annoying Habits: Pickles: is a tire-biter
Pickles, Jr.: barks at shadows

THREE BARREL BREWING COMPANY
DEL NORTE

Founded 2005

Reviving a 120-year-old brewing tradition in Del Norte

Focus on small batch brewing along headwaters of Rio Grande River

Nearly deported, Pickles and Pickles Jr. are immigrants. Originally from Mexico, they are two of five known Mexican Rat Terriers in Southern Colorado. No taco leftovers for these pals, who prefer the more exotic flavors of salmon and halibut. Although from different litters, Pickles, Jr. is truly a little brother to Pickles, Sr., acting as his constant shadow. Oddly, they prefer winter over the dry summer heat of Del Norte, and can spend hours outside rolling in the snow. Bystanders are amazed when brewery owner John Bricker rides by on his horse with Pickles and PJ on his lap. 🐾

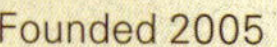

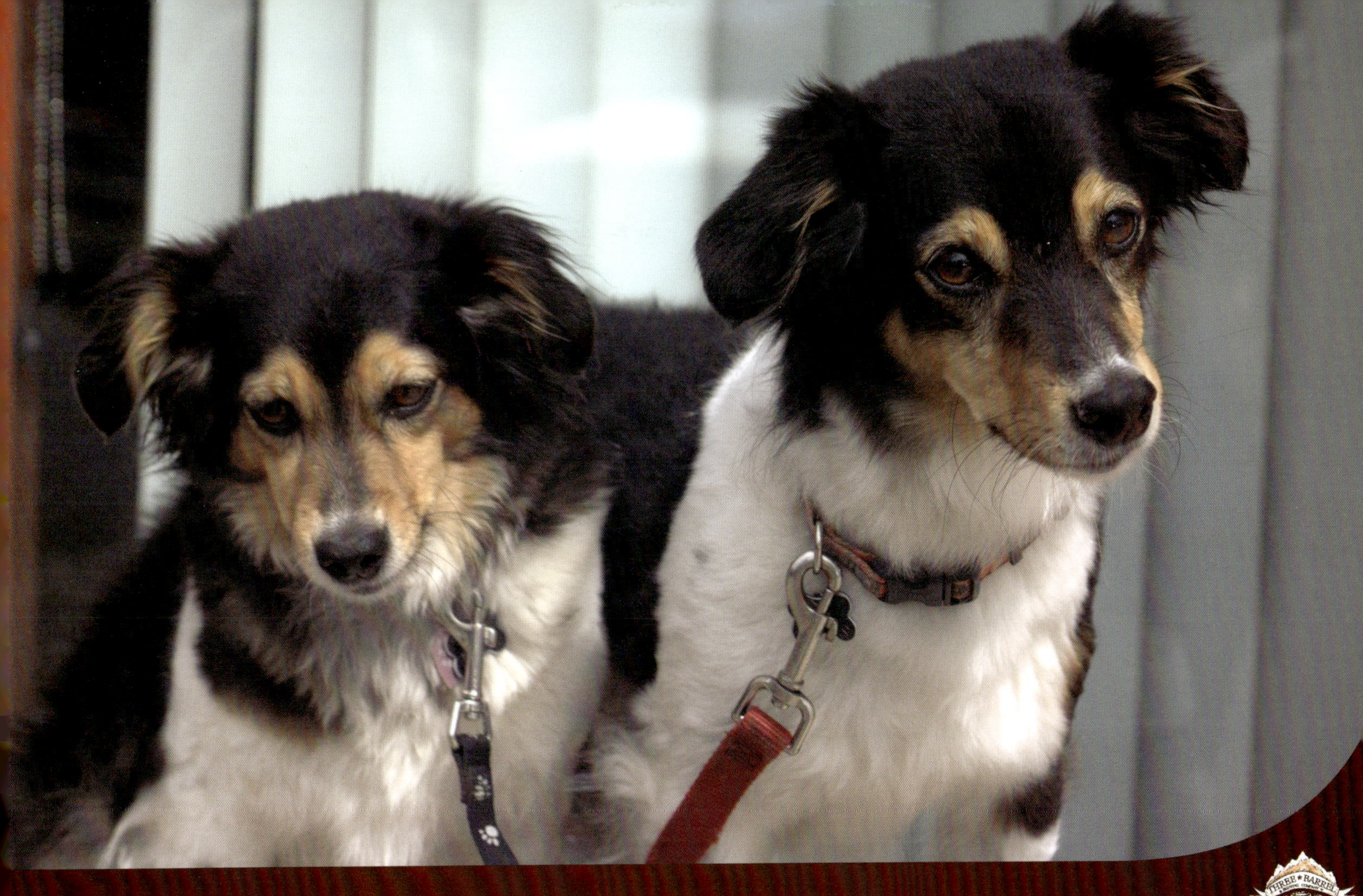

Pickles, 6 & Pickles Jr., 5, Mexican Rat Terriers   Owner: John Bricker

Bunni

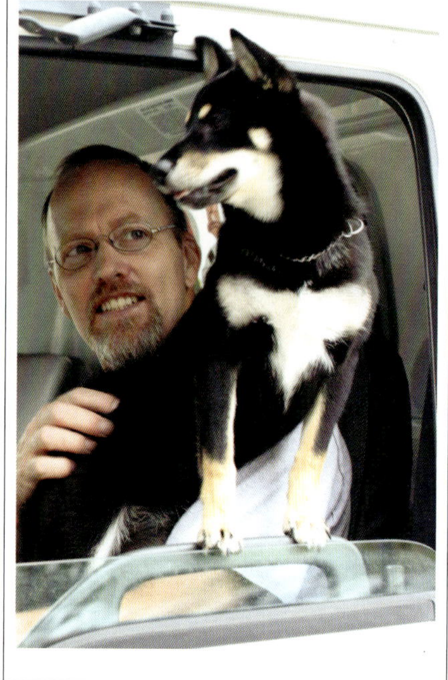

ROCKYARD BREWING COMPANY
CASTLE ROCK

Founded 1999

Double Eagle Ale Gold Medal GABF 2003

As an amateur, brewmaster Jim Stinson won a home brew contest

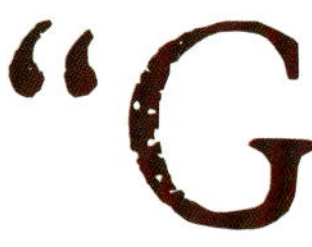

"**G**reed with speed,** mine, mine, mine," describes Bunni. To the cats in her neighborhood, she is Public Enemy Number One. She steals their toys, eats their food, chases them and even raids the litter box – YUK! She is also the household thief, stealing and hiding anything small, including decorative figurines. Rockyard brewmaster Jim has found that taking her on deliveries is the best way to keep this pup out of trouble at home. 🐾

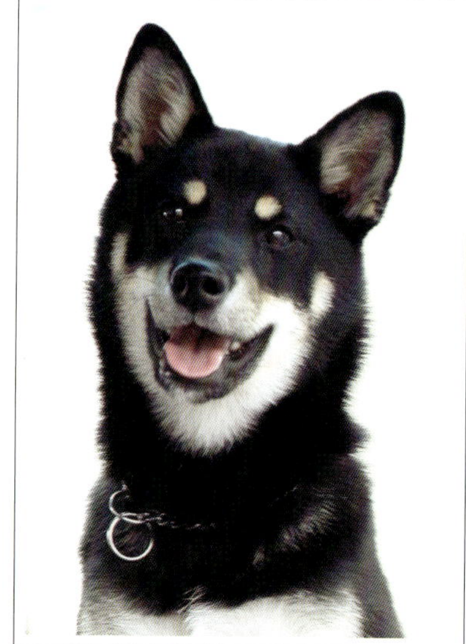

Favorite Food: Anything the cats are eating

Most Excellent Adventure: Poodle pal "Reilly" helped with an escape and they ran away!

Funny Habit: Steals golf balls and bounces them on the wood floors

Favorite Toy: Vibrating mouse cat toy

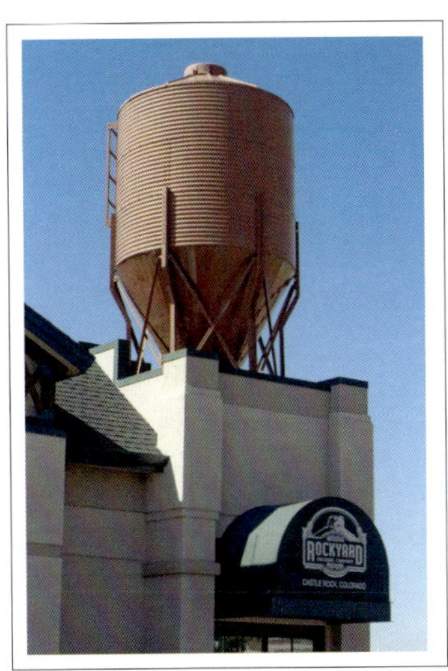

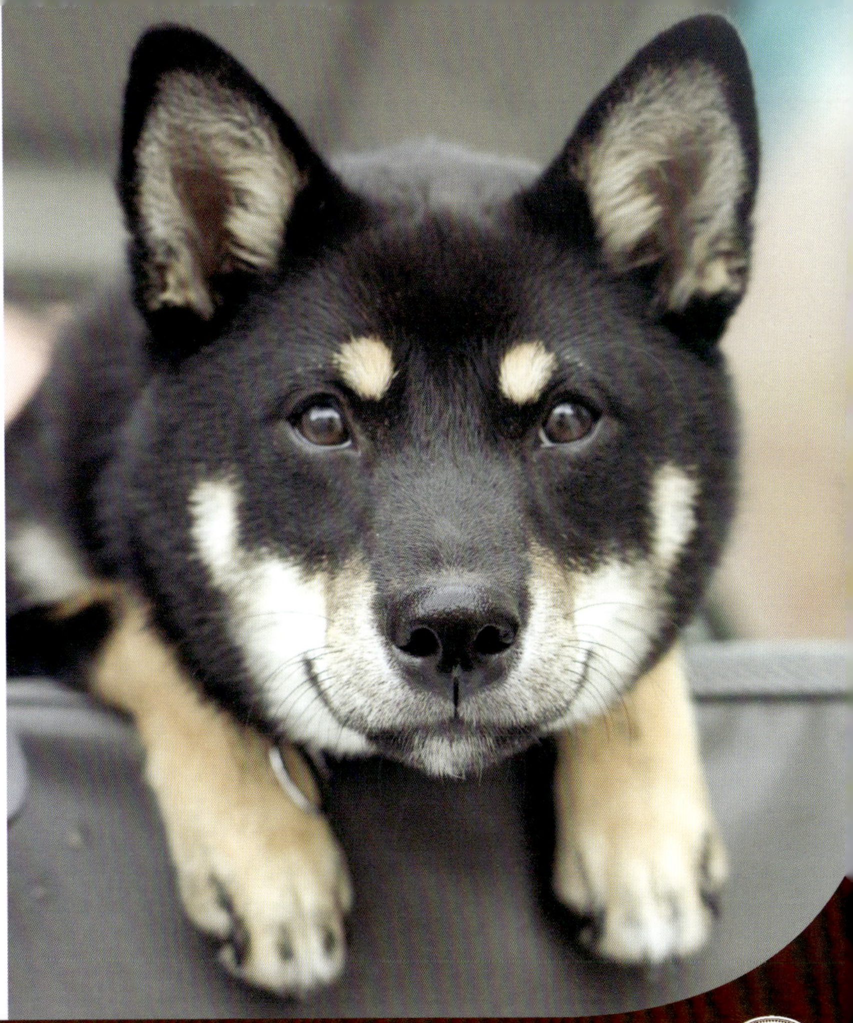

Bunni, 6 months, Shiba Inu   Owner: Jim Stinson

Kaya, Porter and Bailey

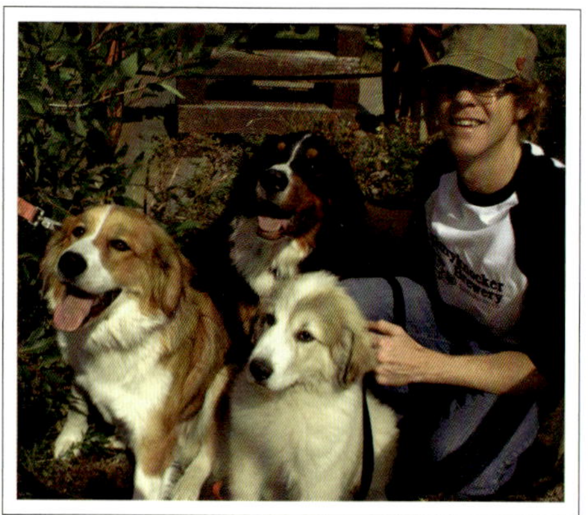

Kaya
Favorite Hangout: In the holes she digs
Favorite Hobby: Plotting escape routes from the yard
Best Friend: Porter
Most Excellent Adventure: Surviving a tornado

Porter
Annoying Habit: Talks too much!
Pastime: Being pretty lazy
Naughtiest Deed: Ate a pile of fireworks
Gets Excited About: Kids

Bailey
Funny Habit: Crawling over the two larger dogs
Favorite Hangout: Behind the wood-burning stove
Most Recent Mishap: Stung by a bee at 9 weeks old, right on the lip
Annoying Habit: Early a.m. barking to be fed

TOMMYKNOCKER BREWERY
IDAHO SPRINGS

Started brewing 1994

Located in an 1859 building, historic to the Gold Rush days

Gold Medal 2009 Colorado State Fair

Starting for Team Lawlor. . . Porter at Quarterback: as team leader, he uses his huge, expressive and talkative personality to call the plays. Off the field though, his "all star" reputation was tarnished by a fireworks-eating incident. Kaya at Running Back: finds the holes…usually the ones she's dug under the fence…and runs as many (neighbor) yards as she can…Bailey the Rookie: at three months, is learning to carry the ball…so far, he just wants to chew on it….needs to get into shape, too. He's always hungry and whining for a nap; a big baby. When not managing his team, Sean stays busy brewing beer. 🐾

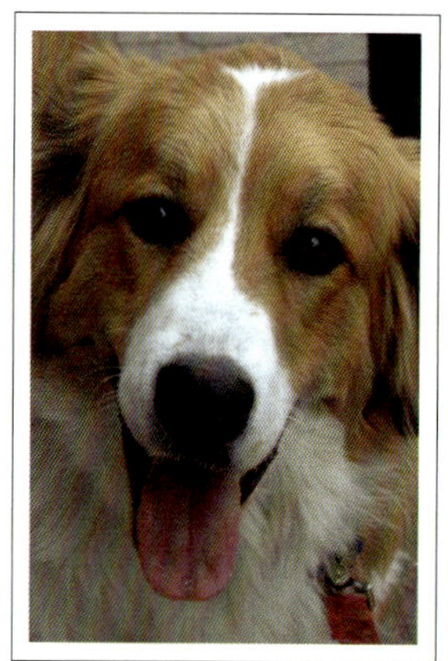

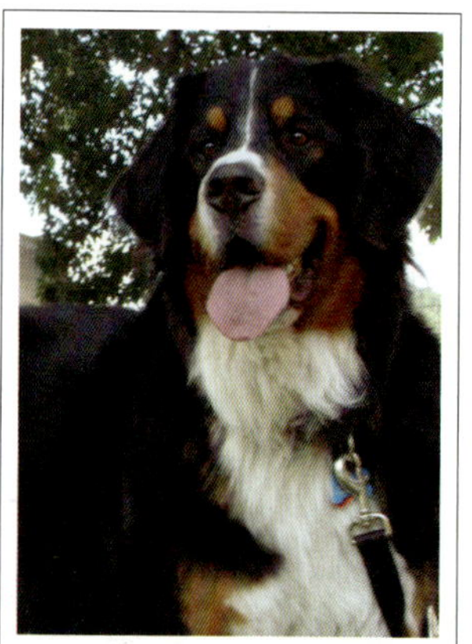

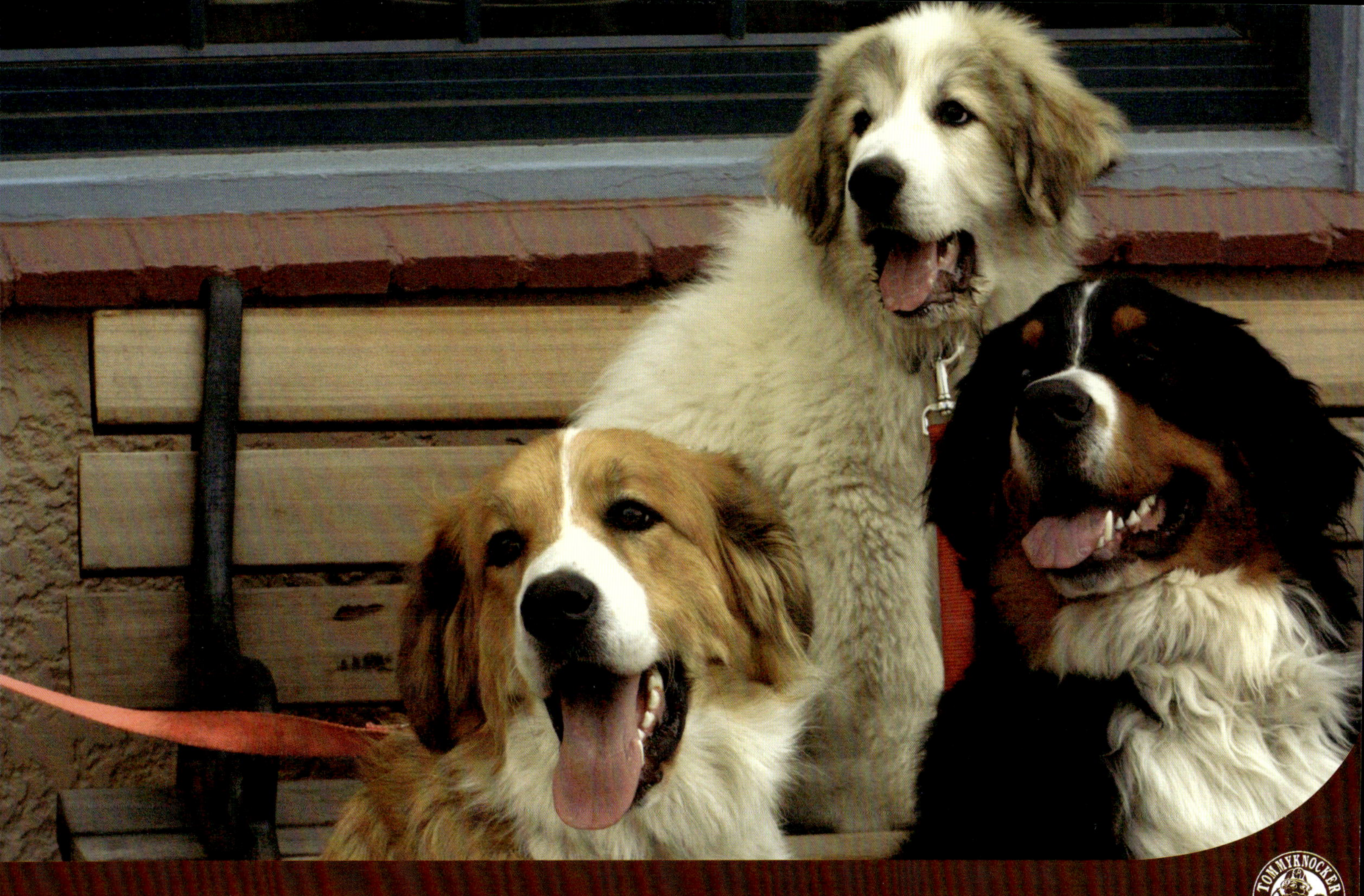

 Kaya, 1; Bailey, 3 months; & Porter, 1   Bernese Mountain Dog/Great Pyrenees, Great Pyrenees, Bernese Mountain Dog   Owner: Sean Lawlor

Bruno

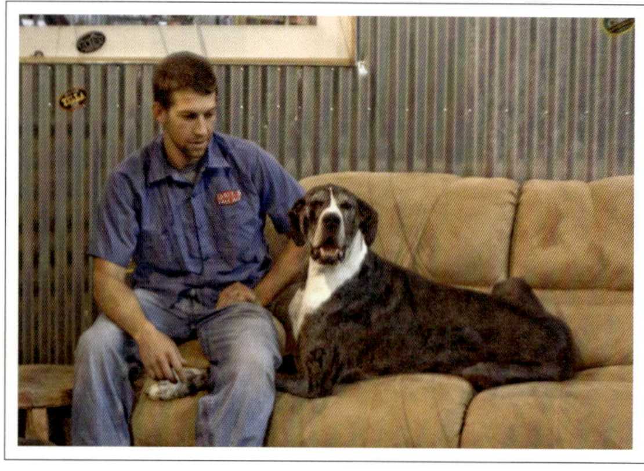

Best Trick: Balancing beer cans on nose

Annoying Habit: Separation anxiety

Gets Excited: About going for a ride or walk

Best Friend: Jeremy

Founded 1997

100-person capacity concert venue, focusing on Blues bands.

Cajun, Creole and Southern-style food featured in Pub

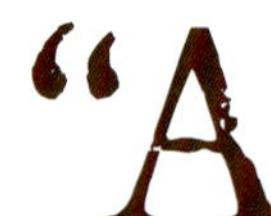

"**A**lways cries at weddings**"** would describe Bruno, a very sensitive fellow who often cries with babies with howls of his own. He even wells up at sad movies or when a baby is crying on the TV. Jeremy, "grandmaster canning department" at the brewery, says "Bruno hates coffee, cigarettes and beer," which might qualify him to be a mascot for the Health Department.

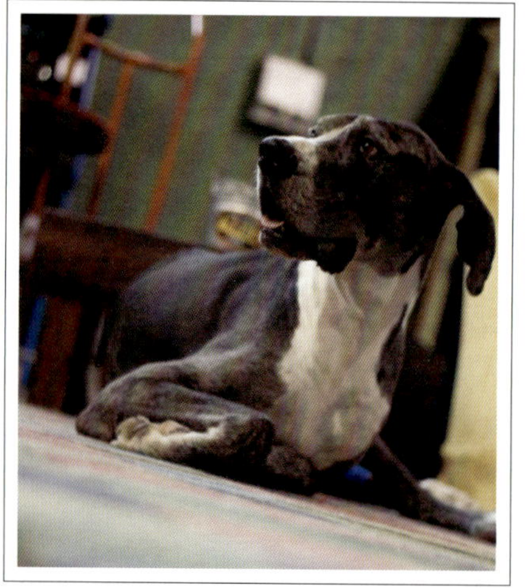

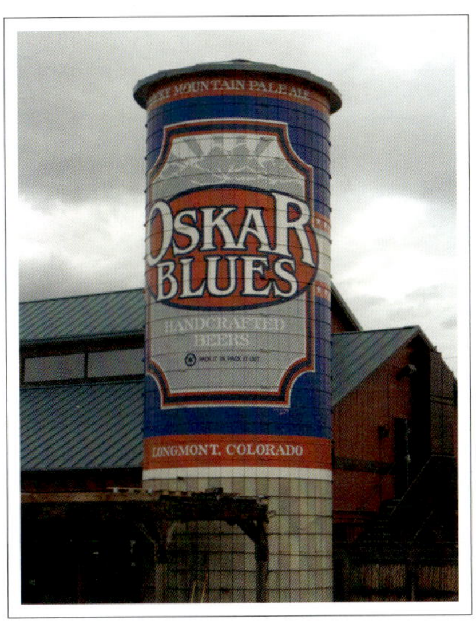

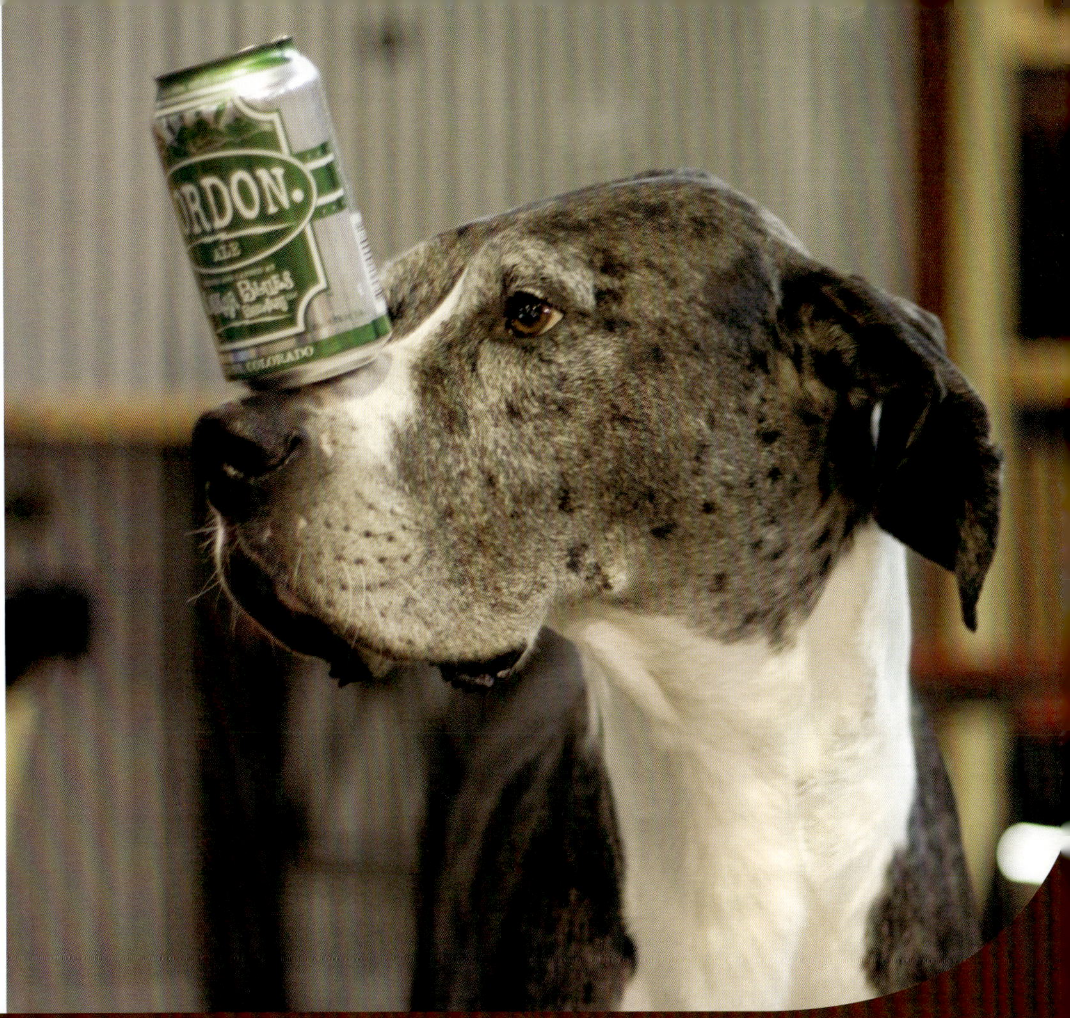

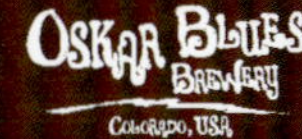

Bruno, 6, Great Dane   Owner: Jeremy Rudolf

Kaley

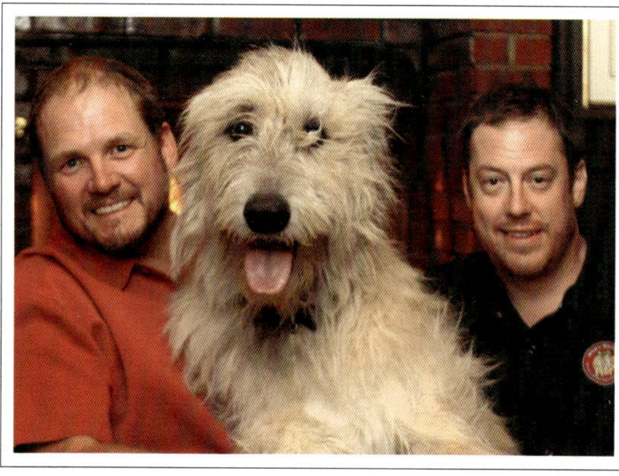

Funny Habit: Sleeps on back; runs in her sleep

Best Friends: "Little dogs" George, a Black Lab, and Aspen, a Golden Retriever

Gets Excited: To ride in David's 1968 Cadillac Fleetwood Limousine

Favorite Hangout: On the porch at the cabin in Grand Lake

BULL AND BUSH PUB AND BREWERY
GLENDALE

Started as English-style pub in 1971, modeled after original 17th-century Bull and Bush in England; Brewery added 1997

GABF Gold Medal 1998

Nation's first "sports bar" with satellite TV

Where does a 170 pound dog sleep? This gentle giant doesn't care, just as long as there is enough room! Usually a long sofa will do just fine. One of her favorite positions is lying on her back, so she can run in her sleep, according to the brewpub's co-owner brothers, David and Erik Peterson. She's probably reliving the day when, much to her amazement, she actually caught that pesky squirrel.

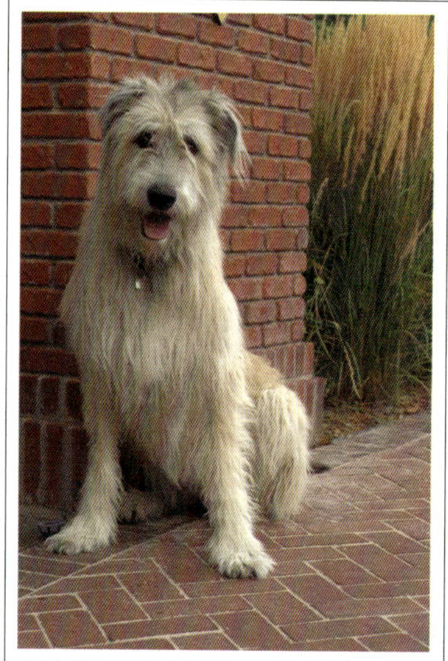

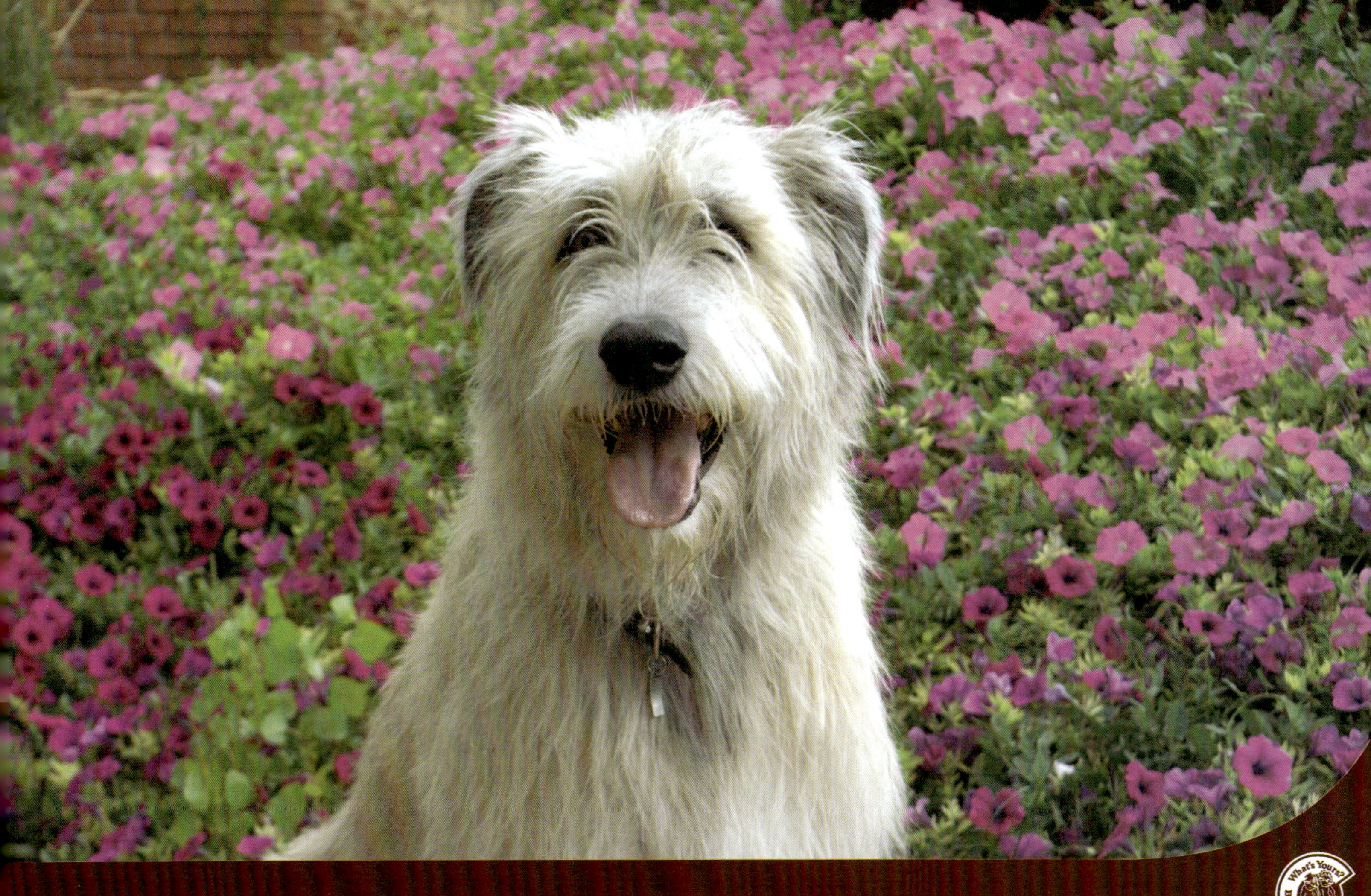

 Kaley, 7, Irish Wolfhound Owners: David and Erik Peterson

Teddy Bear

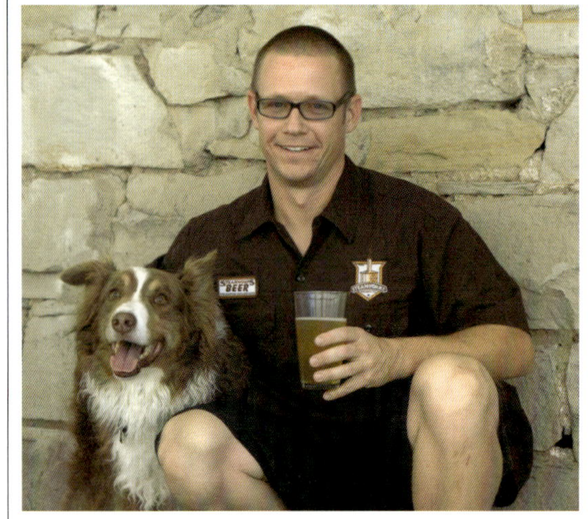

Hobby: Finding the end of his tail

Favorite Food: Deer carcass

Annoying Habit: Whines when riding in car

Favorite Hangout: The brewery with pals Ember & Ruca

Started 1996

Back-to-back GABF Gold Medals (2006-2007) for Steam Engine Lager

Steamworks beer sold in nine states

Whipped cream out of a can and kids are the perfect combination for big, fluffy Teddy Bear. He is a true working dog, brewmaster Spencer Roper relates. Teddy Bear likes to herd Spencer's guests by circling them and gently nudging the backs of their legs. Pretty soon, the unsuspecting company finds they are talking very closely. 🐾

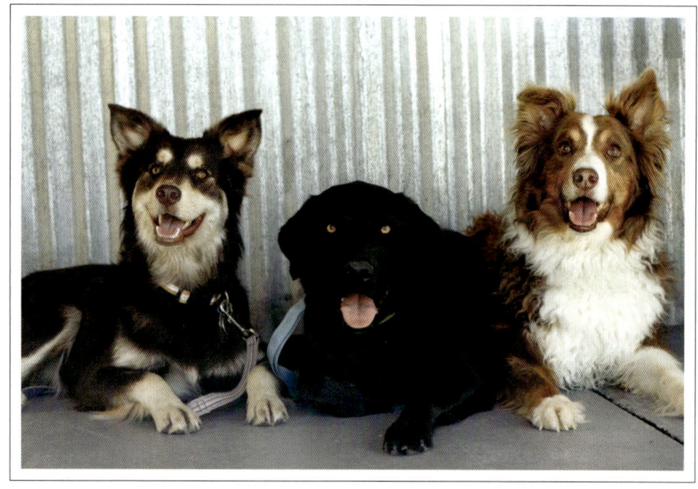

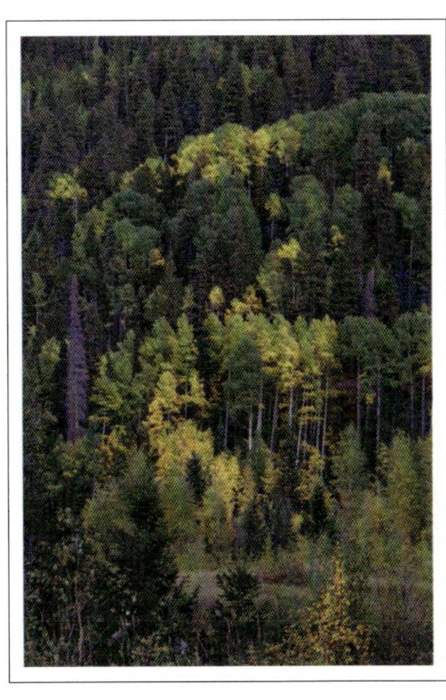

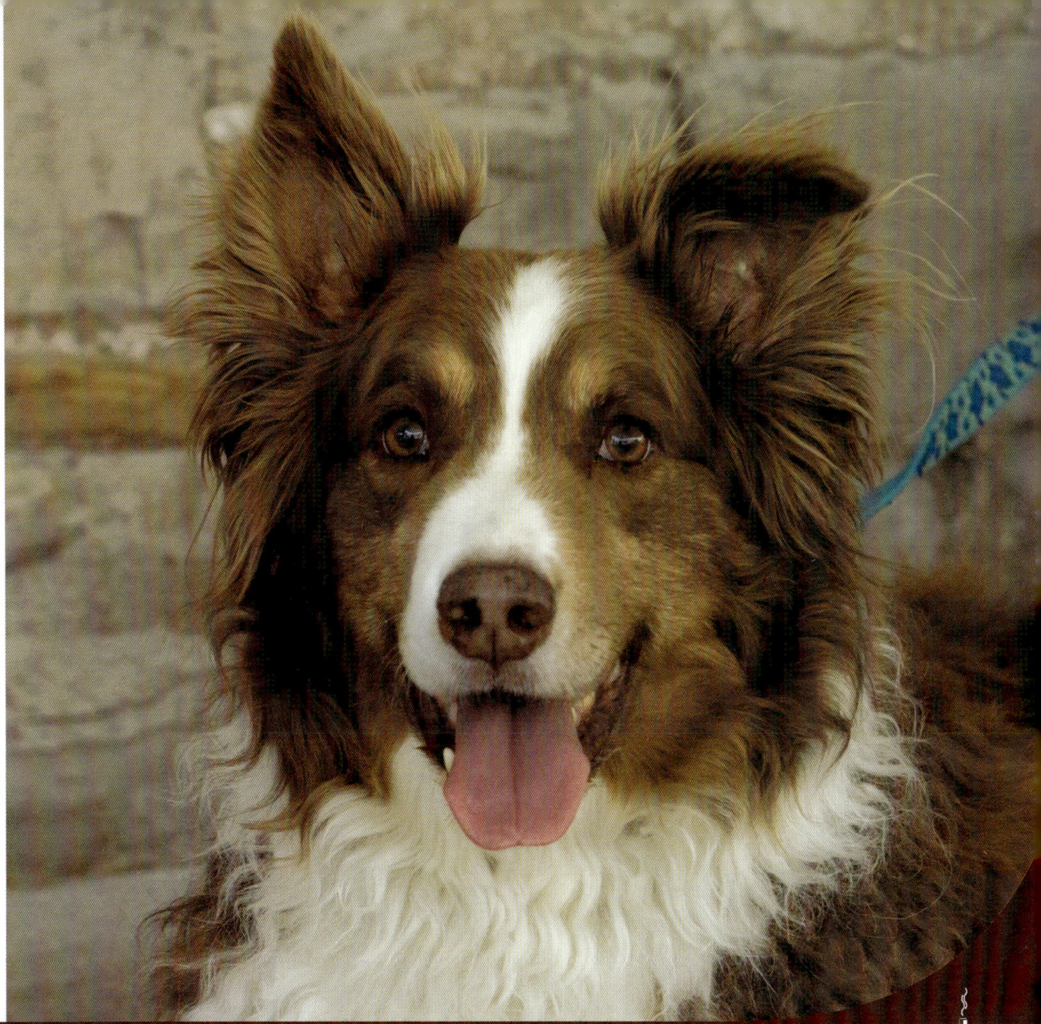

Teddy Bear, 8, Australian Shepherd   Owner: Spencer Roper

Bella

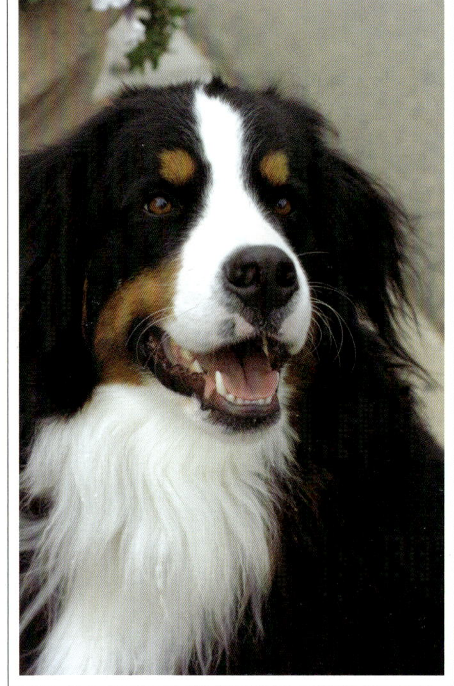

Favorite Toy: Stuffed black bear

Favorite Food: Dog treat with peanut butter

Favorite Hobby: Swimming in lakes

Best Trick: Superman

First beer, CBC-Draft House, debuted Inauguration Day 2009

Host of University of Colorado football coach's show, 2009

Downtown Boulder location

Bella in any language describes this gentle brewdog. With a winning smile and a people-loving personality, Bella lives up to her name. Draft House owner Jim Howser describes her as "ridiculously good" though an inconveniently early riser. True to her breed, Bella is steady-tempered. The only time she is less than compliant is when she refuses to get back in the car after indulging in her favorite pastime of swimming in a lake. Bella is the inspiration for *Big Bella Brown*, one of CBC-Draft House's most popular brews. 🐾

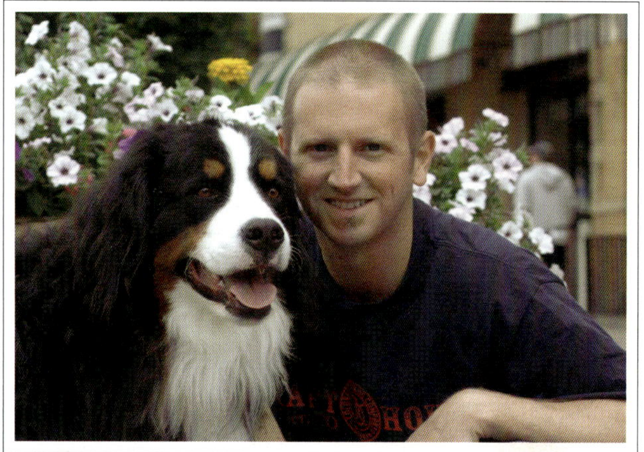

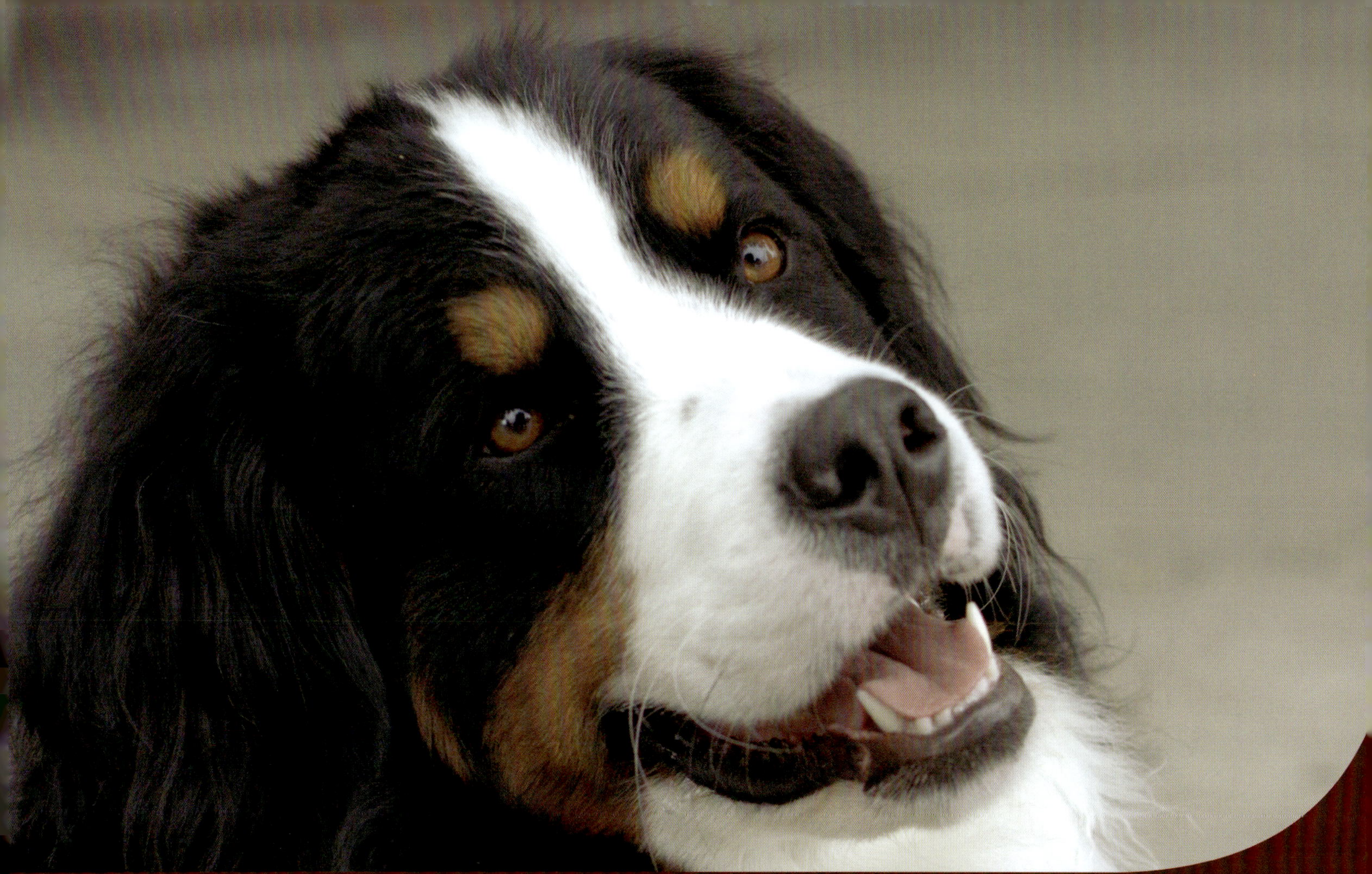

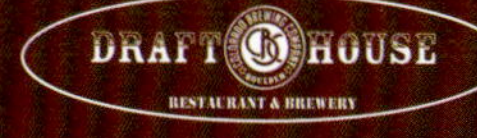

Bella, 3, Bernese Mountain Dog Owner: James Howser

Halifax & Dora

Established 1996

Silver Medal GABF 2009

One of country's highest breweries at 9,097 feet

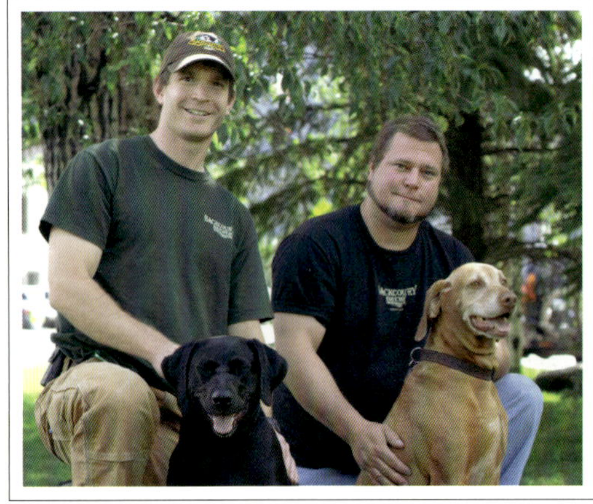

"**M**y dog Halifax can say, 'Earl'. . .but Dora hears, 'squirrel?!'" Those little critters still always manage to get away. Halifax and Dora are great friends who from time to time test boundaries. "They ate a door once," said Kyle, a Backcountry brewer. Halifax loves swimming, while Dora prefers to watch for birds by the feeder on Kyle's deck. By the way, fellow brewer Alan Simons (pictured left) confirms that Halifax doesn't know anyone named "Earl." 🐾

Halifax

Best trick: Can say "Earl"

Naughtiest Deed: Ate a door

Best Friend: Dora

Hobby: Swimming

Dora

Favorite Pastime: Watching birds

Naughtiest Deed: Ate a door

Best Friend: Halifax

Best Trick: Hearing Halifax say "squirrel"

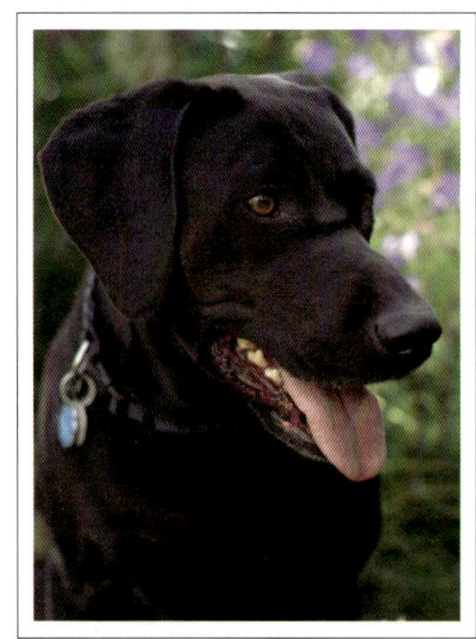

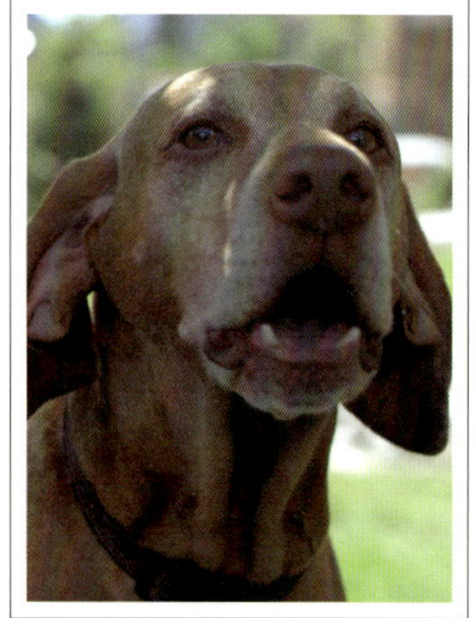

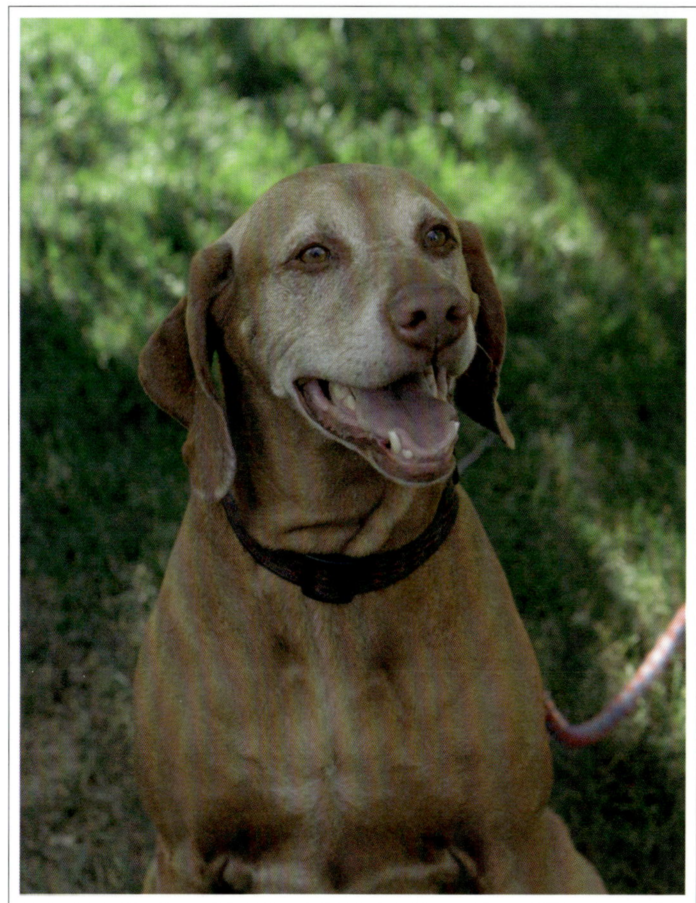
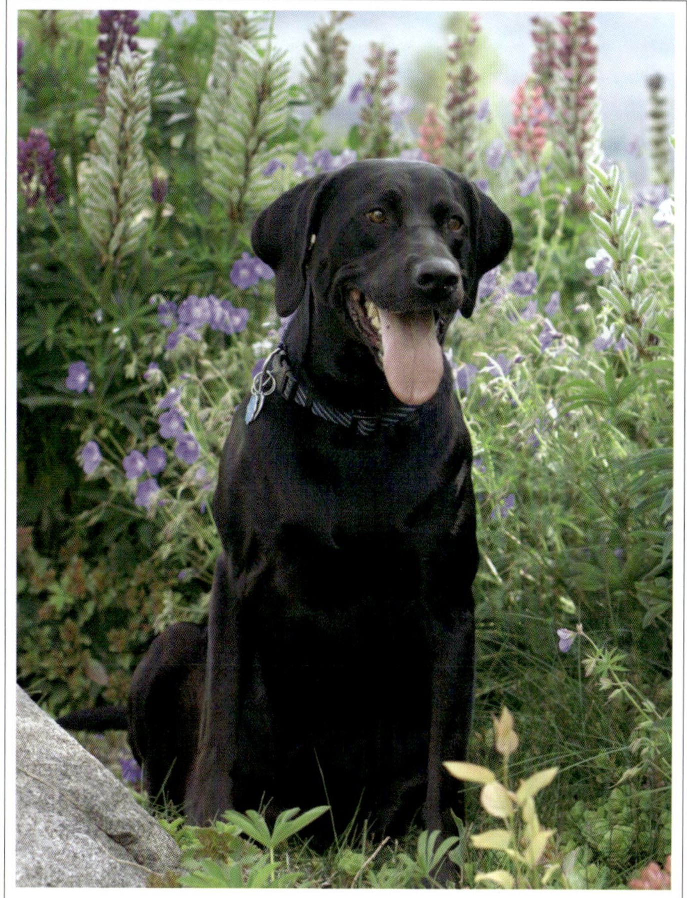

Halifax, 9 & Dora, 3½, Vizla & Black Lab/Vizla Owner: Kyle Carstens

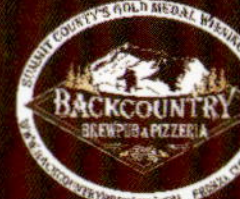

Porter

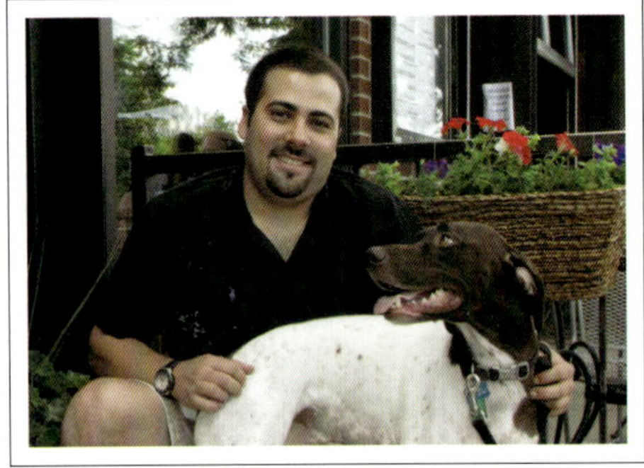

Hobby: Bird watching, hoping one falls from the sky

Favorite Treat: Potato chips

Best Trick: Can catch a fast pitch tennis ball

Annoying Habit: Whining to get outside

First beer, CBC-Draft House, debuted Inauguration Day 2009

44 Pale Ale Silver Medal winner at 2009 GABF

Mike served on the Chicago Brewers Guild

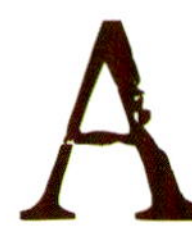

A **pair of shoes...**will be your welcome gift from Porter when you visit brewmaster Mike's house. Porter steals shoes and hides them in the backyard. When guests arrive, he brings them as a present! Living in the present (moment), however, is not such a good idea sometimes, (as Porter found out). While on a hike, Porter got lost when he chased a deer over the mountain and into the next valley. Much to Mike's surprise, Porter was able to find his way back to a friend's house. He is pretty athletic, and can catch a fast pitch tennis ball. Little dogs need to be careful with Porter, who hasn't figured out that he is too big to play rough.

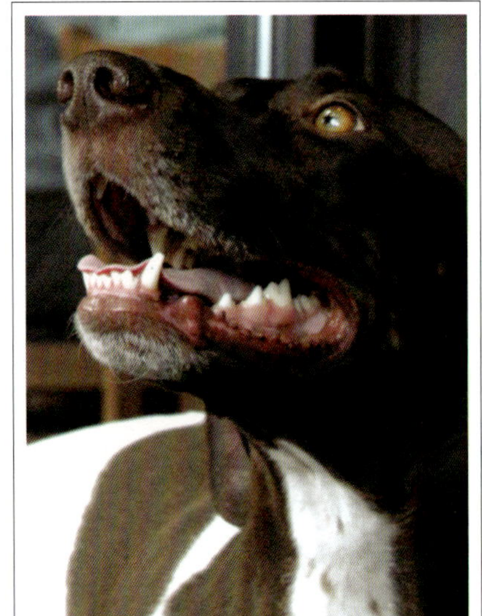

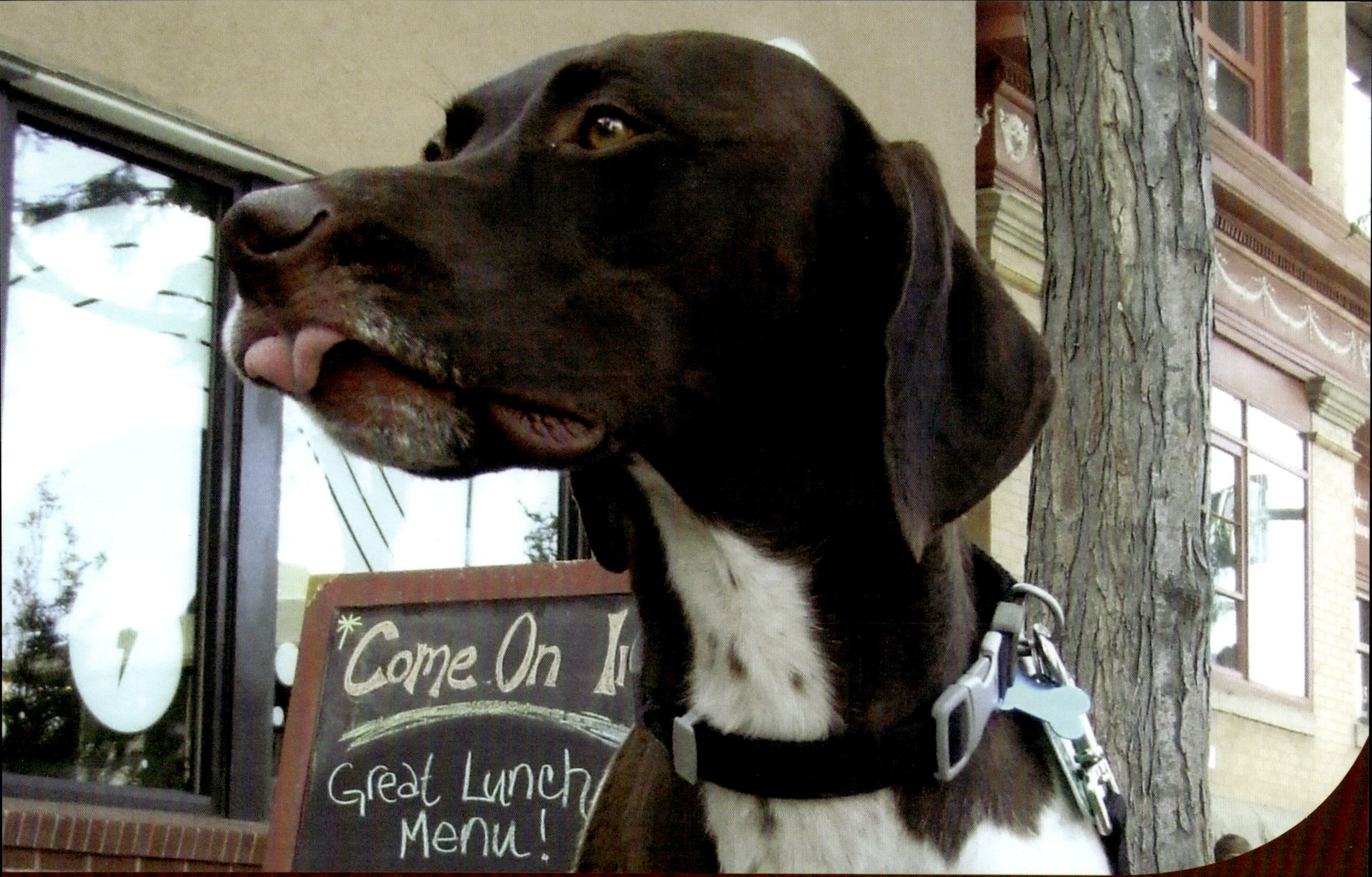

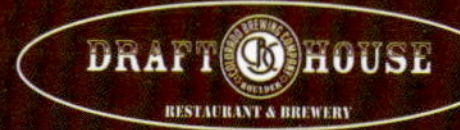

47 *Porter, 4, German Shorthaired Pointer Owner: Mike Kasian*

Coop

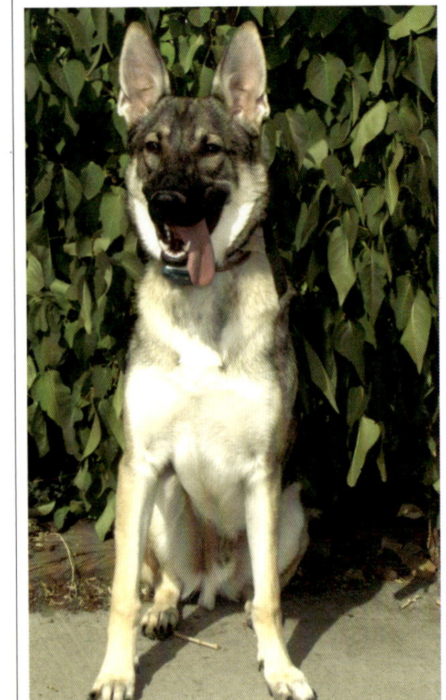

Best Trick: Gathers rocks to play games of solo soccer

Favorite Toy: Whatever he can steal from Harry

Annoying Habit: Wakes up too early

Favorite Hangout: On the sofa with the family

Brewery started in 1994

Historic 1901 Columbine Mill Grain Elevator location

Current owners since 2008

Giggles and barks...are the noises most often heard at the home of Old Mill co-owners, Kathy and Bill Frangiskakis. Their two-and-a-half year old son Harry considers Coop, the family's eight-month-old German Shepherd, to be his little brother. "Coop will do anything Harry wants him to," says Bill, including racing through Harry's play tunnel to chase down a ball. These two are a rolling, hugging, playful pair. 🐾

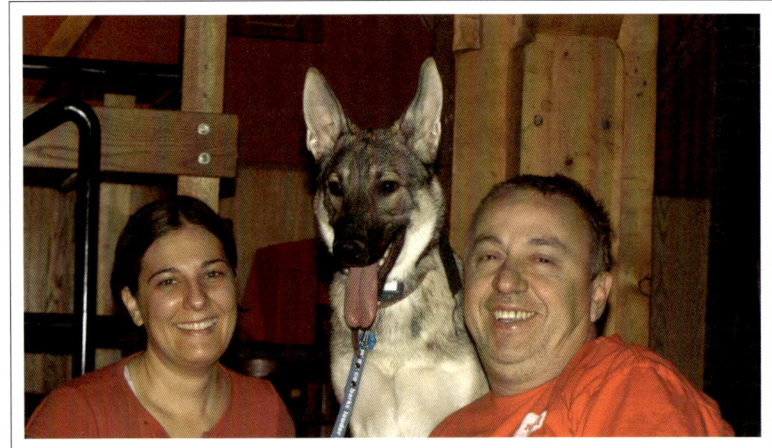

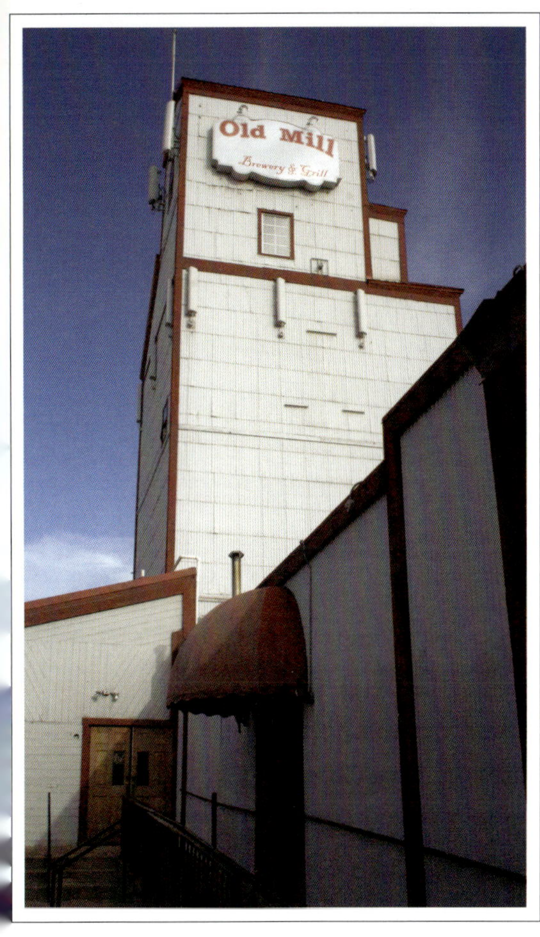

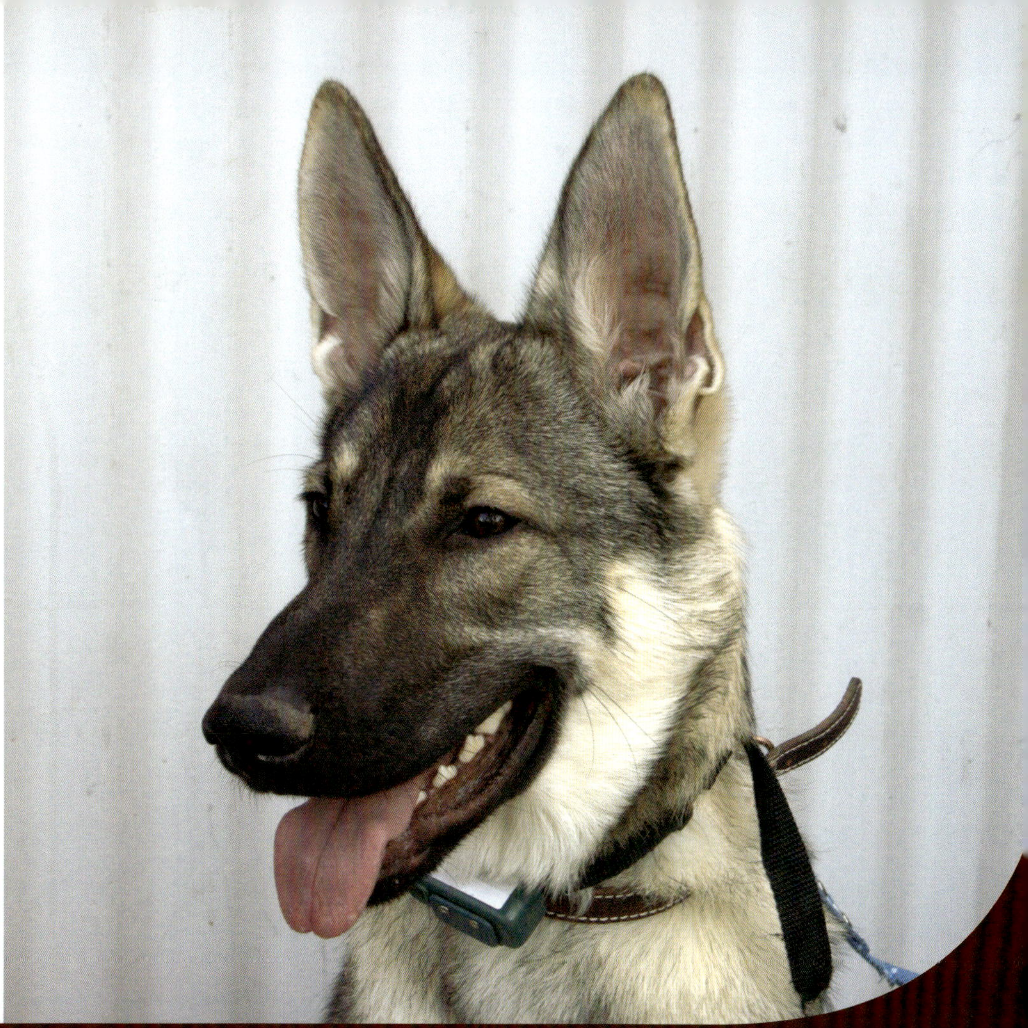

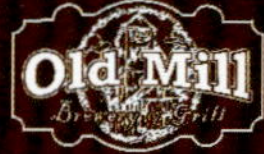

 Coop, 8 months, German Shepherd   Owners: Kathy and Bill Frangiskakis

Gomez

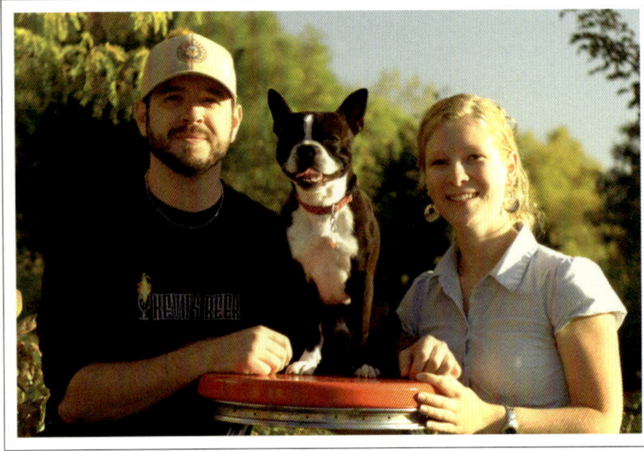

Best Trick: Pulls Soren around on a skateboard

Funny Habit: Sneezes when he wants to go outside

Naughtiest Deed: Sleeps on bed when nobody is home, then acts guilty

Favorite Treat: Prime rib

Began commercial production 1991

Contributed over $470,000 in philanthropic funds in 2008

Corporate mission of sustainability and environmental stewardship

Personals: **Handsome, fun-loving male seeks** well-bred female. Likes long walks in the mountains and naps in the sunshine. Will give kisses on demand, and loves to snuggle. Hobbies include: playing with tennis balls, wrestling non-stop and swinging around at the end of a rope by his teeth. Well-mannered ladies only. Contact: Soren in management, labeling and packaging department, or Sigrid at home. ❧

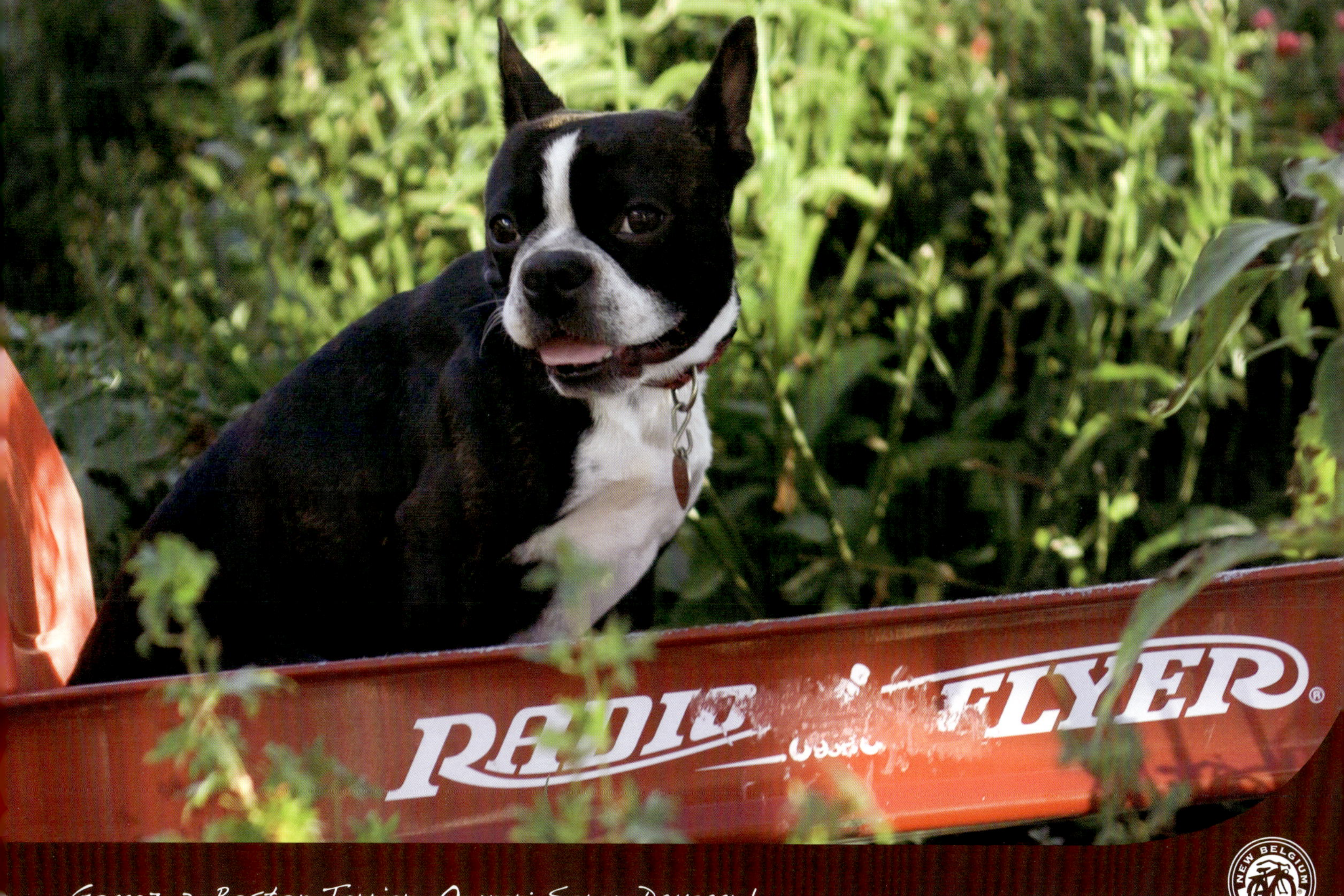

51 Gomez, 3, Boston Terrier Owner: Soren Daugaard

Bear

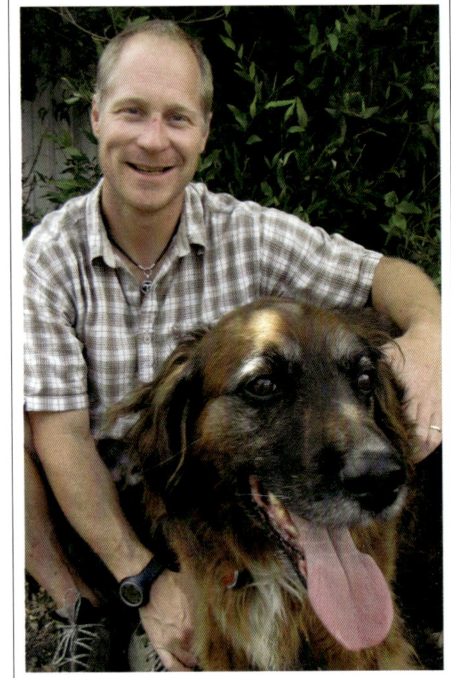

Most Annoying Habit: Following Eric around the house

Gets Excited About: Seeing the car keys

Favorite Treat: Stolen bread off the counter

Best Trick: Looks both ways when crossing the street

ESTES PARK BREWERY
ESTES PARK

Established in 1994

Award-winning India Pale Ale

Site of the Best of the West Brewfest

Bear is a true brewery dog, which is where he loves to hang out, followed closely by the Estes Park police station. It seems that Bear's frequent "dog at large" treks there have led him into a friendship with the local police.

When business owner Eric is out of town promoting his Gold Medal-winning India Pale Ale, Bear sneaks out to go to the brewery. At age 10 however, "old and slow," he just walks up to the police and "gets arrested" which usually results in a free ride. 🐾

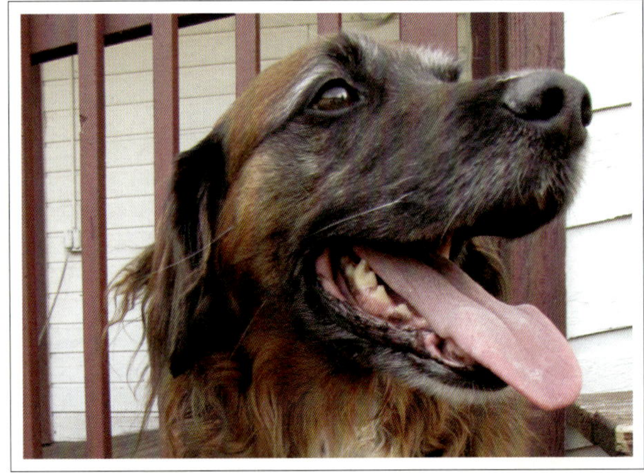

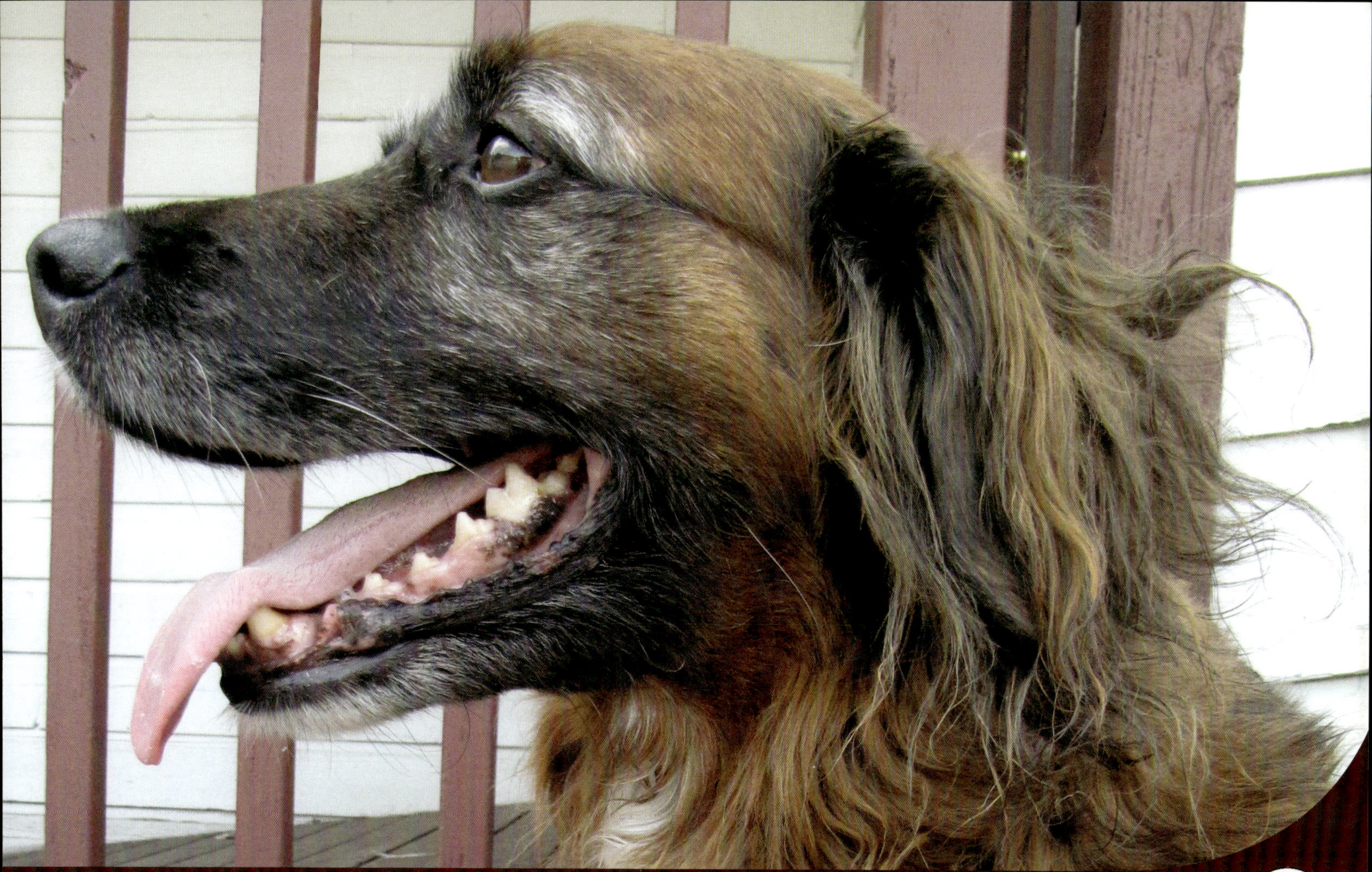

Bear, 10, Collie Mix   Owner: Eric Bratrud

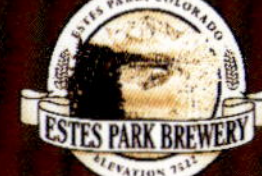

Lucky

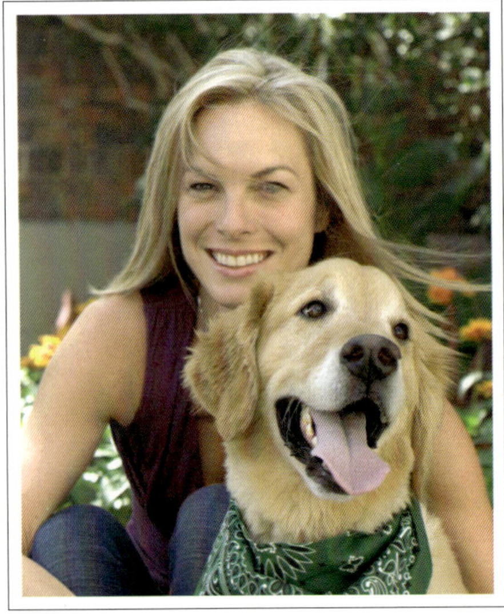

Favorite Treat: Bacon

Most Mischievous Act: Chewed original woodwork

Best Trick: "Staying"

Favorite Hangout: The bed

Founded in 1988

Colorado's oldest brewpub

Produced 4,330 barrels of fresh beer in 1997

Lucky, **the golden Golden from Golden,** Colorado, stays fit running with Jamie, Wynkoop's marketing director, as she rides her bicycle in the abundant open space and trails near their home in Golden. Lucky is a lucky dog because he gets plenty of miles to run with Jamie and husband Bob, who are both avid cyclists. At home, he stays in shape by chasing his tennis ball and hanging out on the bed. 🐾

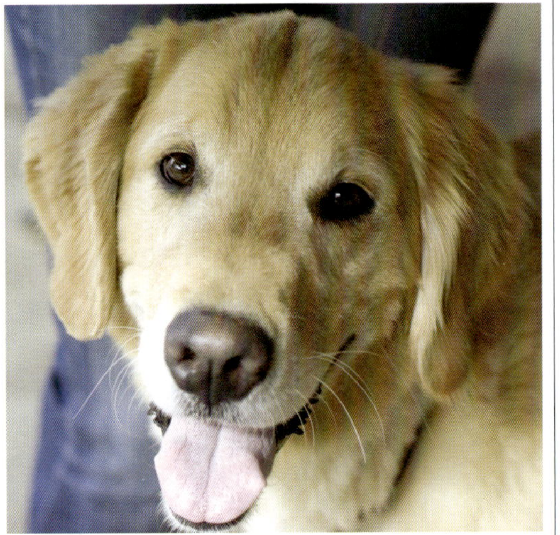

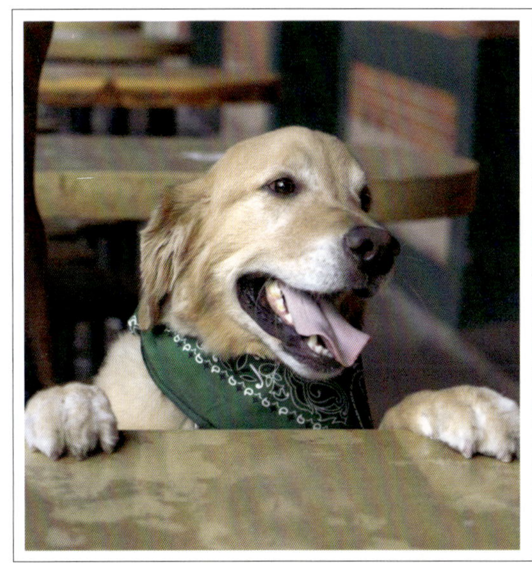

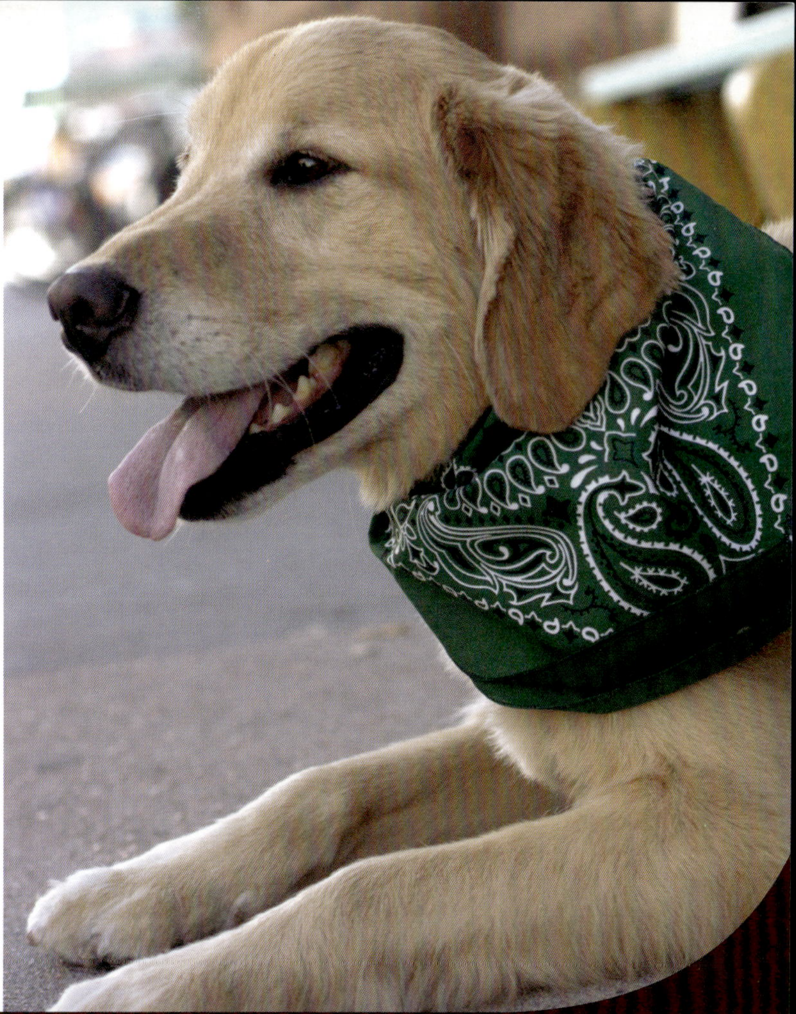

Lucky, 3½, Golden Retriever   Owner: Jamie Webb

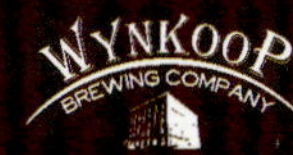

Barley Bear and Maggie Moo

Established October 2005

2009 GABF Best Small Brewing Company award

2009 GABF Brewer of the Year award

GEE! and HAW! are sledding commands that Maggie and Barley know well. When the sled harnesses come out, the excitement begins, and brewer Lachlan McLean has two pals that enjoy back country sledding as much as he. Inseparable friends, Barley and Maggie have different *modus operandi*. Maggie is a chewer and has consumed a deck and couple of chairs, while Barley prefers to beg and steal donuts off the table.

Most Excellent Adventure: Back country sledding

Favorite Hangout: Summer, under the deck; winter, in a snow drift

Best Friend: Anybody with food

Nicknames: Road Block & Mischievous Maggie

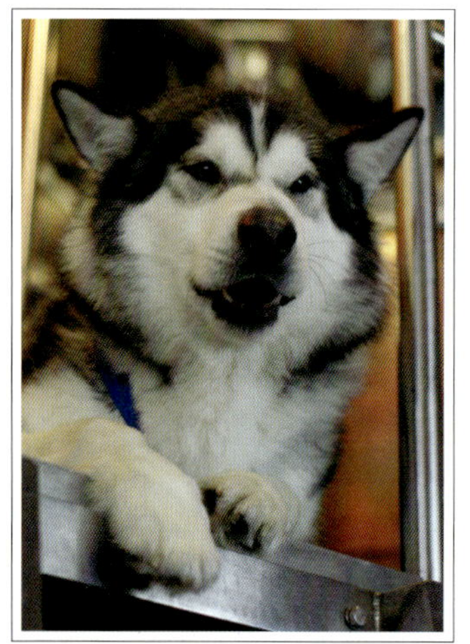

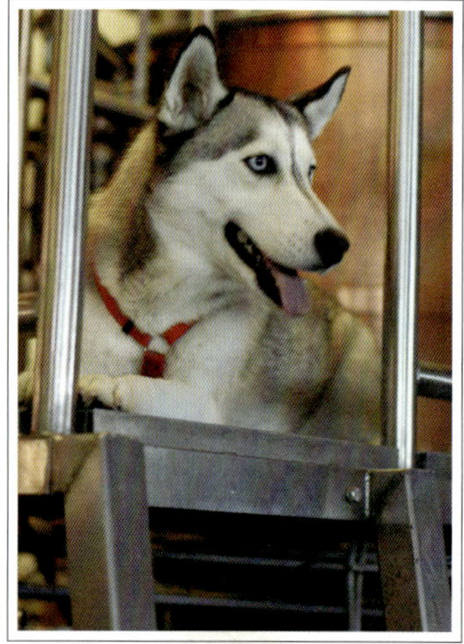

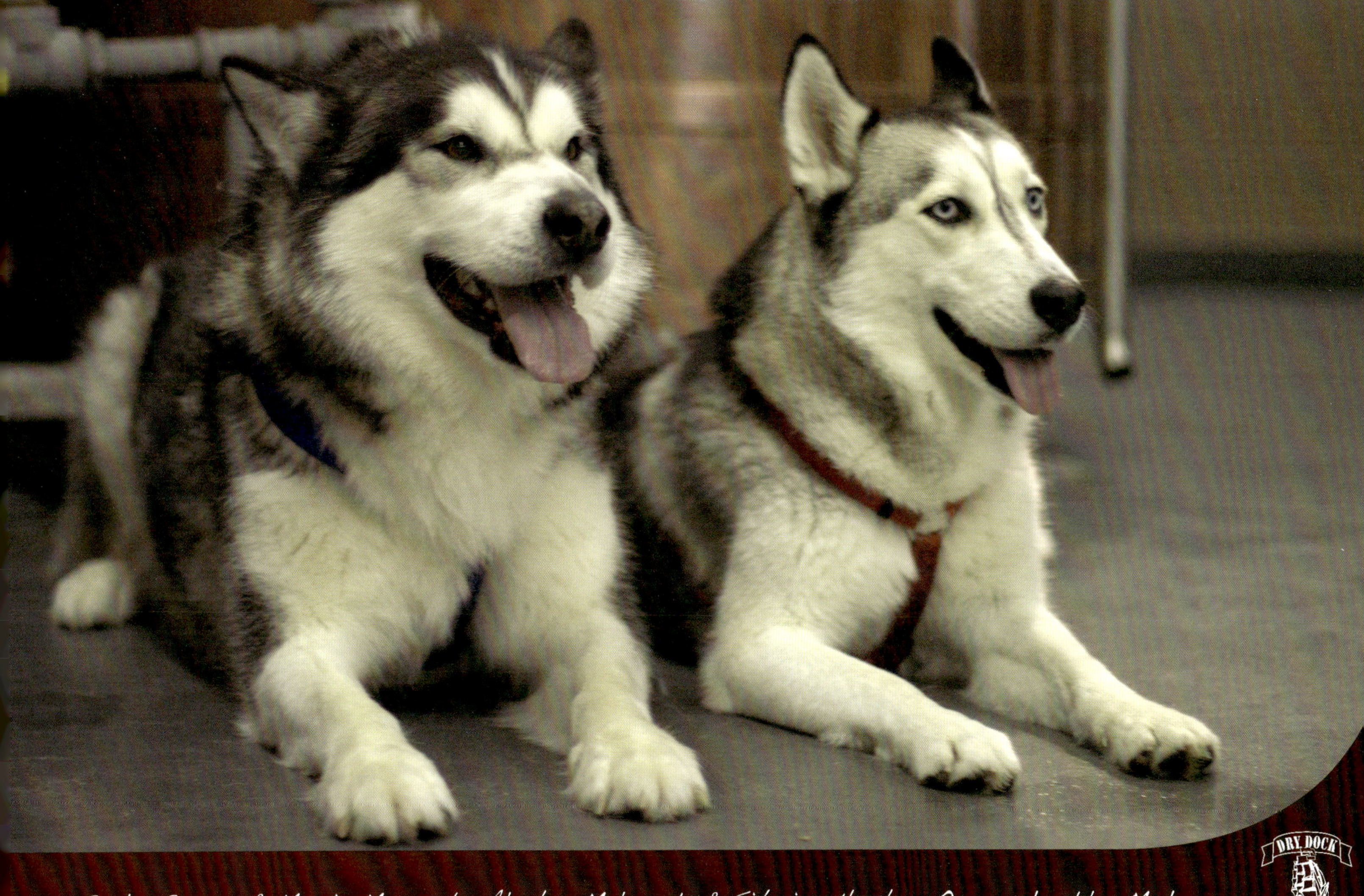

57 Barley Bear, 5 & Maggie Moo, 1½, Alaskan Malamute & Siberian Husky   Owner: Lachlan McLean

Schneider

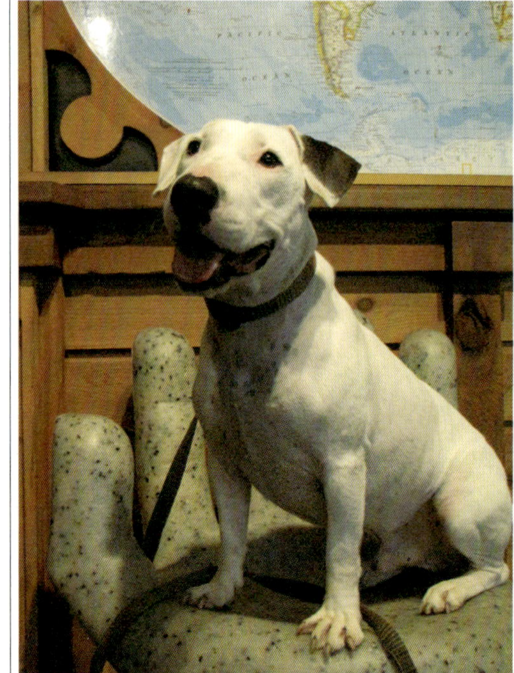

Favorite Food: Raw eggs

Favorite Past Time: Sunbathing (uses sunscreen-prefers SPF30)

Favorite Hangout: Backyard hammock

Annoying Habit: Likes to spoon

Started in 1994

Gold Medal winner first year at Great American Beer Festival

Gold Medal 2009 GABF

Crack an egg, and Schneider comes running. "We can never find our shoes because he throws them around the house," says award-winning brewmaster Ro Guenzel. "I always find my tools and scissors in the backyard." Schneider is also an escape artist, and jumps 6-foot fences to get away. He hates cold weather and in the winter, he has to be forced outside for his morning constitutional. 🐾

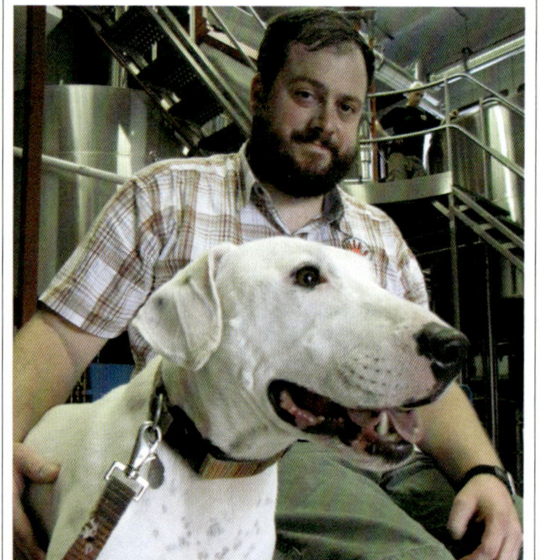

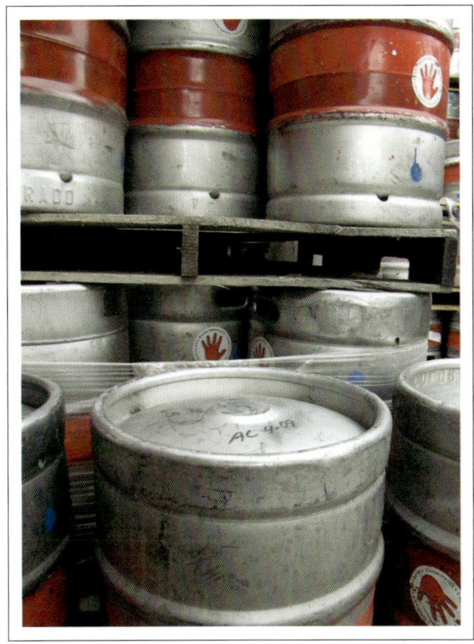

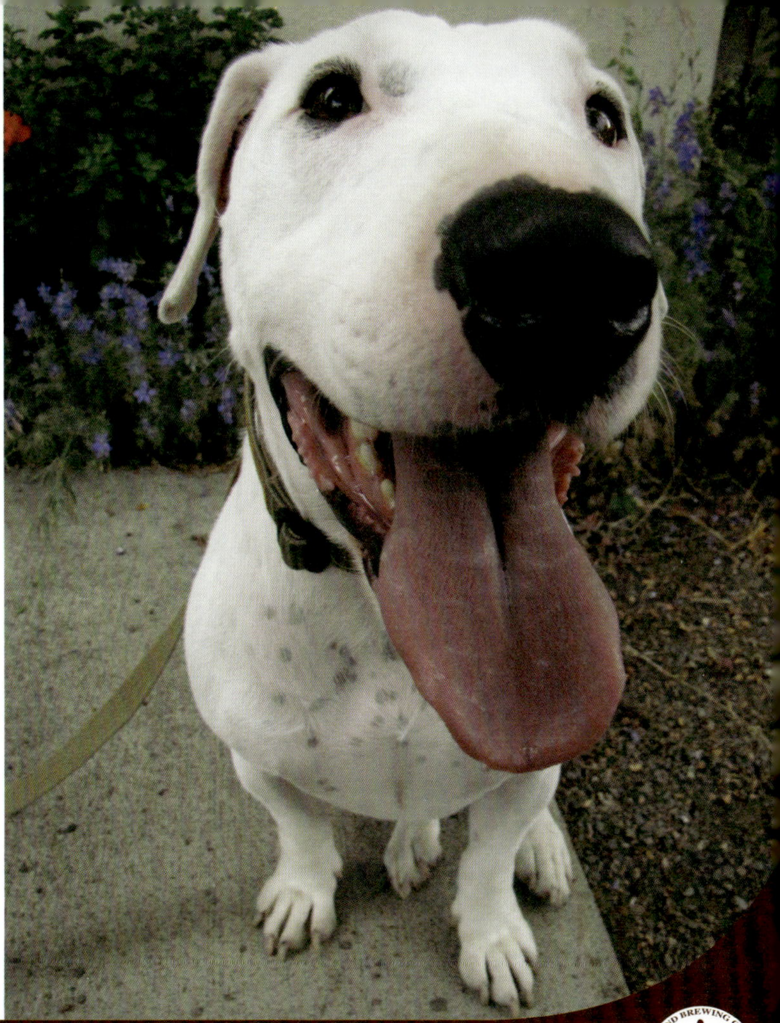

Schneider, 5, Jack Russell/Bull Terrier   Owner: Ro Guenzel

Lacey Gray

Opened 1993

Located in historic 1901 Cheyenne Building

Annual production: 2,800 barrels

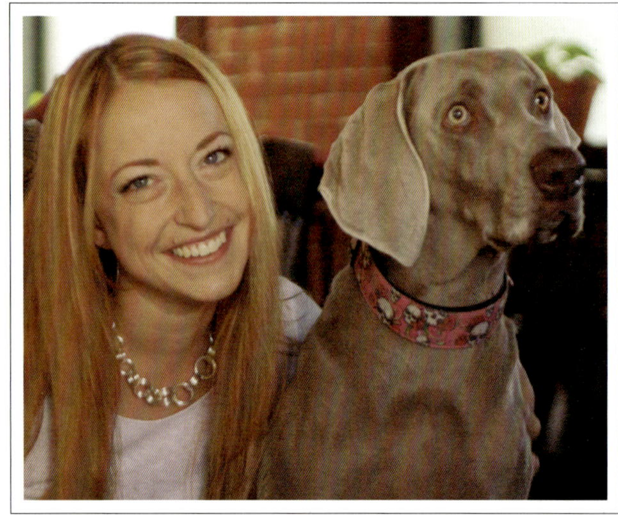

Best Adventure: Finishing a 5.5-mile hike (not a hiker)

Favorite Hangout: Sofa

Favorite Pastime: Sleeping (under the covers)

Favorite Sport: Billiards at Phantom Canyon (not really)

"**L**acey's ears were so long** as a puppy, they had to be pinned up to to keep them out of her dog bowl," remembers Heather, manager at Phantom Canyon. She's grown into them now, and goes for more fashionable accessories. Lacey is a model at heart, and will let Heather dress her up to pose for pictures. She has a taste for the finer things, and once ate an entire box of chocolates, which resulted in an emergency trip to the vet. Lacey loves to sleep under the covers, keeping them warm, and is described by Heather as "the best dog ever." 🐾

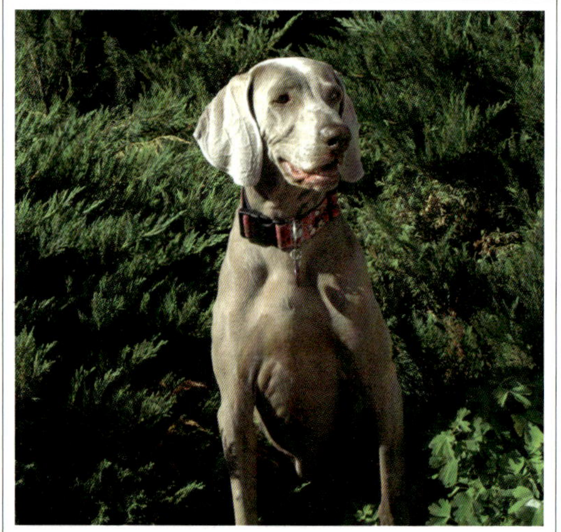

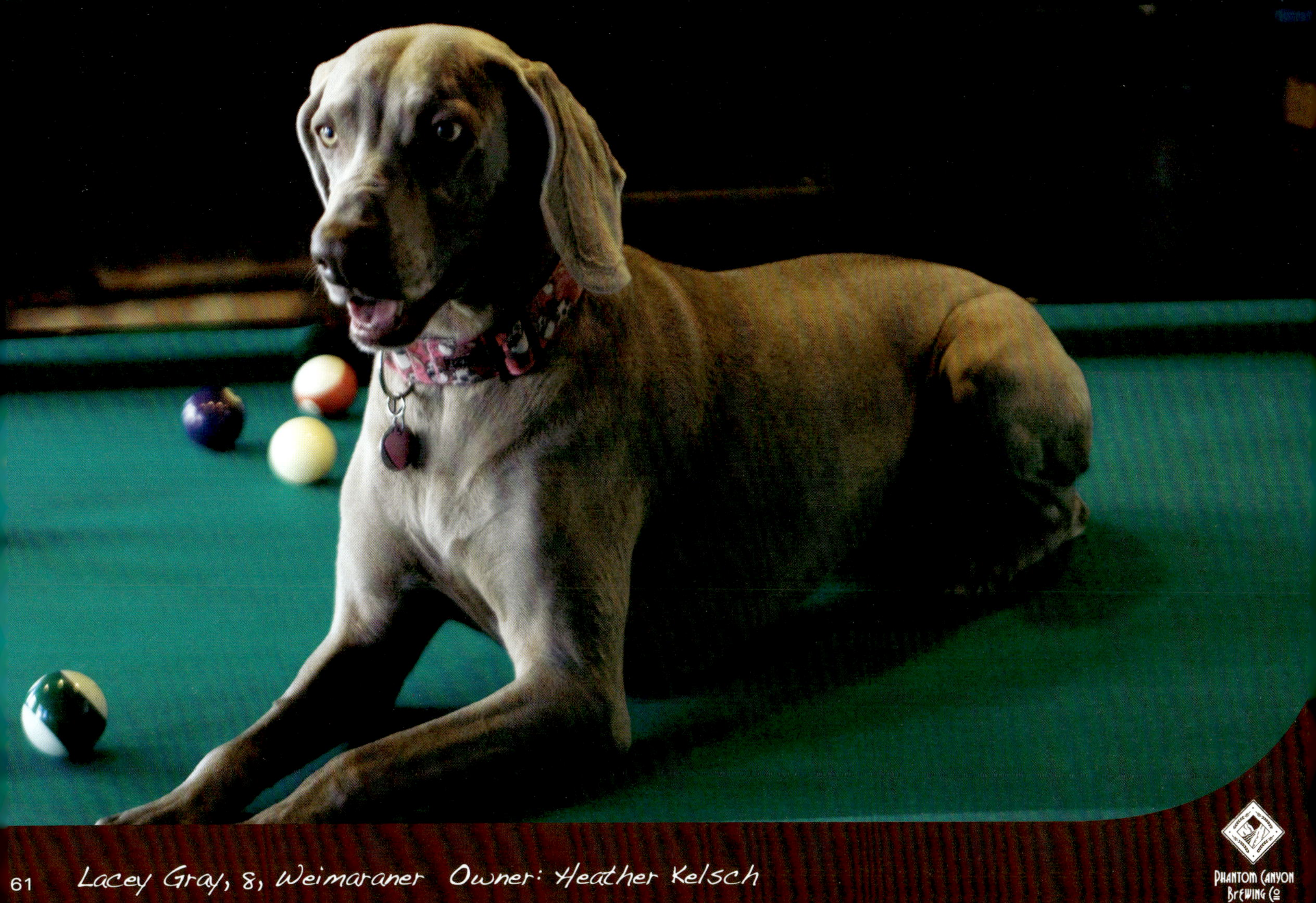

61 *Lacey Gray, 8, Weimaraner Owner: Heather Kelsch*

Allee

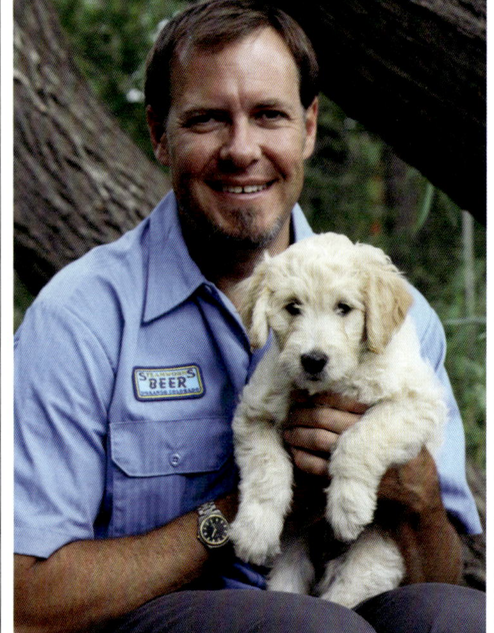

Best Trick: The Triple Lindy

Favorite Hangout: Steamworks, of course

Favorite Treat: Peanuts

Annoying Habit: Chewing on everything

Opened in September 1996

Steamworks refurbished an automotive building that was built in 1920, giving it an industrial-chic look

Added Bayfield branch in 2005, which expanded the brewing capacity threefold

"**A**llee is a Gemini** who loves people, other dogs and Colorado," says Kris Oyler, CEO of Steamworks Brewing Company. At eight-weeks-old, she already has a mind of her own. She prefers to make friends by licking people's toes and stealing kids' sand toys at the lake, a technique that seems to work for her. Full of energy, Allee shows off by performing somersaults while chasing her tail. She will nibble on anything and loves belly-rubs. 🐾

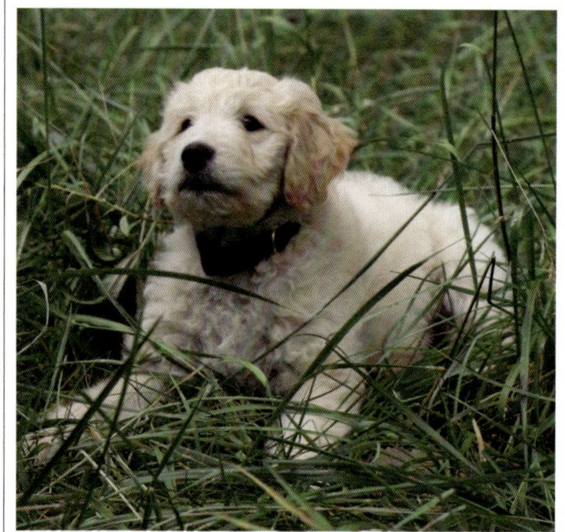

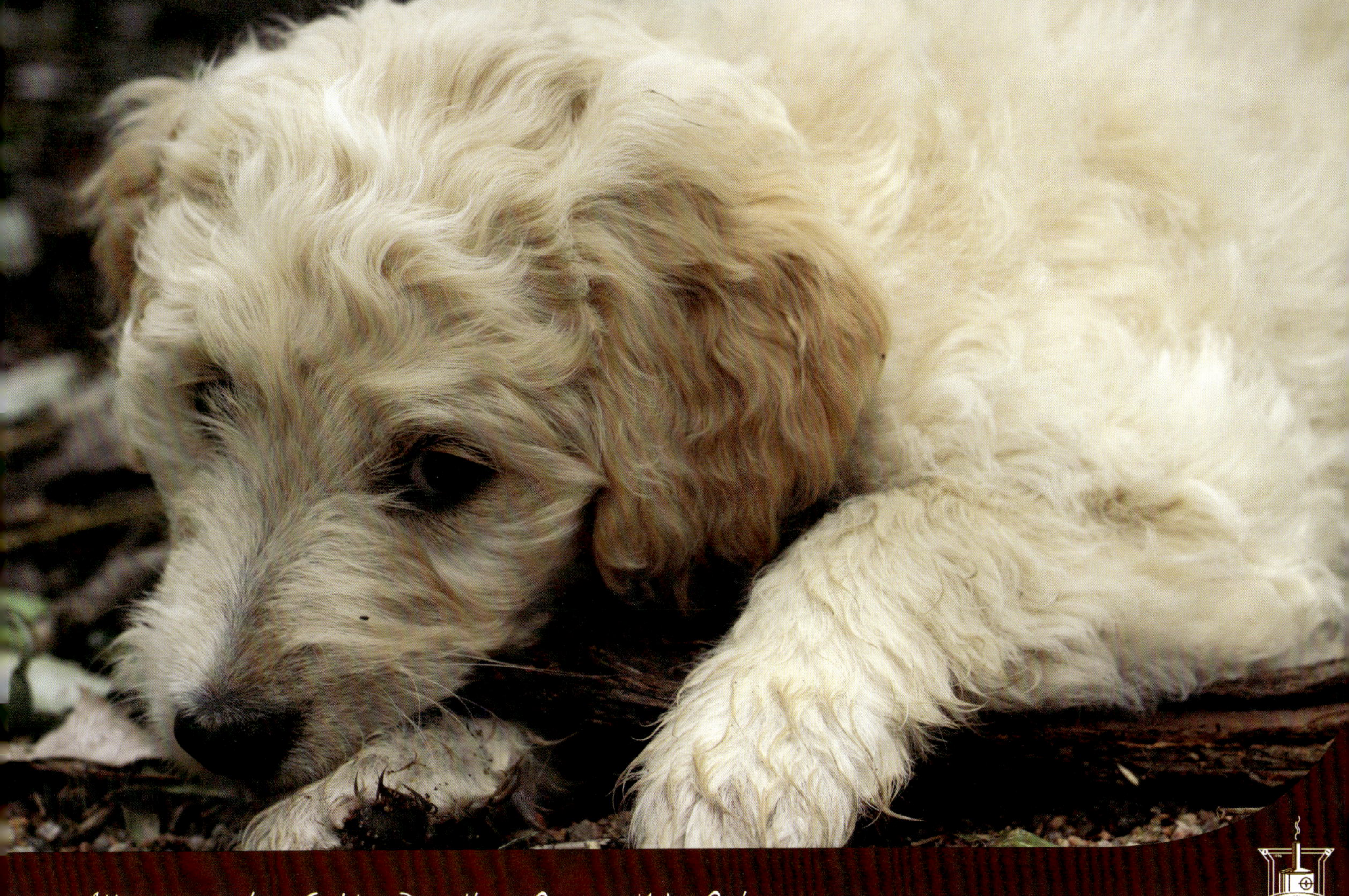

Allee, 8 weeks, Golden Doodle   Owner: Kris Oyler

Guinness

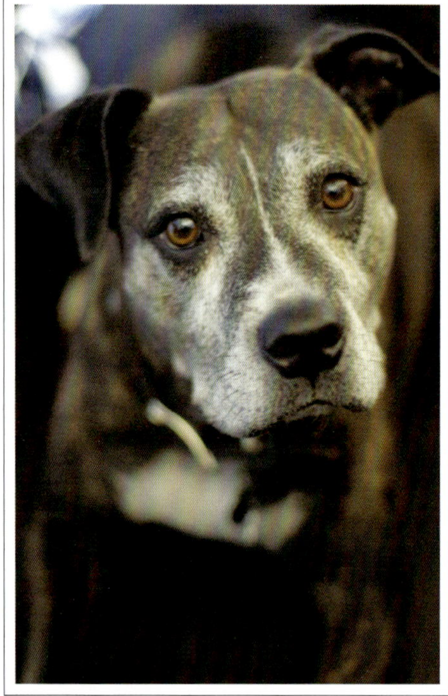

Favorite Toy: Rope with knots

Favorite Food: Anything off of the floor

Funny Habit: Escaping from kennel

Greatest Accomplishment: Destroying five chairs in one year

13 Great American Beer Festival medals and 4 World Beer Cup awards

Established in 1994

Historic Lower Downtown (LoDo) Location

Extreme is the theme that earns Brew Ninja Allen Johnson's reluctant admiration of Guinness' capabilities. Chewing on things, eating anything that hits the floor and displaying a keen ability for escapism are just a few of her more notable skills. Allen also notes that Guinness is not a middle-of-the-road dog. "She's either completely chill or hyper—no in between." When not engaged in these questionable activities, Guinness occupies her favorite hangout: right under Allen's feet.

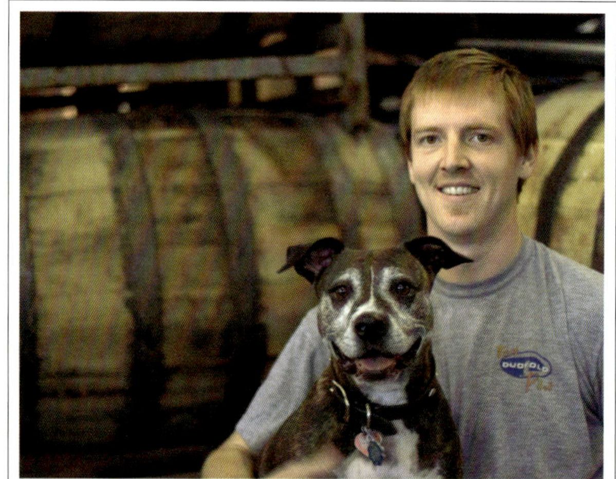

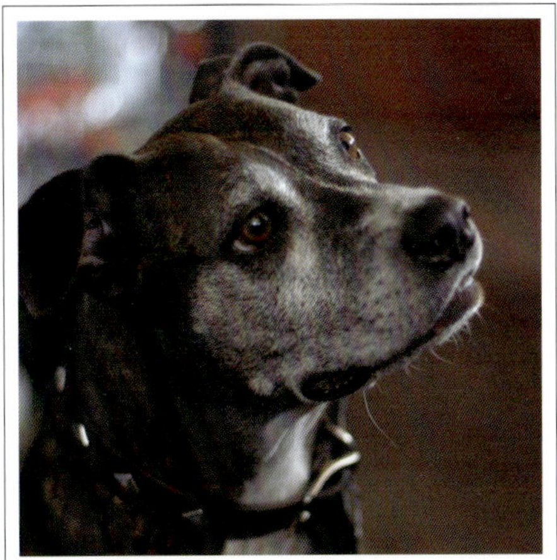

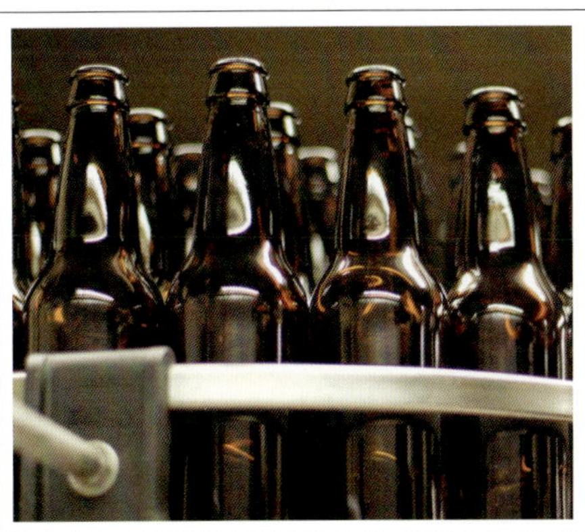

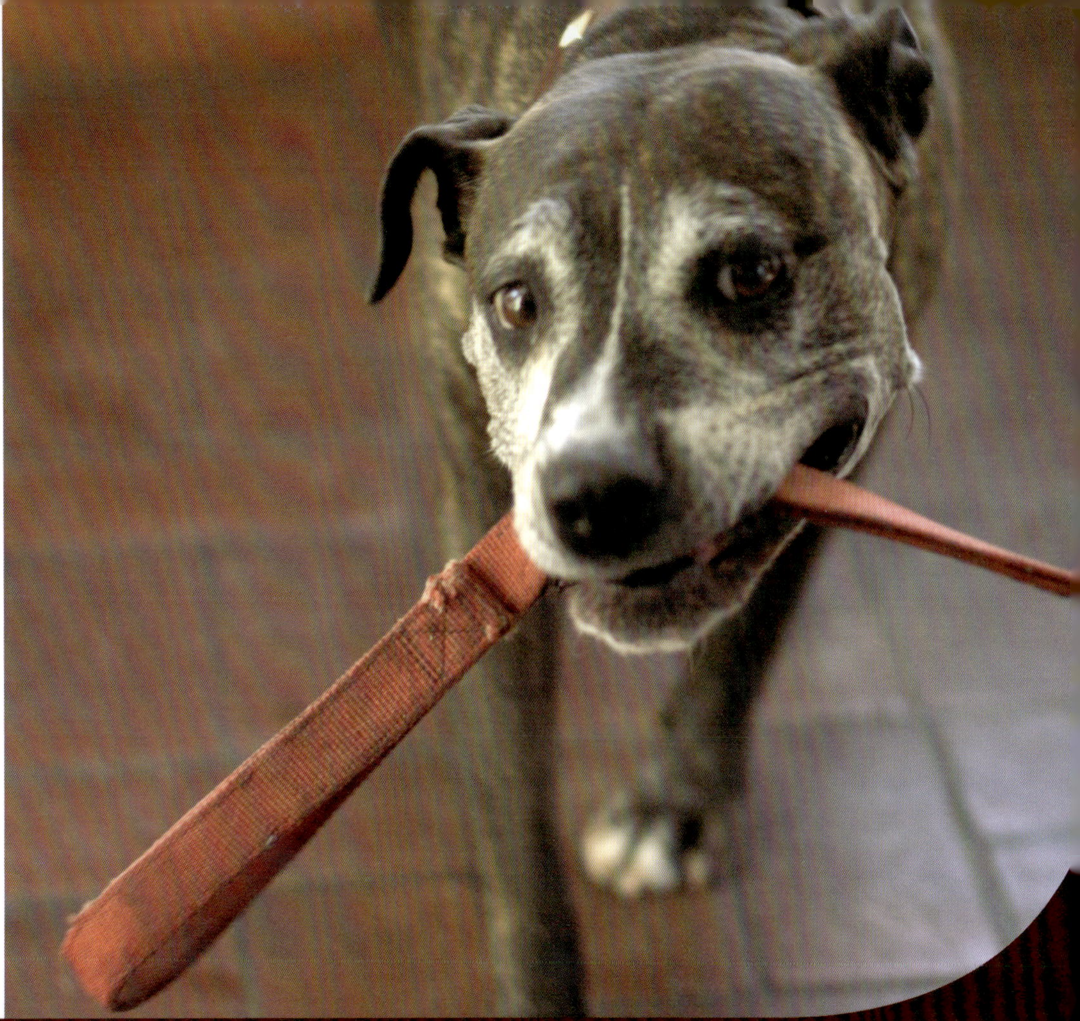

Guinness, 6, Bull Terrier Mix   Owner: Allen Johnson

GREAT DIVIDE BREWING CO

Whiskey

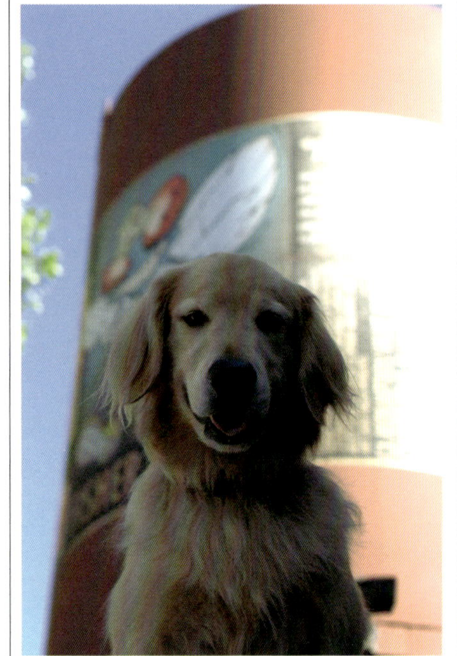

Sold first beer in December 1997

Fly Fisher Ale is an award winner

Beers are named after sports enjoyed in the Colorado mountains

Whiskey is a Southern transplant from New Orleans, and moved to Colorado because his asthma couldn't handle the heat and humidity. Brewery owner Jim Errant notes that Whiskey is a very people-oriented, very "human" sort of dog and a true homebody who really enjoys lounging. He sometimes covets other dog's toys, but Whiskey has a technique to get them. He will grab a toy from his basket, take it to the other dog, paw theirs away and push the new toy toward them. Everyone is happy. 🐾

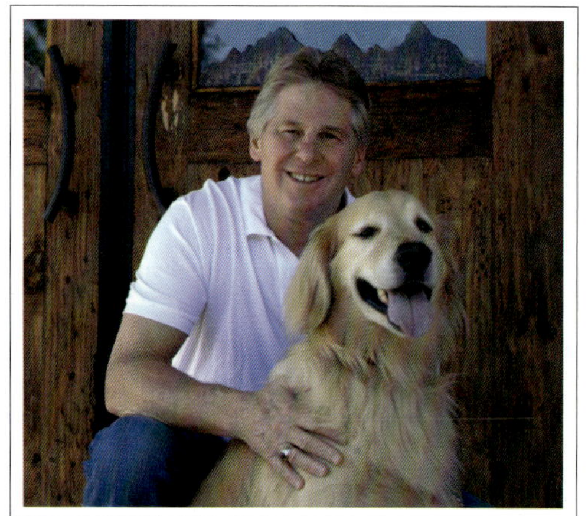

Greatest Achievement: Once ate a cell phone

Favorite Hobby: Swimming in the pond

Best Trick: A "phenomenal" catcher

Hangout: The theatre recliner chair to watch movies with the family

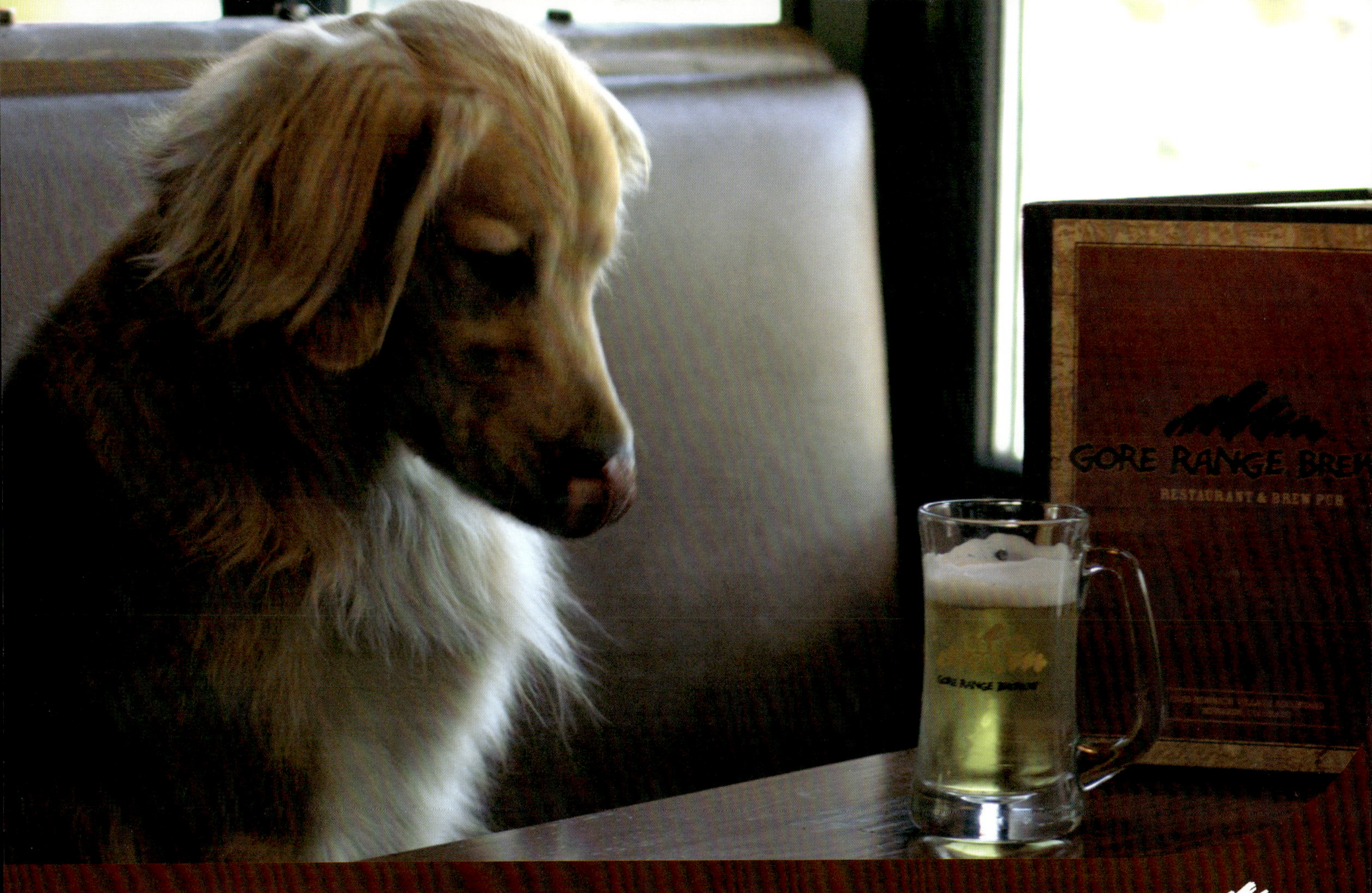

67 Whiskey, 5, Golden Retriever   Owner: Jim Errant

Ella

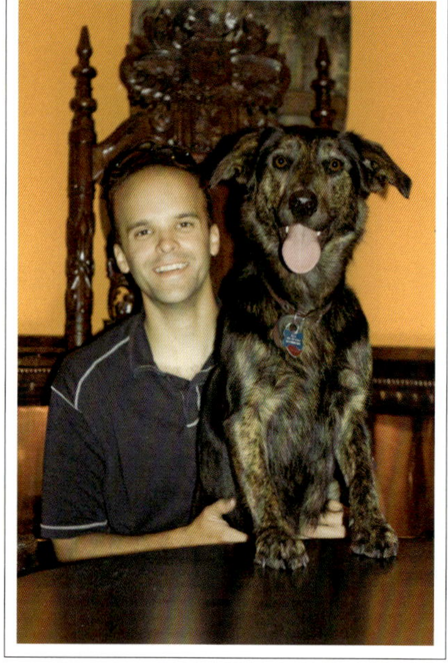

Naughtiest Deed: Eating squirrels

Favorite Hangout: Under the bed

Most Excellent Adventure: Mountain biking in Moab

Gets Excited About: Dinner

Began bottling in 1993

Out of Bounds Stout was a Gold Medal winner at GABF in 1994

Brews over 20 different ales

High five Ella and she will gladly slap paw to hand with anyone. Running shoes never stay in the back of the closet, because Ella drops them by the front door to motivate her owners. Ted Whitney brewed his first batch of beer in the dorms while a student at the University of Colorado---not a bad way to meet your neighbors. He now enjoys selling great Colorado microbrew professionally, and of course, he knows his product well. 🐾

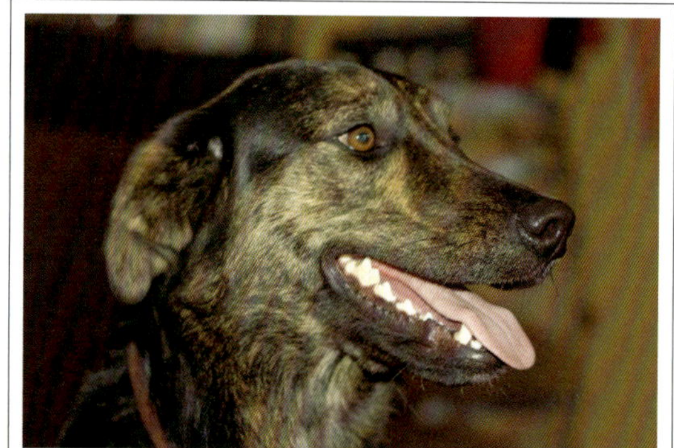

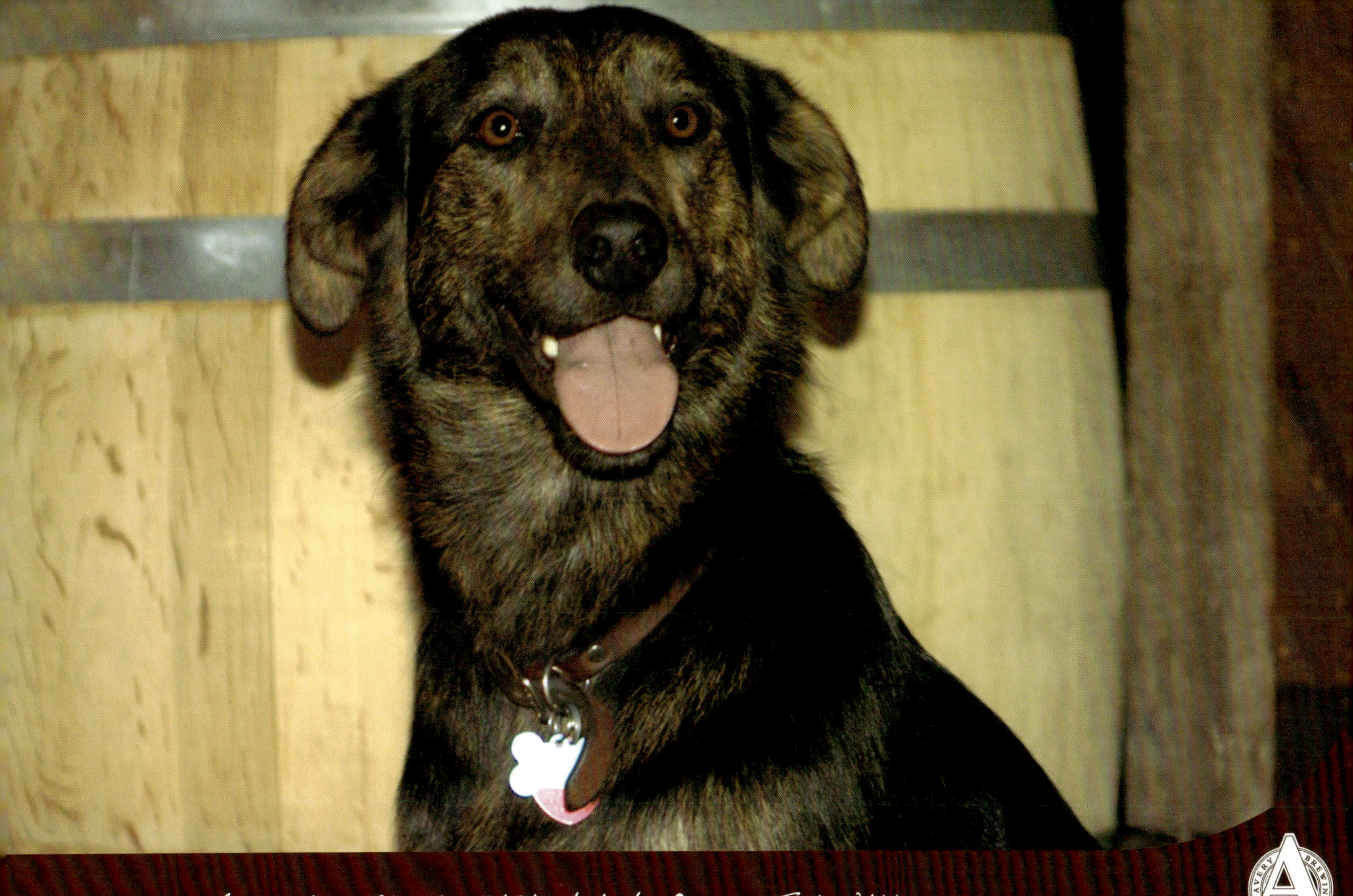

Ella, 2½, Australian Shepherd/Black Lab Owner: Ted Whitney

Mala and Jager

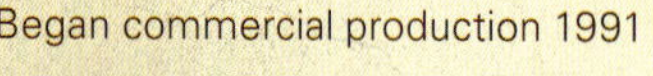

Began commercial production 1991

Silver Medal 2009 GABF

Wind-powered electricity since 1999

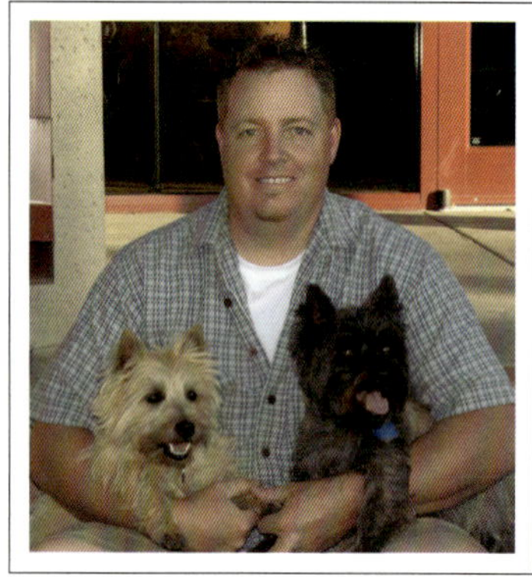

Mala

Funny Habit: Howls like a wolf

Best Friend: Jager

Favorite Toy: Golf ball

Mischievous Act: Hides clothing under bed

Jager

Best Trick: Plays dead

Favorite pastime: Lying in the sun

Best Friend: Mala

Annoying Habit: Gets impatient and starts crying

She climbs trees trying to catch squirrels. In fact, she has been a climber since she was a pup, scaling her baby gate barrier with ease. Fair-haired Mala does have a stubborn streak, owner V.J. Hartman observes. Her naughtiest deed, (or perhaps from Mala's point of view, greatest accomplishment) is the time she dug up a sprinkler line, including the head as a bonus. She loves her family and is always an enthusiastic greeter when they return home. 🐾

It's an obsession. . .with stuffed animals, and Jager wants them all for himself. V.J. Hartman, New Belgium's lead mechanical technician, recalls the time when Jager ripped open all the gifts at a family baby shower, because they contained stuffed animals! With a gleam of focused determination in his eyes, he will stop at nothing to snatch, capture and steal one more to add to his collection. Our photographer discovered this firsthand, when Jager sprang from nowhere in an attempt to wrestle away the stuffed frog prop from her grasp. 🐾

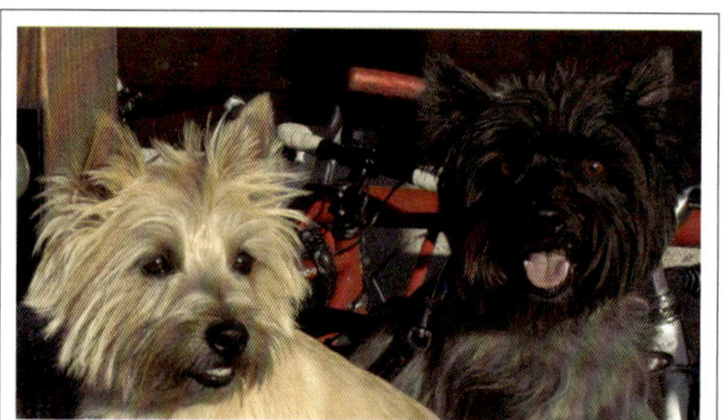

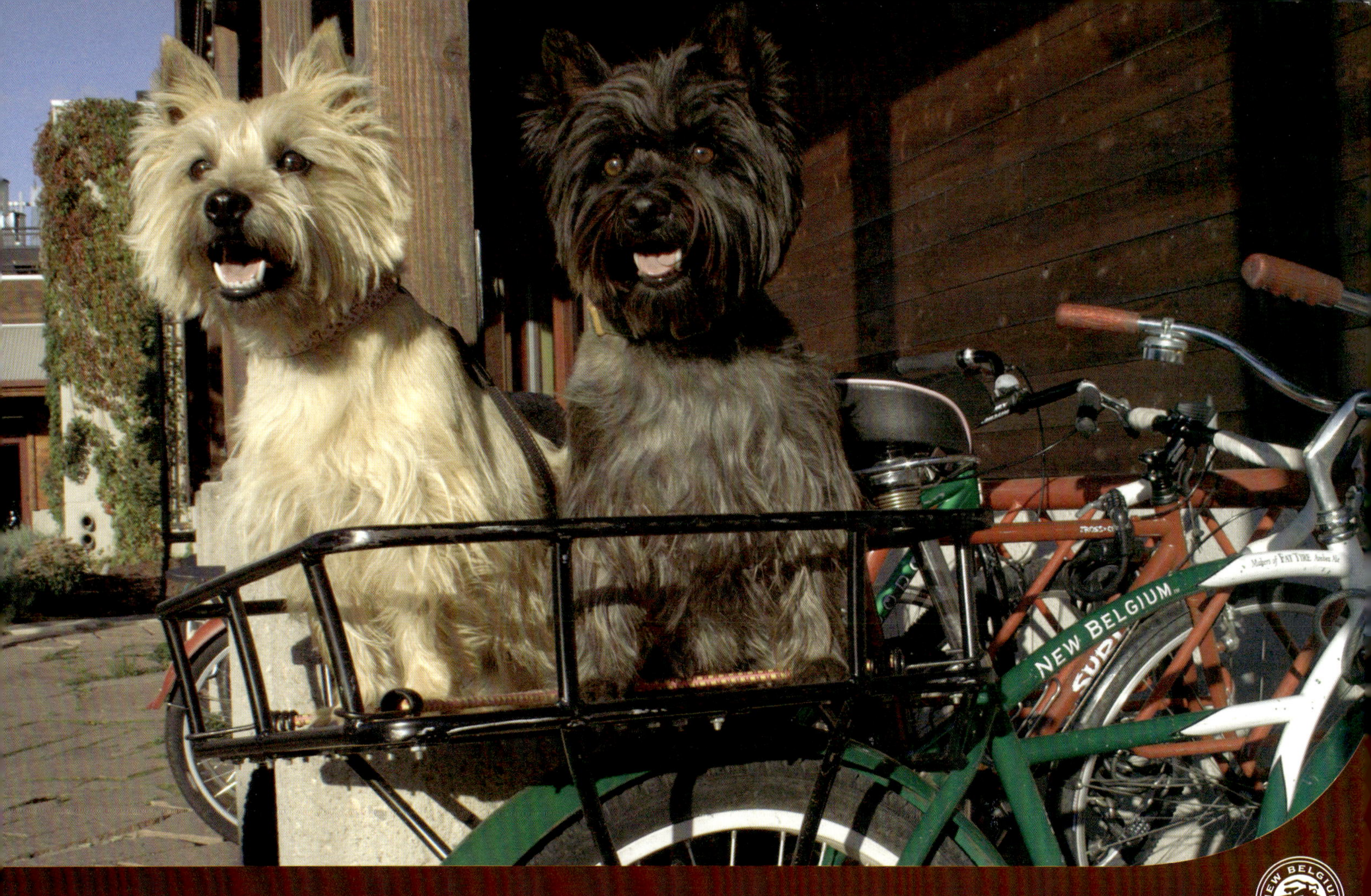

71 Mala, 3 & Jager, 5, Cairn Terriers   Owner: V.J. Hartman

"We realize brewing a fine beer isn't exactly nuclear physics...

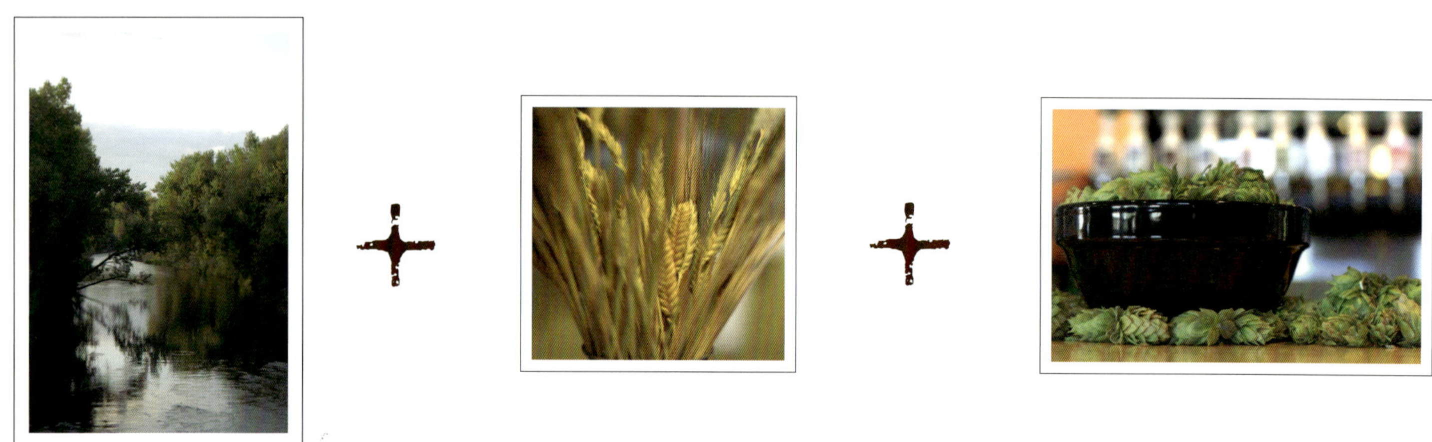

it's something far more important."

Bob Baile, Twisted Pine Brewing Company

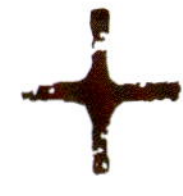

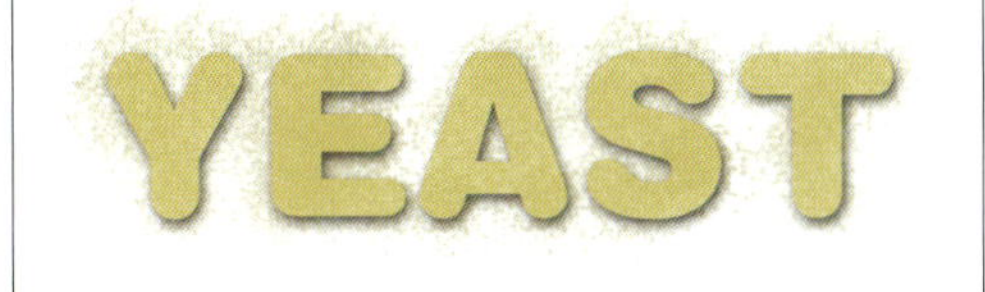

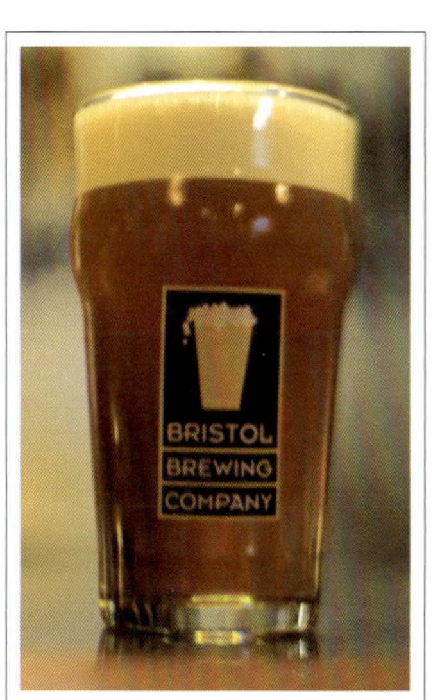

Halifax (Hali)

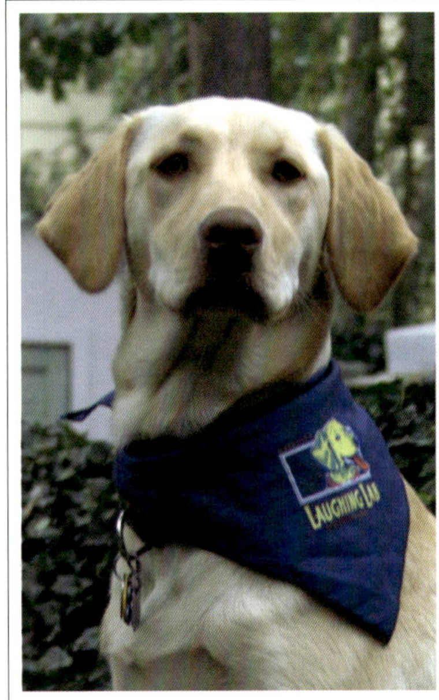

Best Friend: Camden

Favorite Pastime: Likes to run alongside mountain bike

Favorite Toy: Frisbee or rubber tire

Naughtiest Deed: Chewed up a vintage Blues festival poster

Founded in 1994

Over 20 proprietary brews

Silver at the 2009 GABF

Can there ever be another Laughing Lab? No one is talking, but Hali might be an heir apparent. Just seven months old, she is full of energy, but (the original Laughing Lab) Camden, 14 years her senior, "keeps her in line," says Mike Bristol, founder of the Bristol Brewing Company. With a growing family, it makes sense to have two "Laughing Labs." 🐾

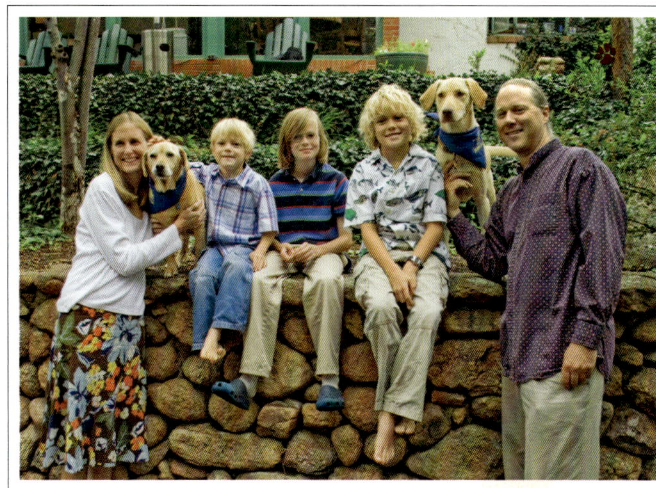

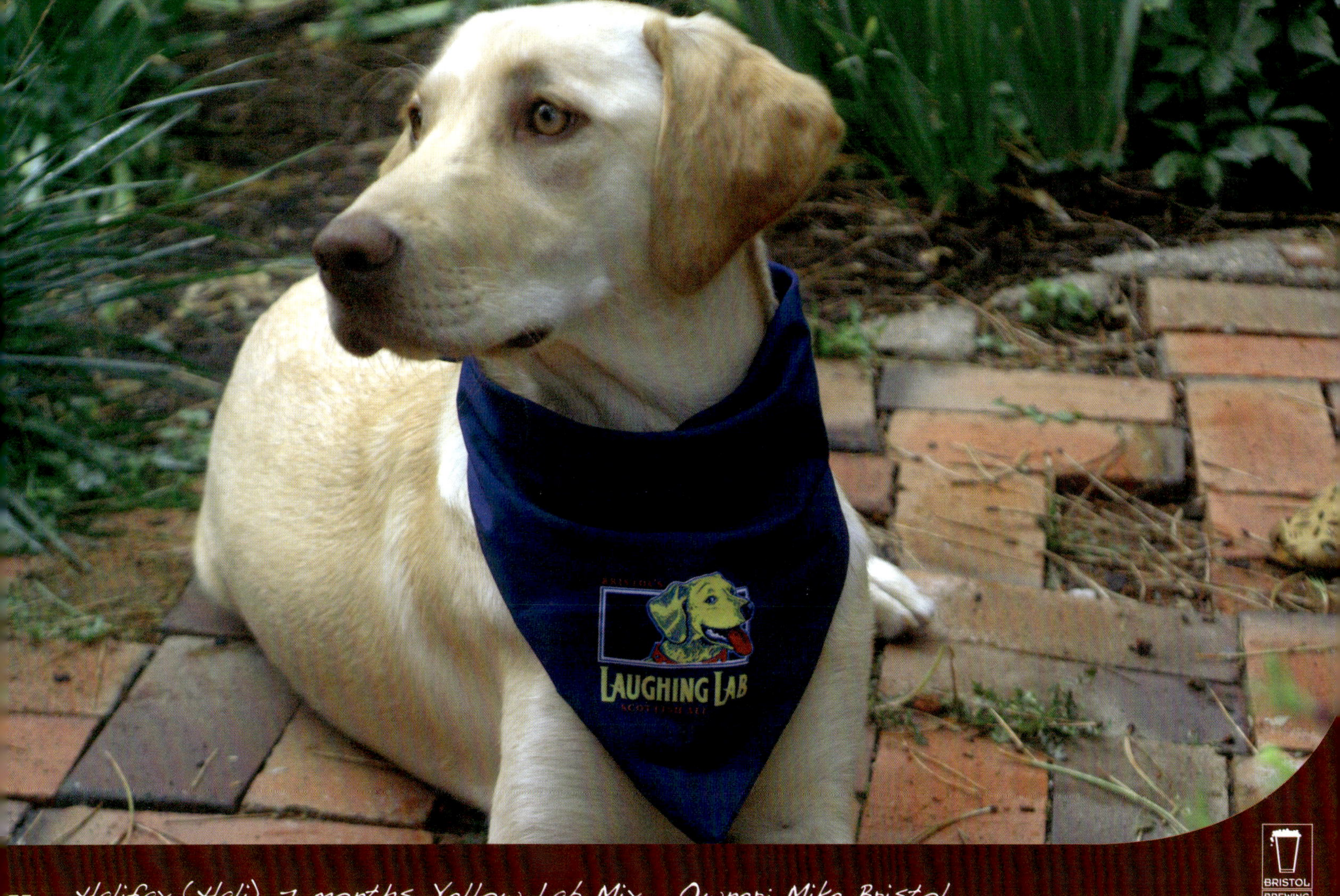

75 Halifax (Hali), 7 months, Yellow Lab Mix   Owner: Mike Bristol

BRISTOL BREWING COMPANY

George

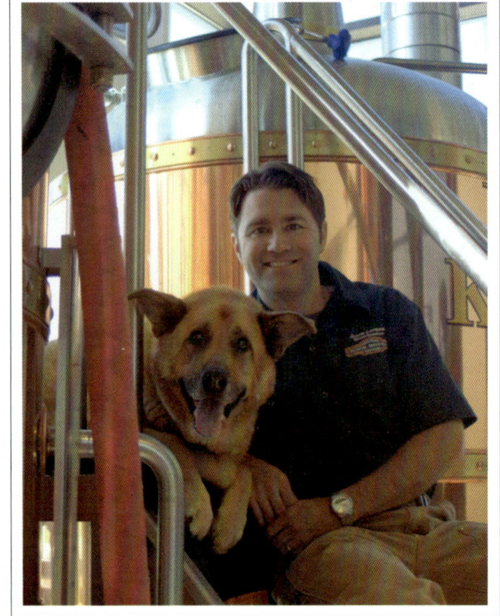

Colorado Springs location opened in January 2006

Rock Bottom Foundation supports hunger relief efforts

3 Gold Medals Colorado State Fair 2009

Retired frisbee catcher George has been a large part of brewmaster Jason Leeman's family. After ACL surgery, George has slowed down, but is still a youngster in spirit. He once rode shotgun on a non-stop motorhome trip from Boston to Colorado without sleeping. Constantly on guard, he is the family's protector, and when Jason puts the kennel in the pick-up, he knows an adventure is in the works. ❖

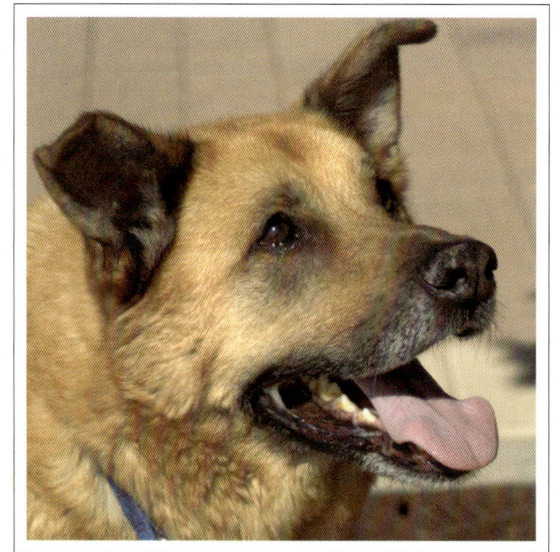

Best Friend/Accomplice: Ferris the cat (now deceased)

Best Trick: Playing tag with children

Favorite Pastime: Herding children

Naughtiest Deed: Opening screen door to let cats escape – net: two lost cats

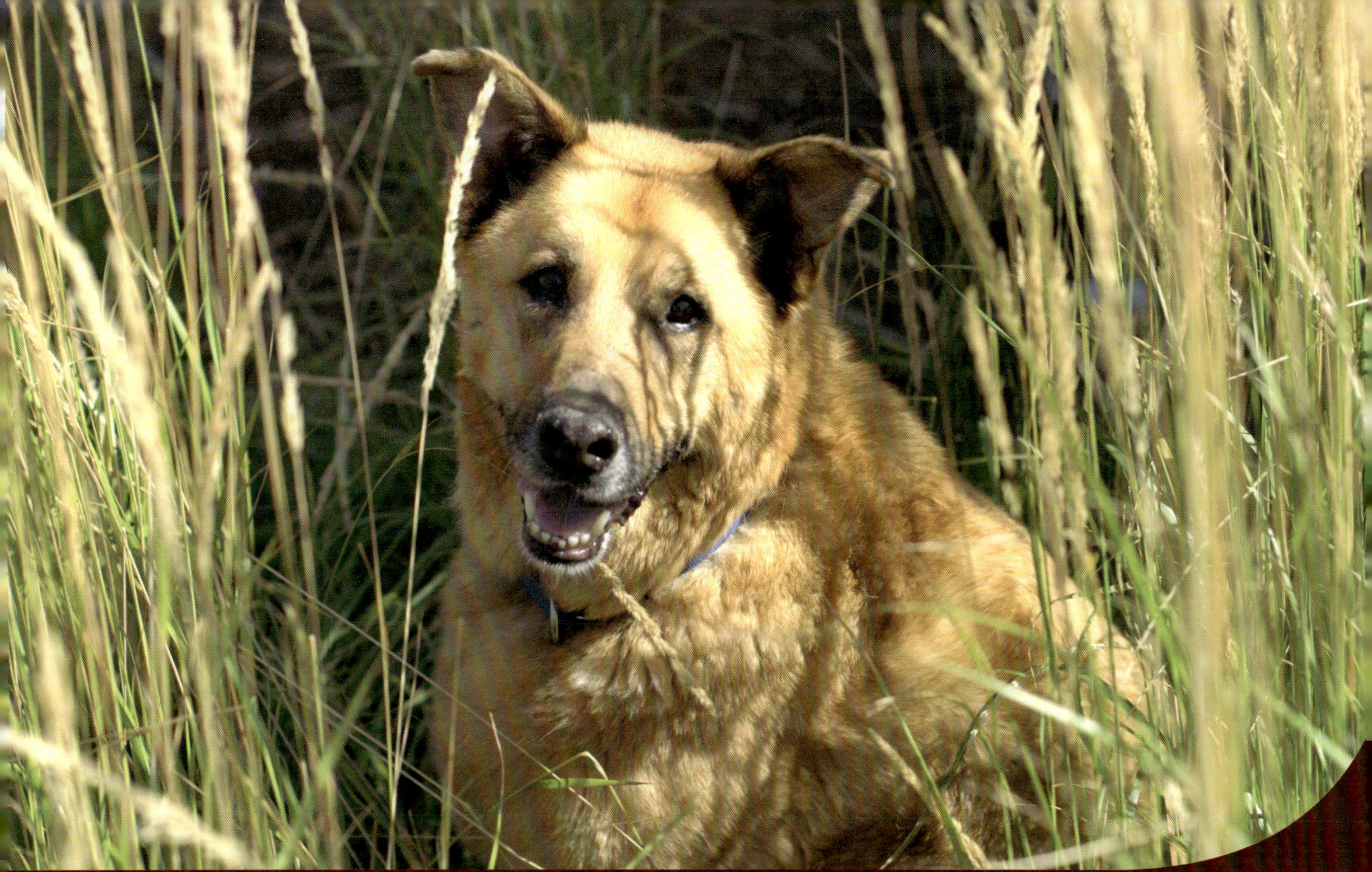

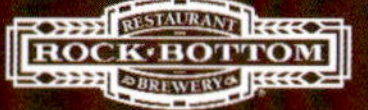

 George, 9, Shepherd Mix Owner: Jason Leeman

Blue and Bailey

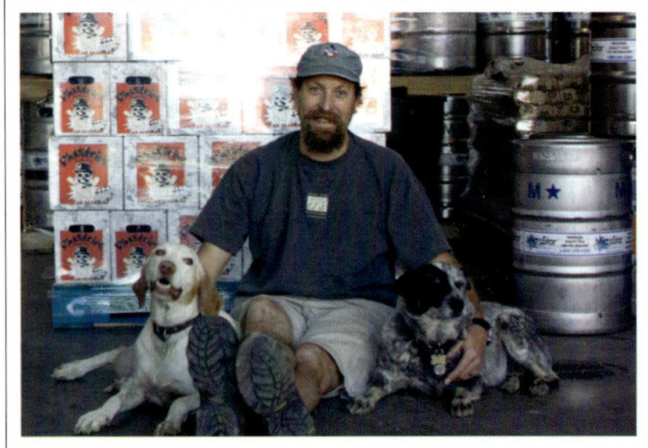

Best Friend/Accomplice: Each other

Pastime/Hobby: Bailey runs and Blue tries to herd her

Favorite Toy: Blue likes a stuffed squirrel; Bailey likes a squeaky toy

Naughtiest Deed: Blue got into the groceries on the way home; Bailey ran away all day

Founded 1997

2008 expanded into new 24,000 sq. foot production facility

Silver Medal 2009 GABF for "Buster Nut" Brown Ale

A **picnic by the river would** suit Blue and Bailey just fine. Blue's favorite treat is hot dogs, and Bailey loves potato chips and peanuts. Both are swimmers and their favorite hangout, of course, is the park by the Animas River that runs through Durango. That suits Bill, one of SKA's three co-founders, just fine too, since he loves to fish. At home, both are guard dogs. Blue guards Bill's two-year-old, while Bailey watches the chicken coop.

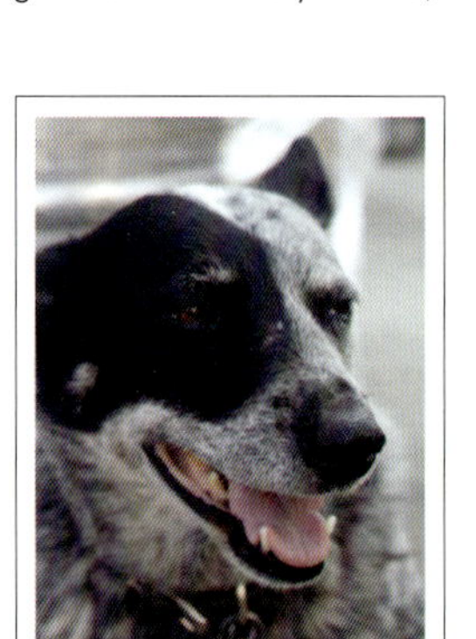

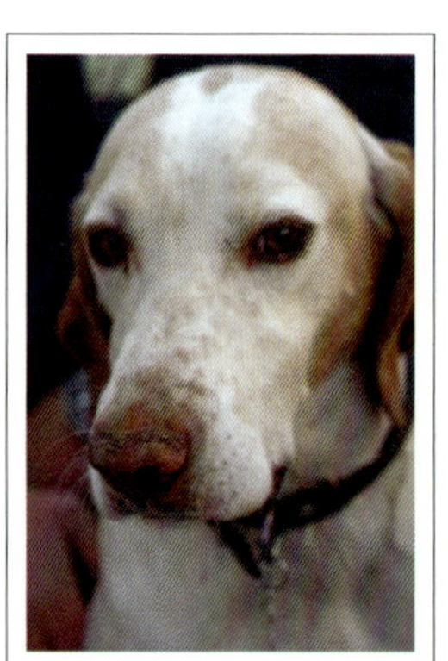

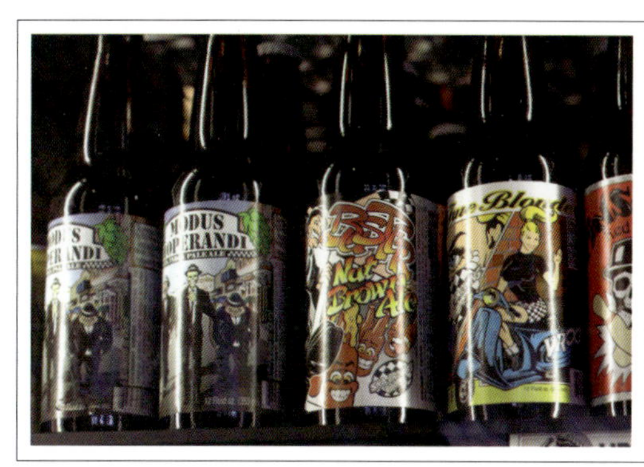

 Blue, 11 & Bailey, 7, Blue Heeler & English Pointer   Owner: Bill Graham

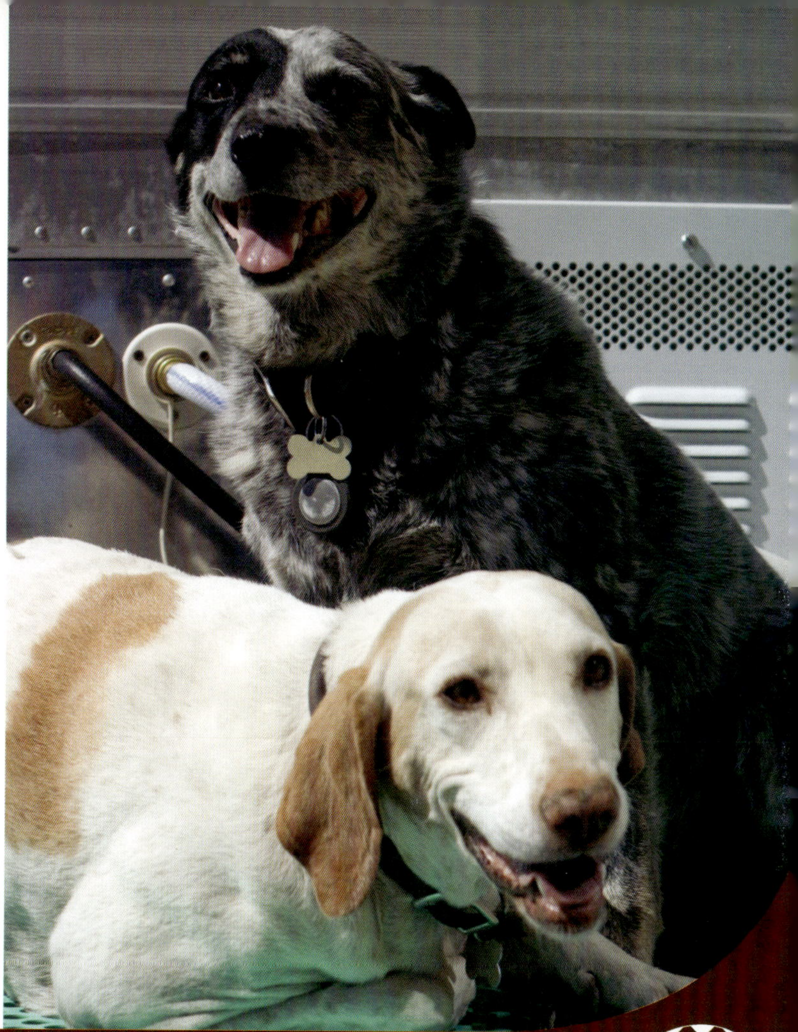

Reilly

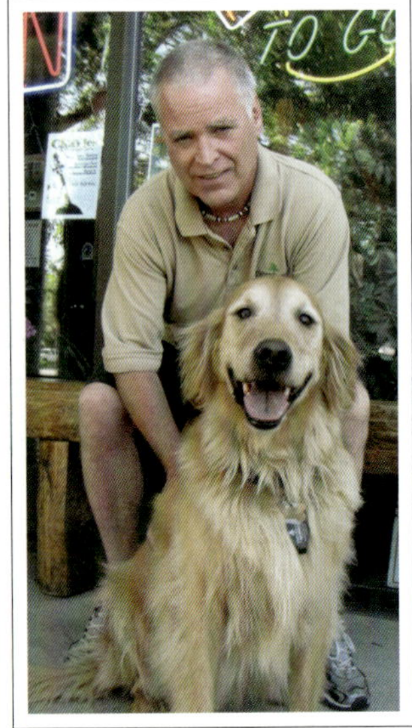

Favorite Treat: Carrots

Best Trick: Sit

Gets Excited About: Squirrels

Best Friend: Bob

Established in 1995

Merged with Peak to Peak Brewing in 1996

Won several awards at the Great American Beer Festival

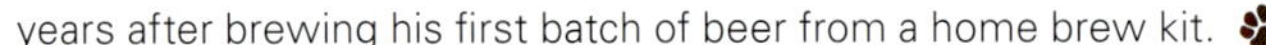

A squirrel's worst nightmare is Reilly the Backyard Predator, who actually brings his trophies home. Most of the time, however, he just likes hanging out at the brewery with his best friend, brewmaster Bob Baile, "It's a hobby gone wild," says Bob, who founded Twisted Pine in 1995, just two years after brewing his first batch of beer from a home brew kit. 🐾

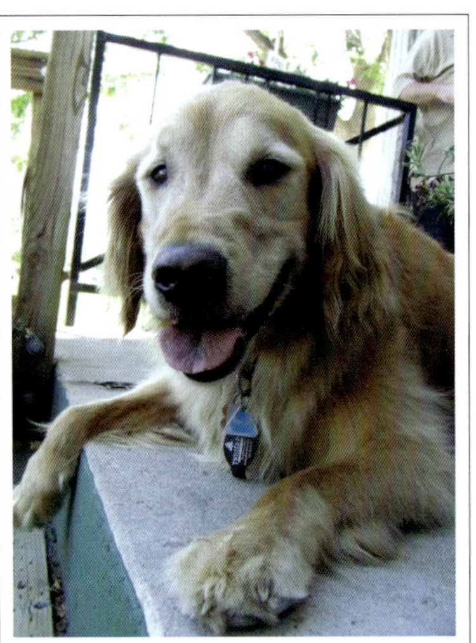

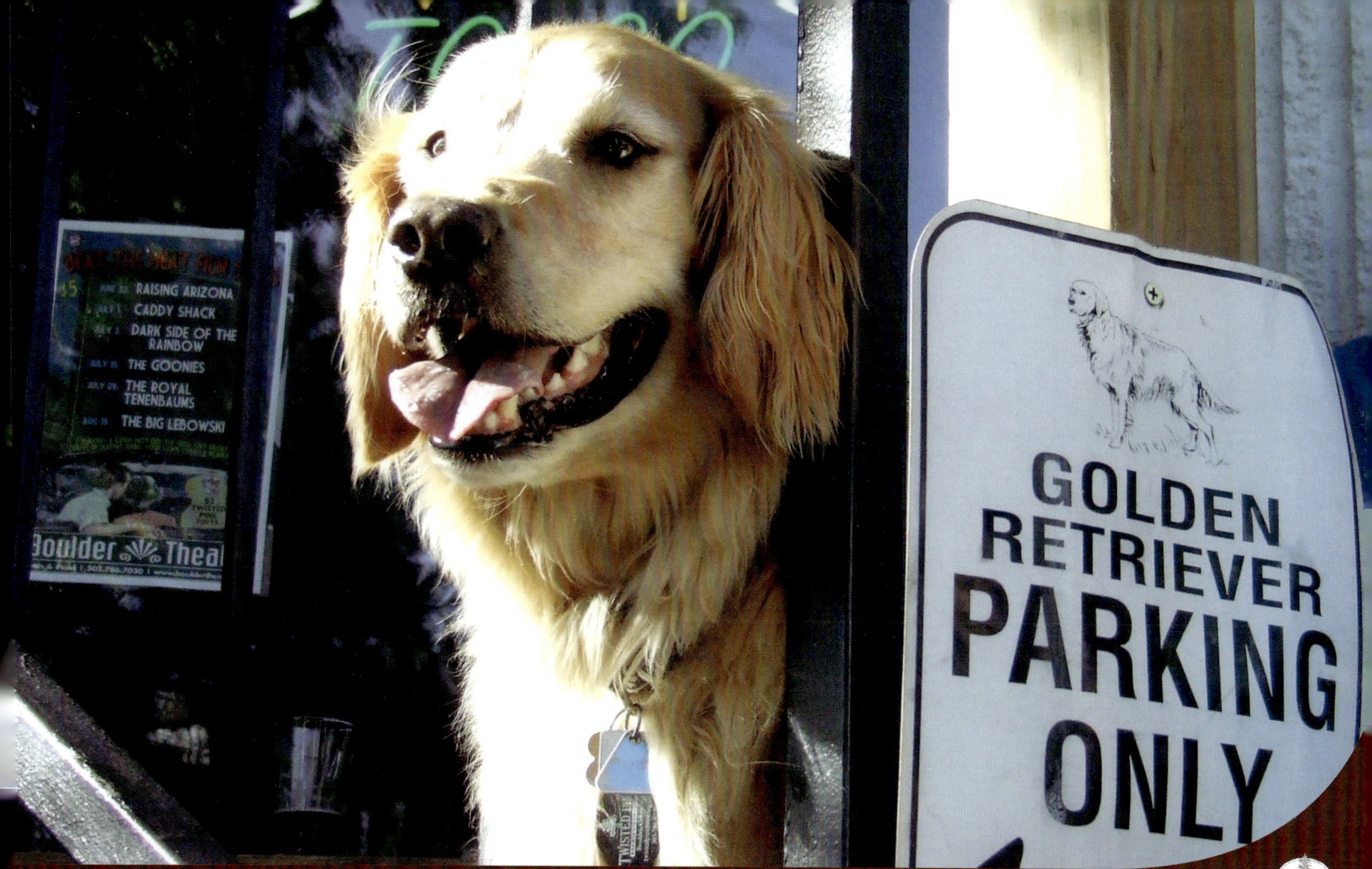

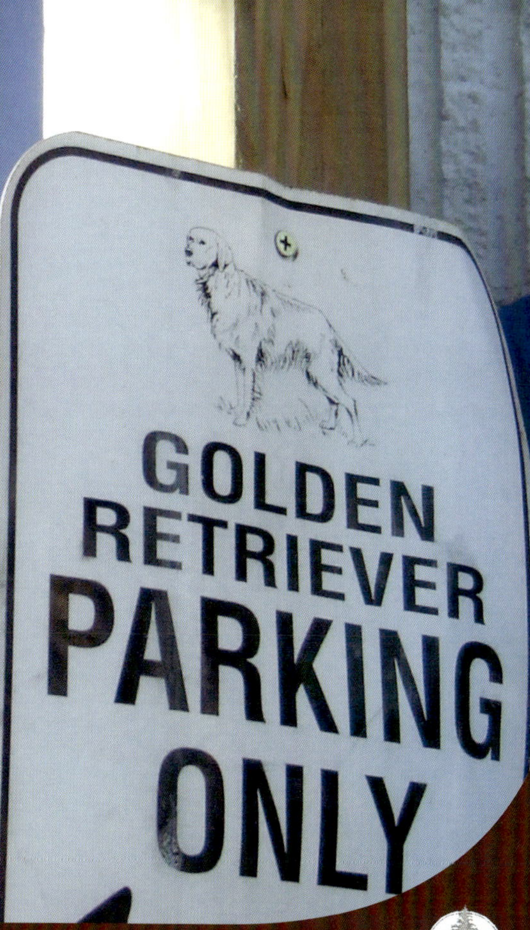

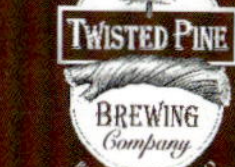

Reilly, 8, Golden Retriever   Owner: Bob Baile

Barley

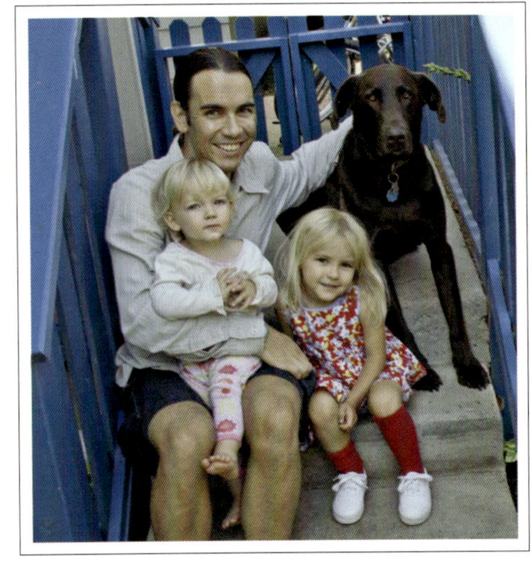

Favorite treat: Venison from Grandpa's hunting trips

Best Friend/Accomplice: Jupiter the cat

Favorite toy: Frisbee

Naughtiest Deed: Chewed all four corners off the coffee table as a puppy

Opened brewery in 1988, first in Four Corners region since Prohibition

Brews 1,000 barrels annually

Award-winning Pilsner

"**H**e's the big brother** to my daughters," says Michael, one of Carver's owners, "and my first born." This lovable, mellow pal even snuggles with Jupiter the cat! With all of that going for him, his "trash diving" habit is tolerated. Barley is a smart, athletic dog, who plays a clever game with the backyard magpies. He lures them in with a bone used as bait, and then pounces from his hiding place to chase them. He also plays catch with himself by propelling a tennis ball against a step and catching the rebound. Barley might be the best Christmas gift Michael has received from his wife Lauren. 🐾

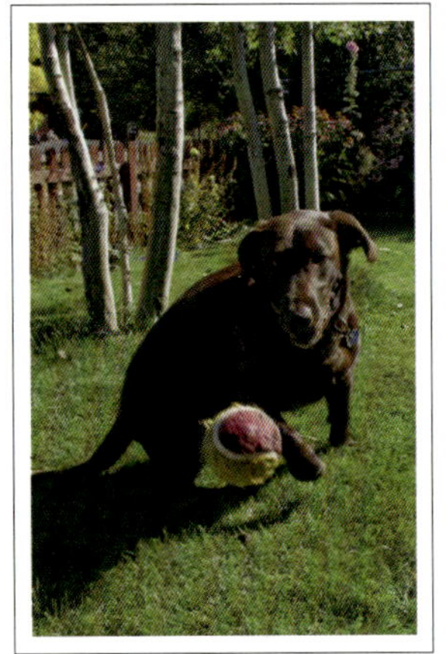

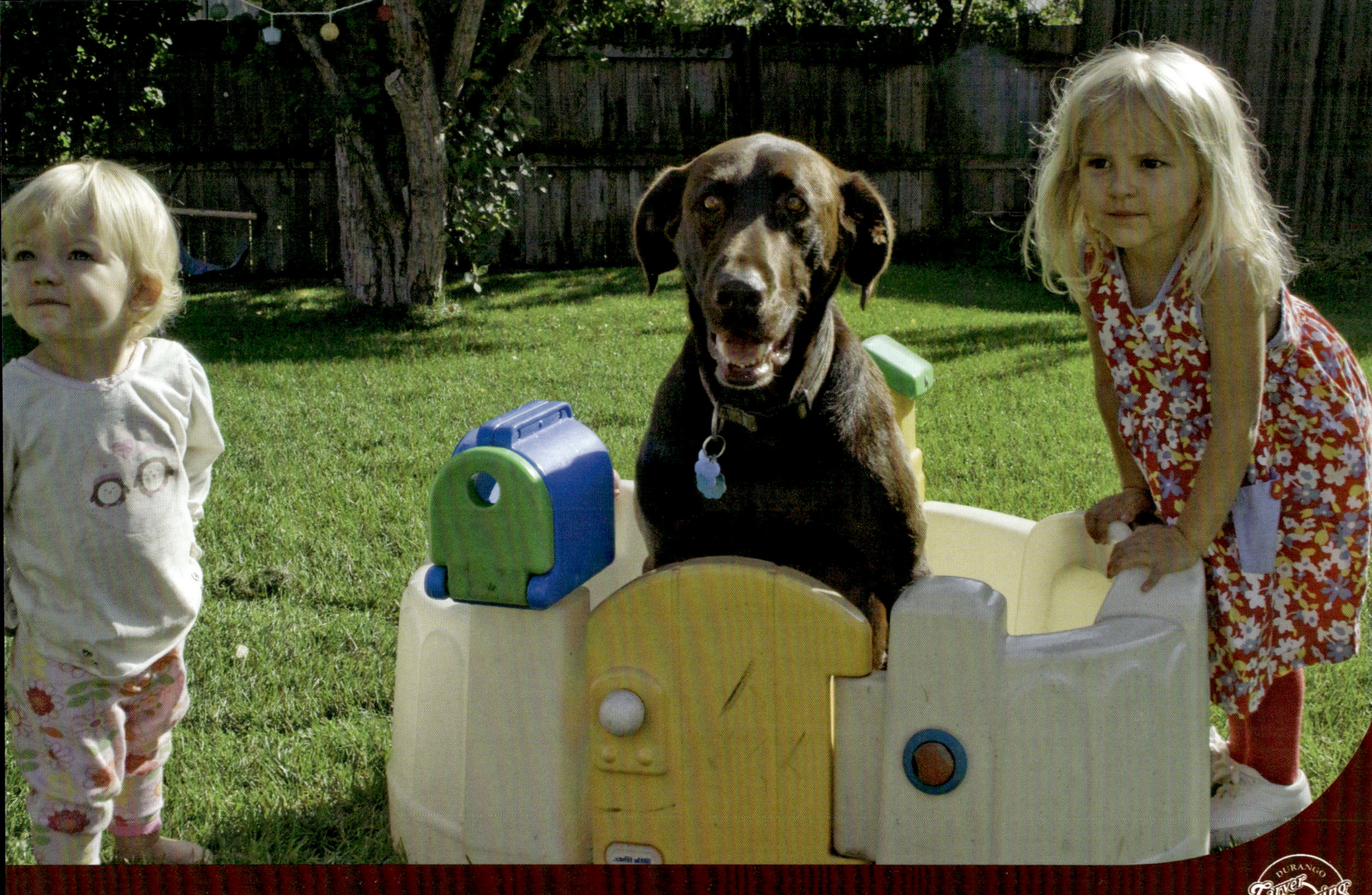

Barley, 5, Brown Labrador Owner: Michael Hurst

Zack

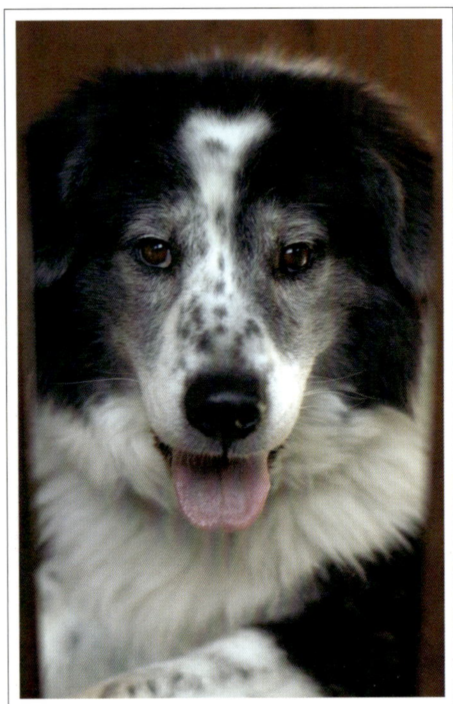

Favorite Pastime: Sleeping

Favorite Hangout: Couch

Favorite Toy: Couch

Most Mischievous Act: Pretending NOT to sleep on couch

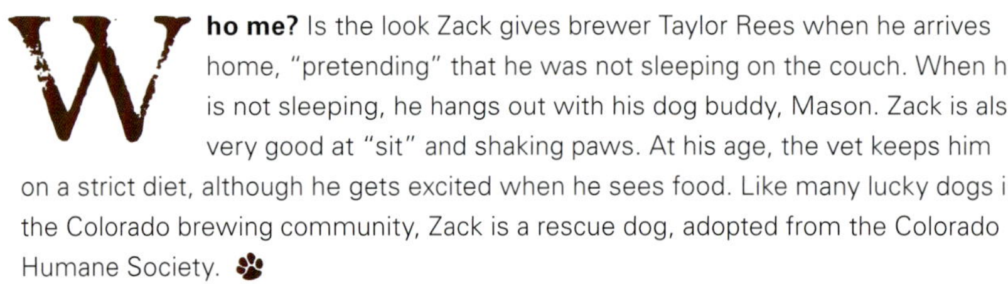

Established in 1994

Brewery ranked 7th in *Beer Advocate's* "All-Time Top Breweries on Planet Earth" 2008

2 Bronze, 1 Silver GABF 2009

Who me? Is the look Zack gives brewer Taylor Rees when he arrives home, "pretending" that he was not sleeping on the couch. When he is not sleeping, he hangs out with his dog buddy, Mason. Zack is also very good at "sit" and shaking paws. At his age, the vet keeps him on a strict diet, although he gets excited when he sees food. Like many lucky dogs in the Colorado brewing community, Zack is a rescue dog, adopted from the Colorado Humane Society.

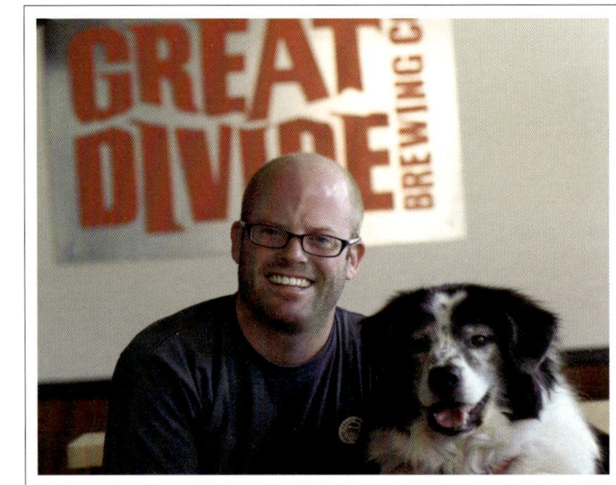

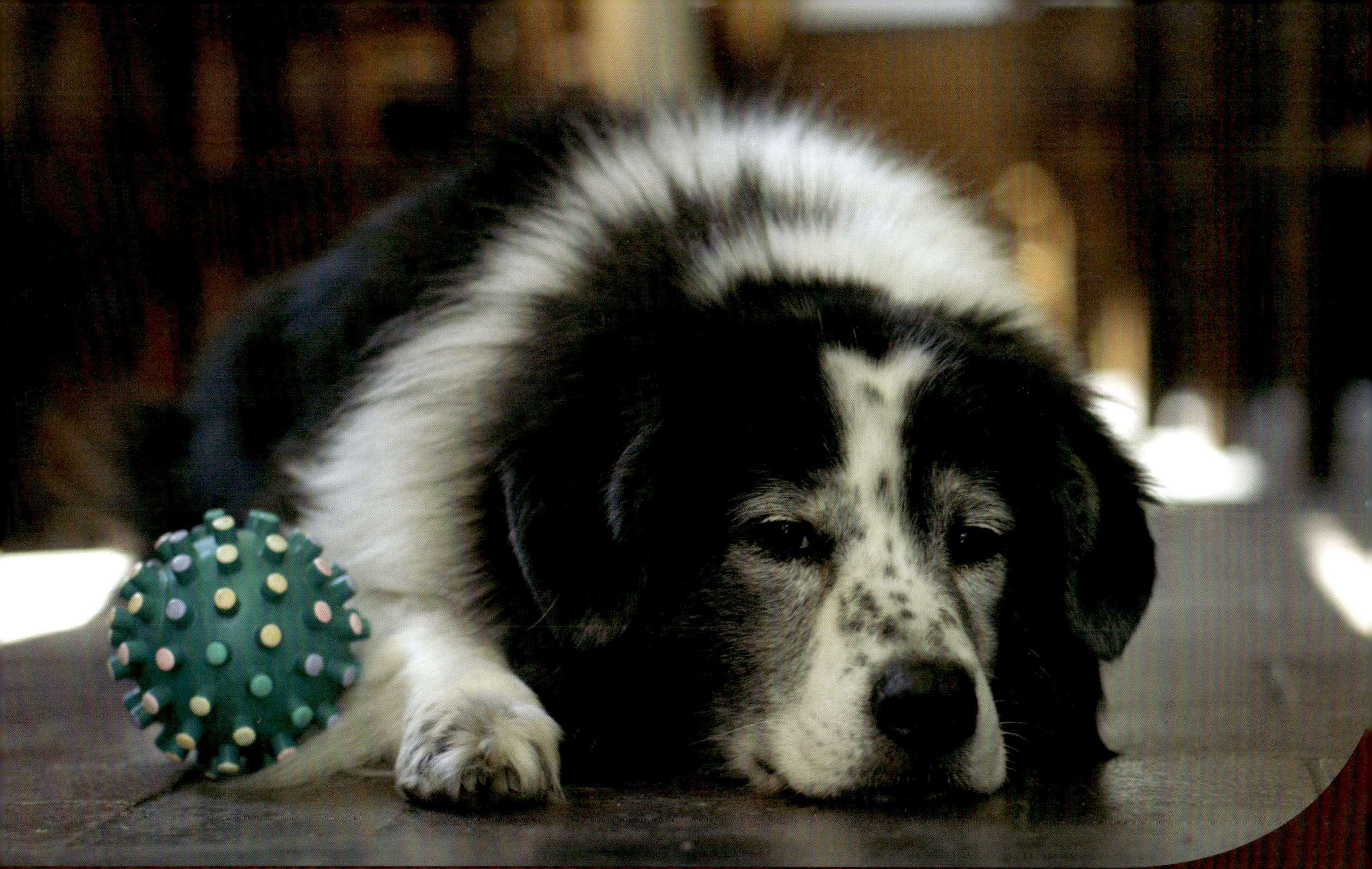

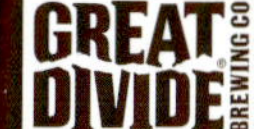

Zack, 10, Border Collie Mix   Owner: Taylor Rees

Comet

Established 1990

Consecutive GABF Gold Medals "Derail Ale" 2007, 2008

Originally was Durango Beer and Ice Company, est. 1886

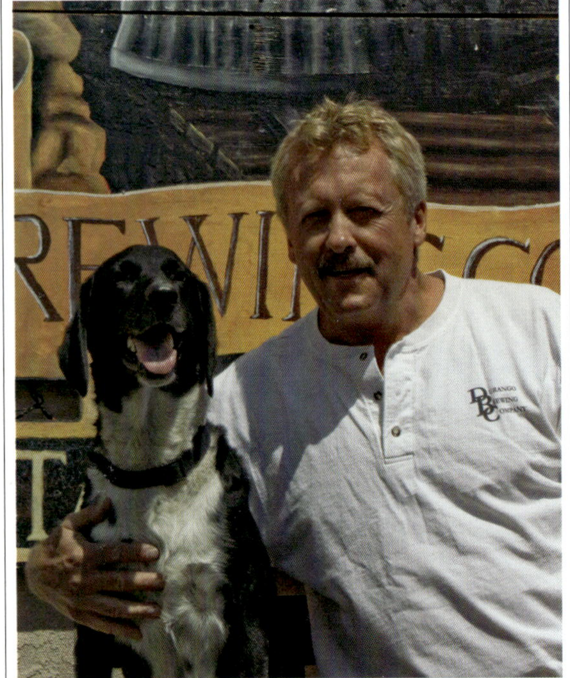

Favorite Toy: Chew rope

Naughtiest Deed: Chewed up a table

Annoying Habit: Flatulence

Favorite Hobby: Chasing lizards

"**H**e chose me on Christmas Eve,"** says brewery owner Mark. "I liked a different dog in the litter, but he just came over and lay on my shoe." He continues, "That night, we came home to find our new puppy had left a 'doggy deposit' under the Christmas tree and it was wrapped in a bow!" Mark is still trying to explain how that happened. Comet is an athletic Frisbee dog, often leaping high to make the catch. 🐾

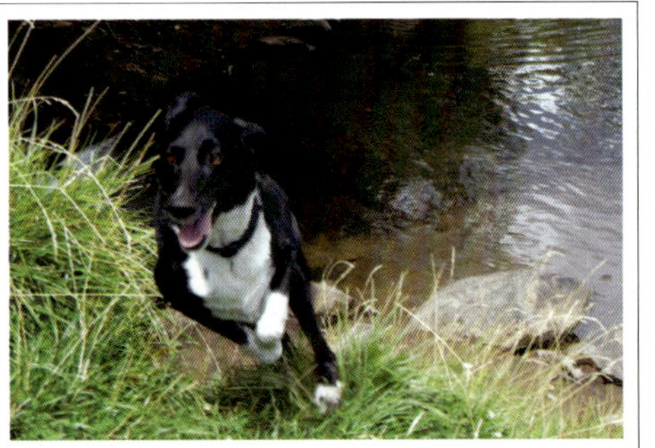

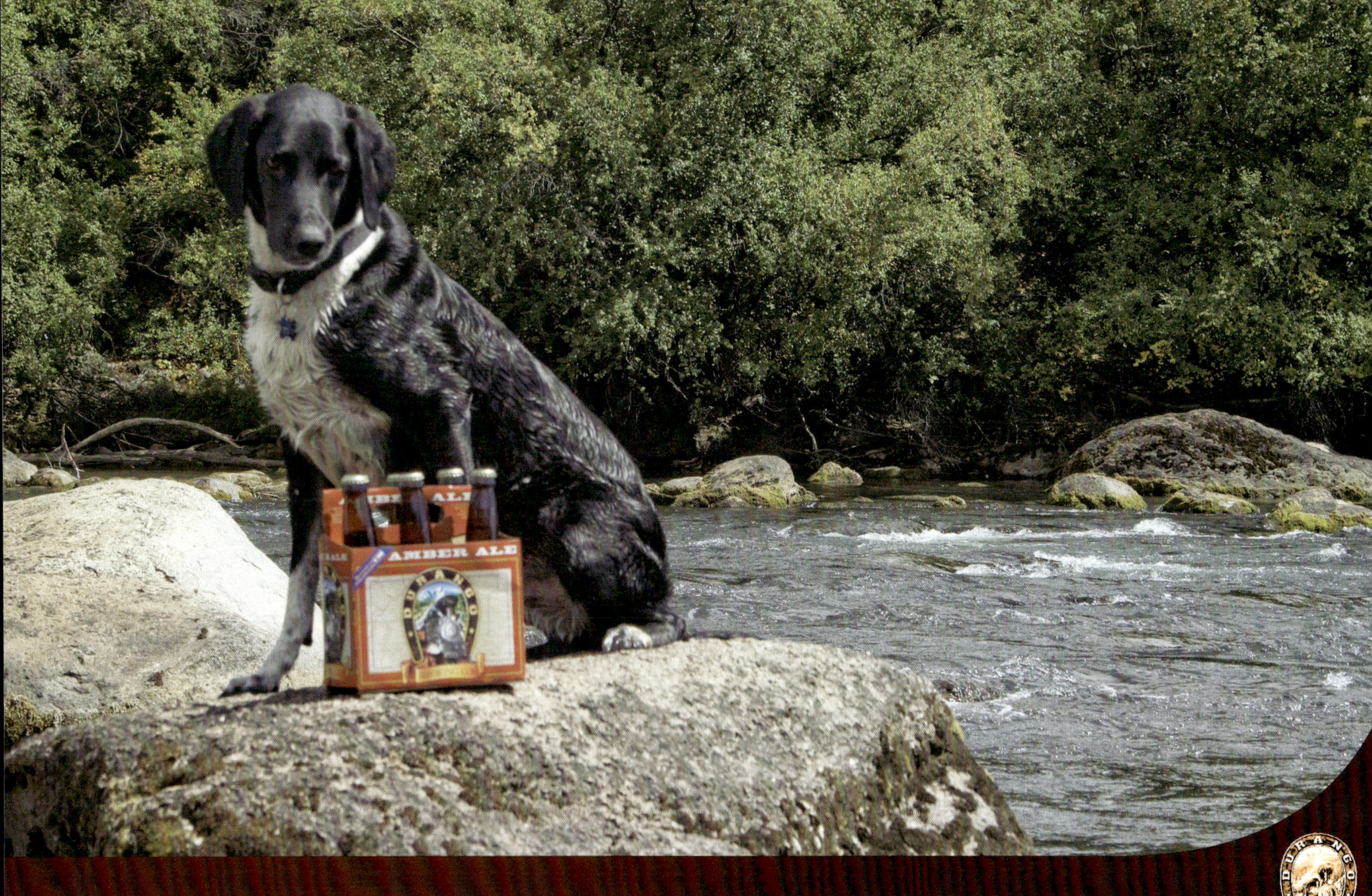

 Comet, 7, German Shorthair/Border Collie   Owners: Mark and Karen Harvey

Ember

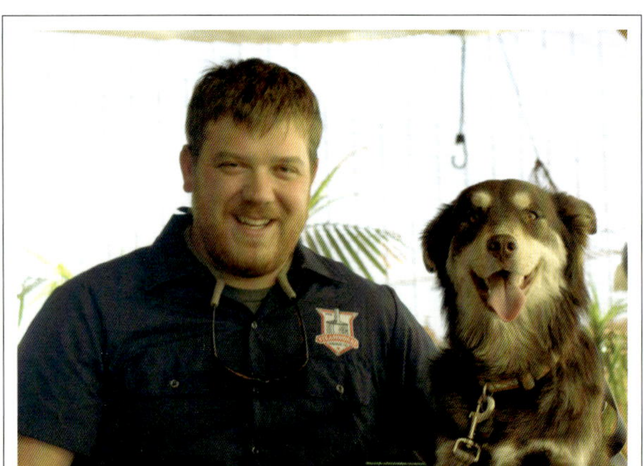

Favorite Toy: Anything she can destroy

Most Excellent Adventure: Ate a mole

Best Trick: Roll over

Favorite Hangout: Falls Creek near Durango

STEAMWORKS BREWING COMPANY
DURANGO

Established 1996

Five Medals 2009 Australia Intl. Beer Competition

Honored by Durango Chamber of Commerce as Business of The Year 2005

She's psycho, in a crazy sort of way," says brewmaster Patrick. "She is also friendly and lovable," he continues. Barely past the puppy stage, Ember still chews anything and everything. The kiddie pool and grill cover are history, and she seems to be looking for the next thing to destroy. When Ember isn't chewing up Patrick's house, she enjoys "partying" with other dogs. 🐾

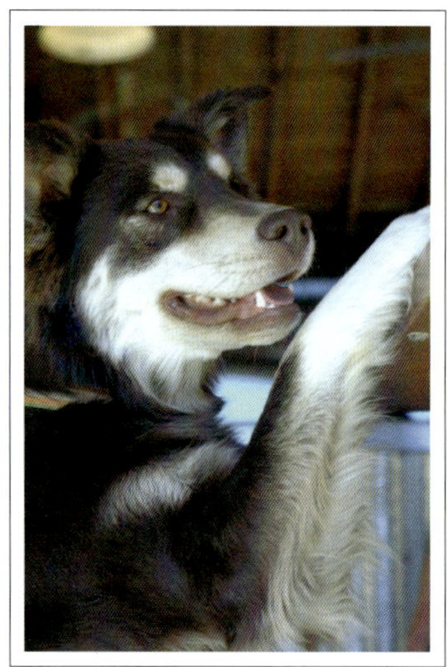

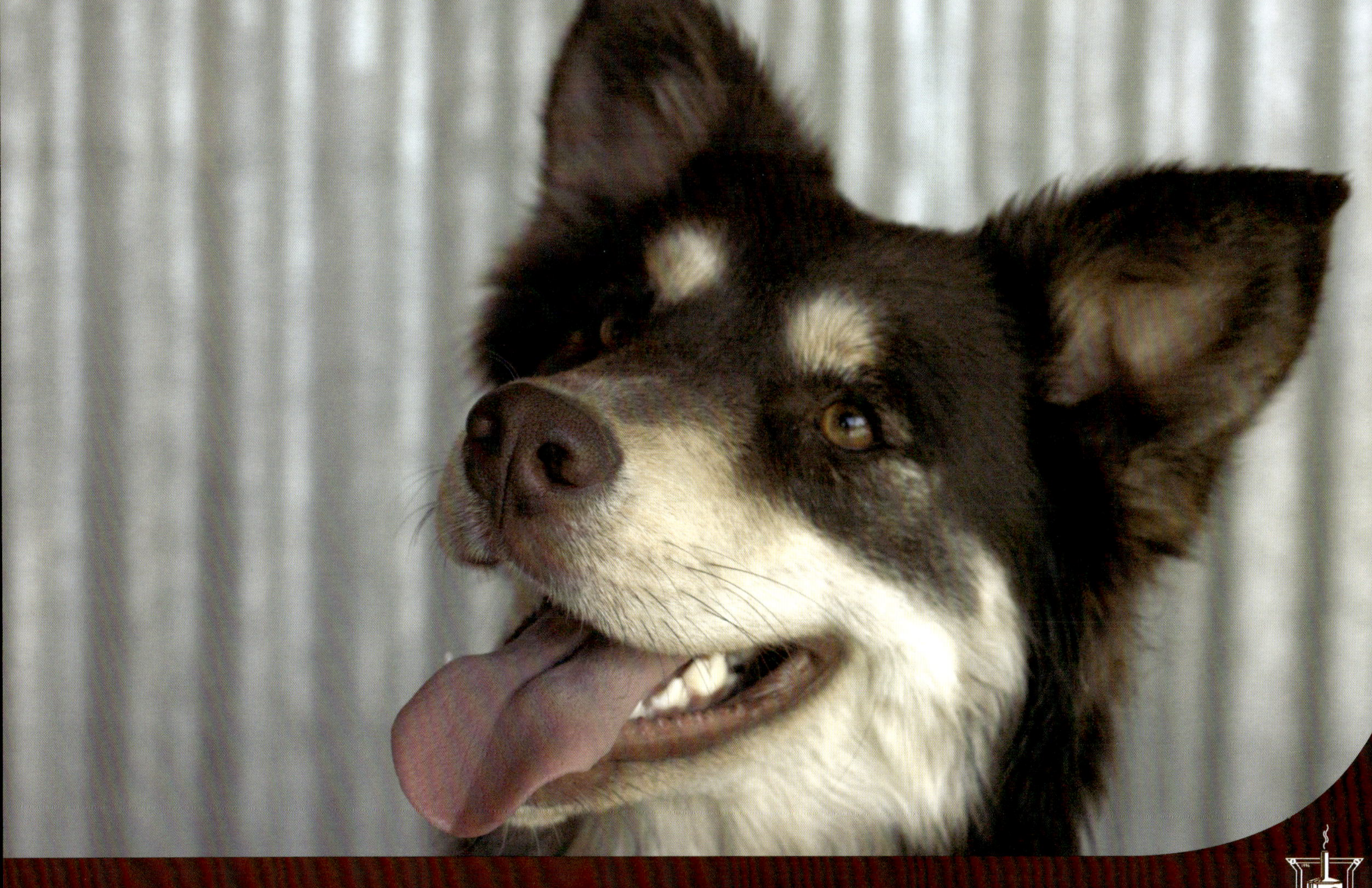

Ember, 17 months, Lab/Husky/Golden Retriever   Owner: Patrick Jose

Max

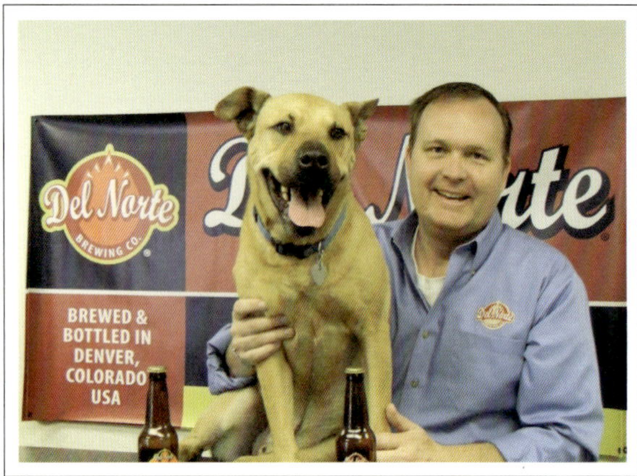

Most Excellent Adventure: Dawn coyote chase that lasted 30 minutes

Happiest Moment: "Dream Power" rescue from New Mexico roadside and subsequent adoption

Favorite Hangout: Wherever the sun is shining

Favorite Hobby: Hiking fourteeners

Began operations in 2004

Only U.S. brewery specializing in Mexican-style lagers

2009 Gold Medal Colorado State Fair

Hot sauce and Gingersnaps for breakfast, yippee! Max needs to get his fuel for hiking Colorado fourteeners with Del Norte owner/brewer, Joe. Before they head out for an adventure, Max will run circles around the house and has even been caught peeling back the screen to the backyard. If treats are really what he's looking for, though, he will try trading by dropping toys at Joe's feet. Joe is a private pilot and flight instructor and enjoys flying Cessnas. Unfortunately, Max can't get his license. 🐾

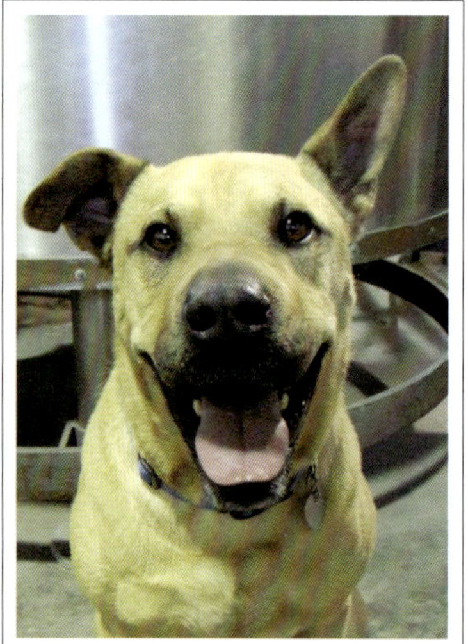

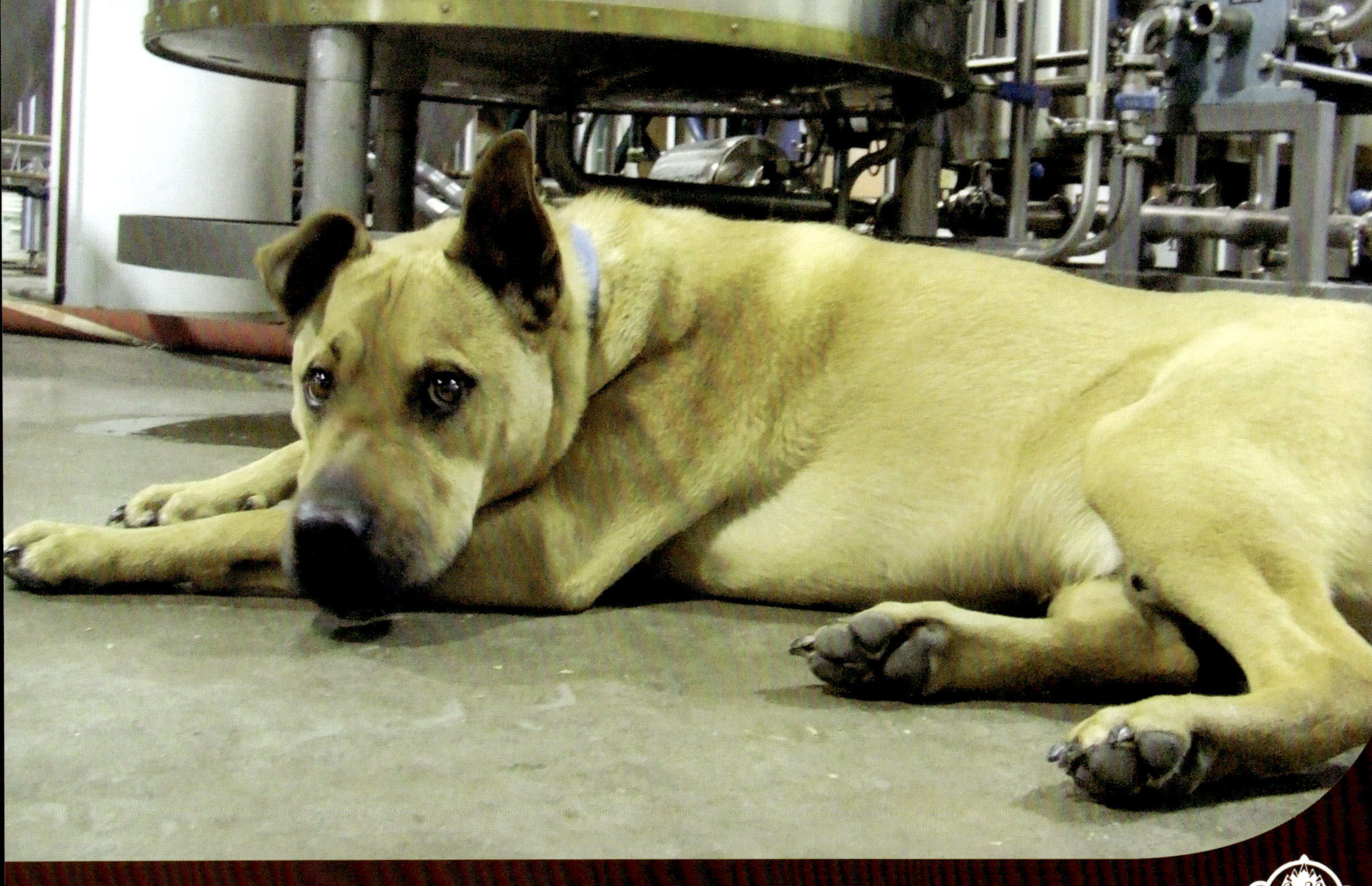

Max, 5, Sharpei Mix Owner: Joe Fox

Feisty

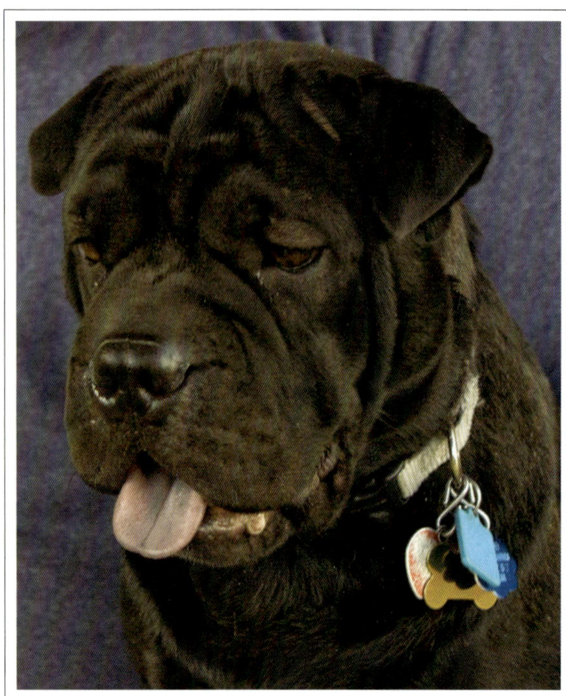

Naughtiest Deed: Chewed up three comforters

Funny Habit: Chasing his tail

Favorite Hangout: The recliner

Best Trick: Runs up walls to catch ball

Opened 2002

The highest packaging microbrewery in the United States at 8,369 feet

Slogan: "It's all downstream from here."

He eats anything plastic, say brewery owners Richard and Karen Wood. So far, Feisty has stolen and eaten: a pair of sunglasses, several pens, plastic balls, soda caps, water bottles and two remotes! Fortunately, no trips to the vet...yet. Feisty also plays a unique game when welcoming his family home. When he sees them arriving, he races around to the back door, then through the house to greet them at the front door. 🐾

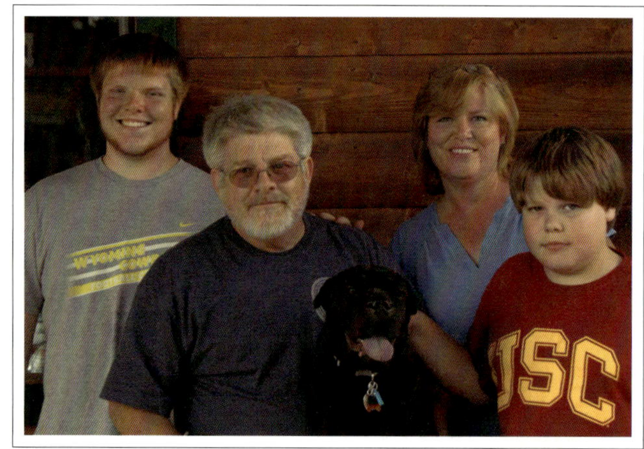

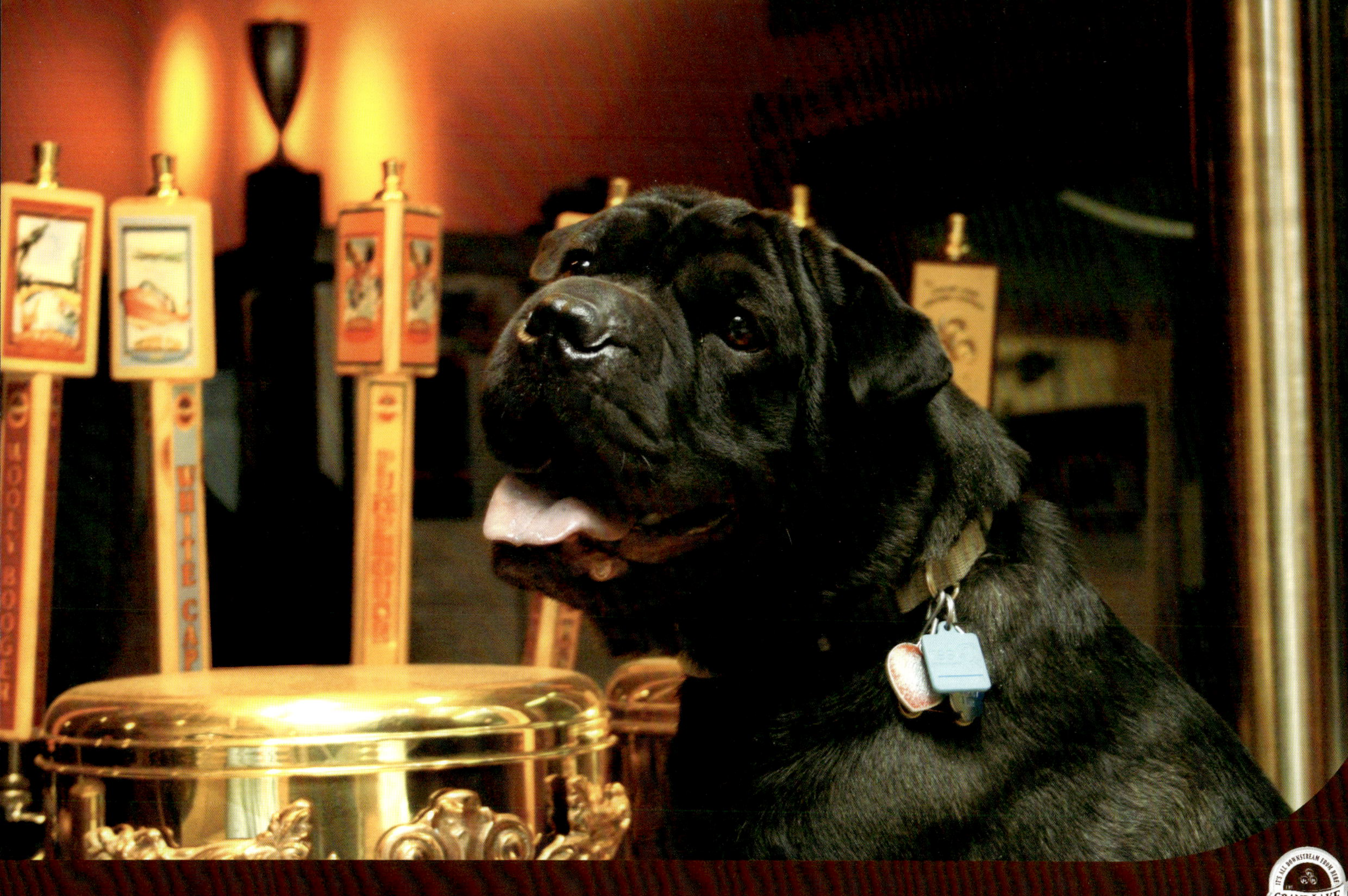

 Feisty, 2, Pug/Sharpei   Owners: Richard and Karen Wood

Bailey

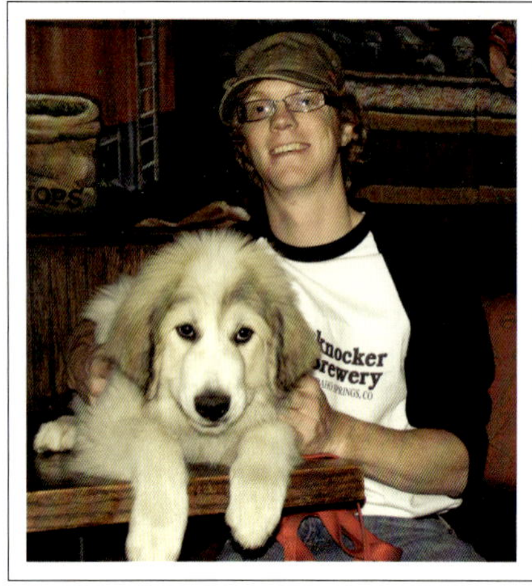

Best Friend: Kaya

Favorite Hangout: Behind the wood-burning stove

Naughtiest Deed: Ate two pairs of shoes

Favorite Toy: Anything to chew on

Brewing since 1994

Produced 9,000 barrels in 2008

11 award-winning beers

Wake up very early...bark at Sean...hungry, must eat now...play, roll, bite the big dogs...hmm, shoes, chew...tired, nap...dig in the dirt with Kaya...eat a bee, ouch!...chew, chew some more... hungry, eat... tired, good-night. Sean, a brewer at Tommyknocker, is the proud new papa to Bailey. Other canine family members include Kaya, a one-year-old female Bernese/Great Pyrenees; and Porter, a male Bernese Mountain Dog, also one year. 🐾

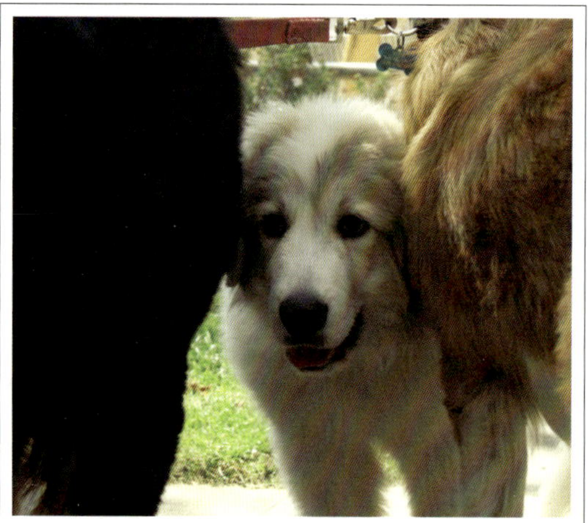

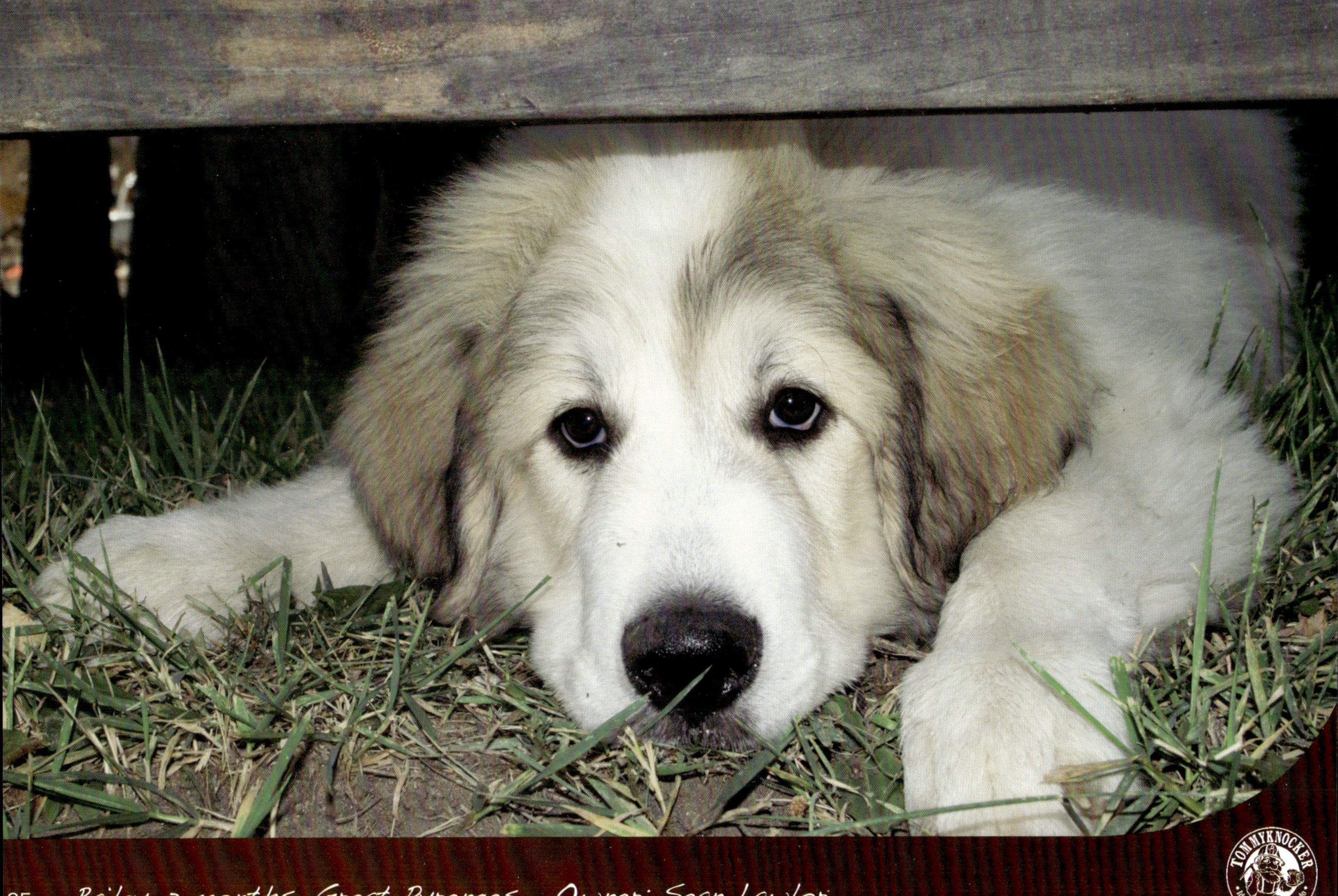

95   Bailey, 3 months, Great Pyrenees   Owner: Sean Lawlor

Daisy

Began 1988

Two Gold Medals 2008 GABF

Fall 2009, "Railyard Ale" first beer to be released in cans

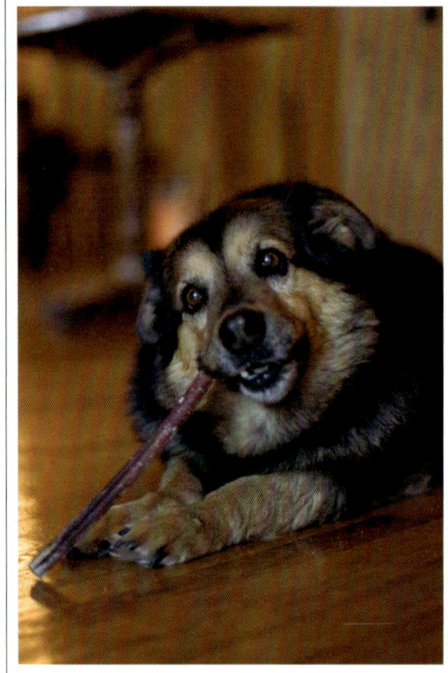

Daisy is a one man brewdog, says brewmaster Andy, of his 13-year-old buddy. Cute toys don't compare to Daisy's favorite "sticks"-crunchy, munchie, delicious, sticks, which she eats right down. She also has a fascination with canned cat food. Daisy is sometimes spotted sneaking to the basement with the stolen goods in an attempt to pry open her prize. So far. . .no success. 

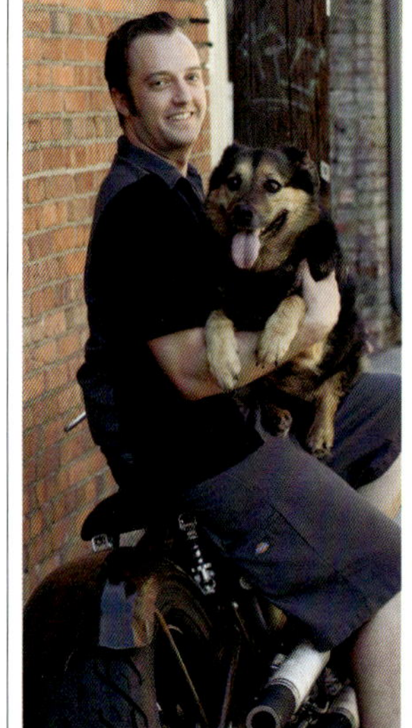

Funny Habit: Bugs eyes when she gets excited

Naughtiest Deed: Chewed a hole in Andy's first nice new leather jacket

Favorite Food: Parmesan cheese rind

Most Excellent Adventure: Riding the road with Andy on his home-built motorcycle

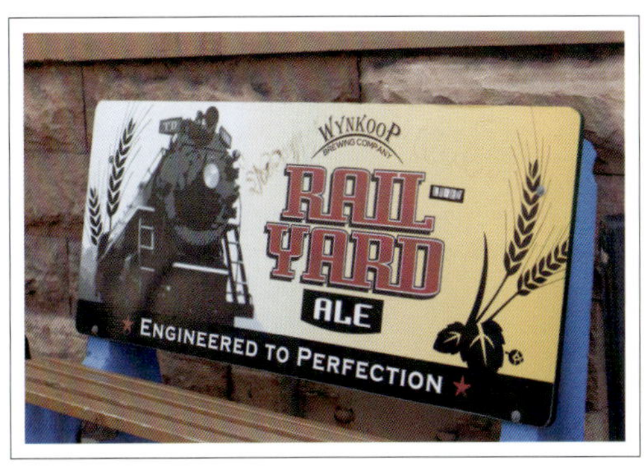

 Daisy, 13, Chow/Rottweiler Owner: Andy Brown

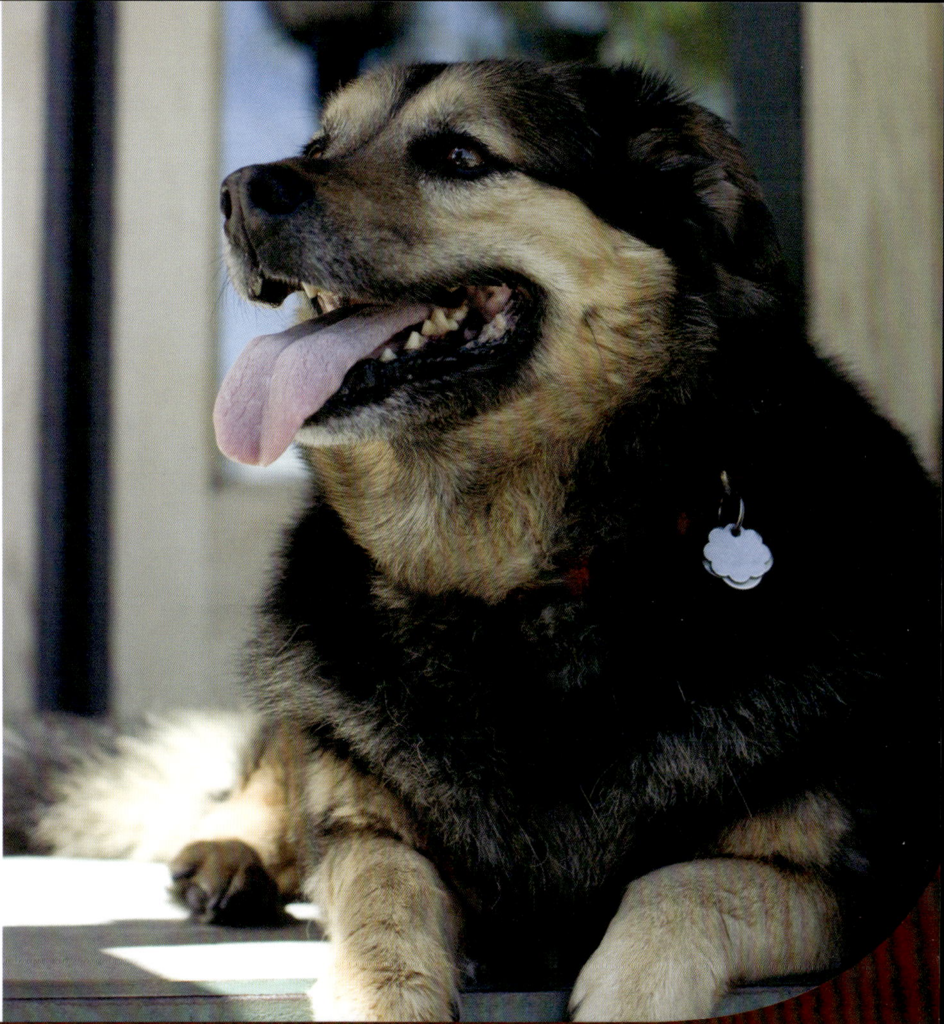

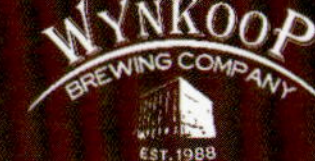

Quincy

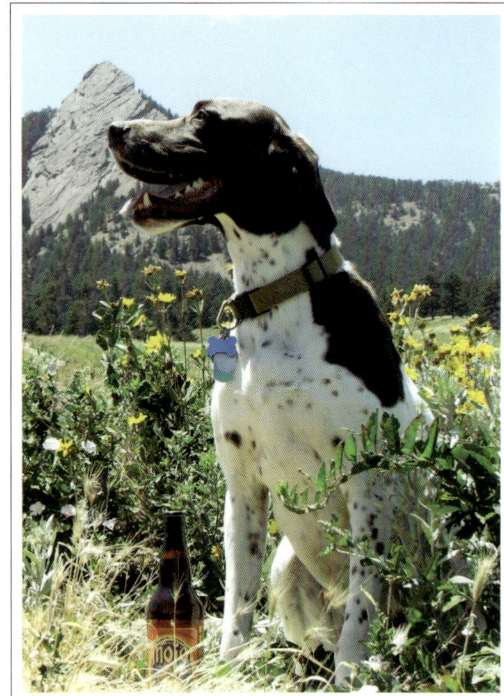

Annoying Habit: Wet nose whip – seeking attention

Most Excellent Adventure: Spending time in the "Big House"

Funny Habit: Moans and sighs to communicate – doesn't bark

Naughtiest Deed: Tore curtains down while looking at a squirrel

BOULDER BEER
BOULDER

Founded in 1979

Colorado's first microbrewery

Production capacity: 43,000 barrels annually

Quincy's story begins in a prison cell in Colorado's Buena Vista Reformatory as part of a dog training therapy and rehab program for inmates. "Quincy is the only member of the family that's been in rehab," says brewmaster David Zuckerman. If you are a squirrel, stay out of Quincy's backyard. He lives to chase squirrels, loves to relax with people and run with David when he is riding his mountain bike. 🐾

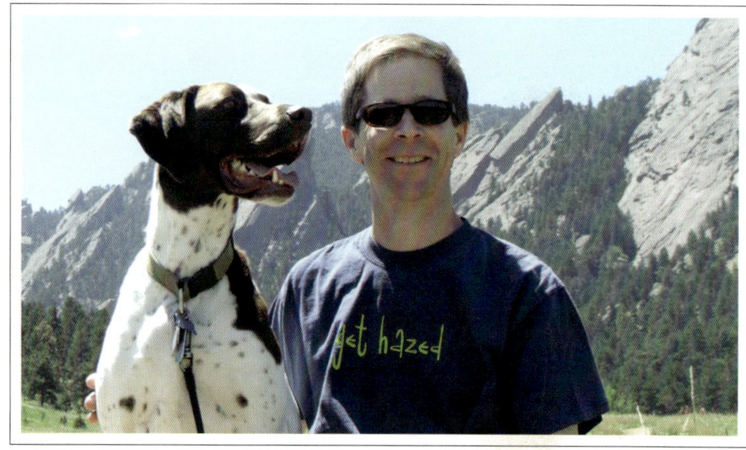

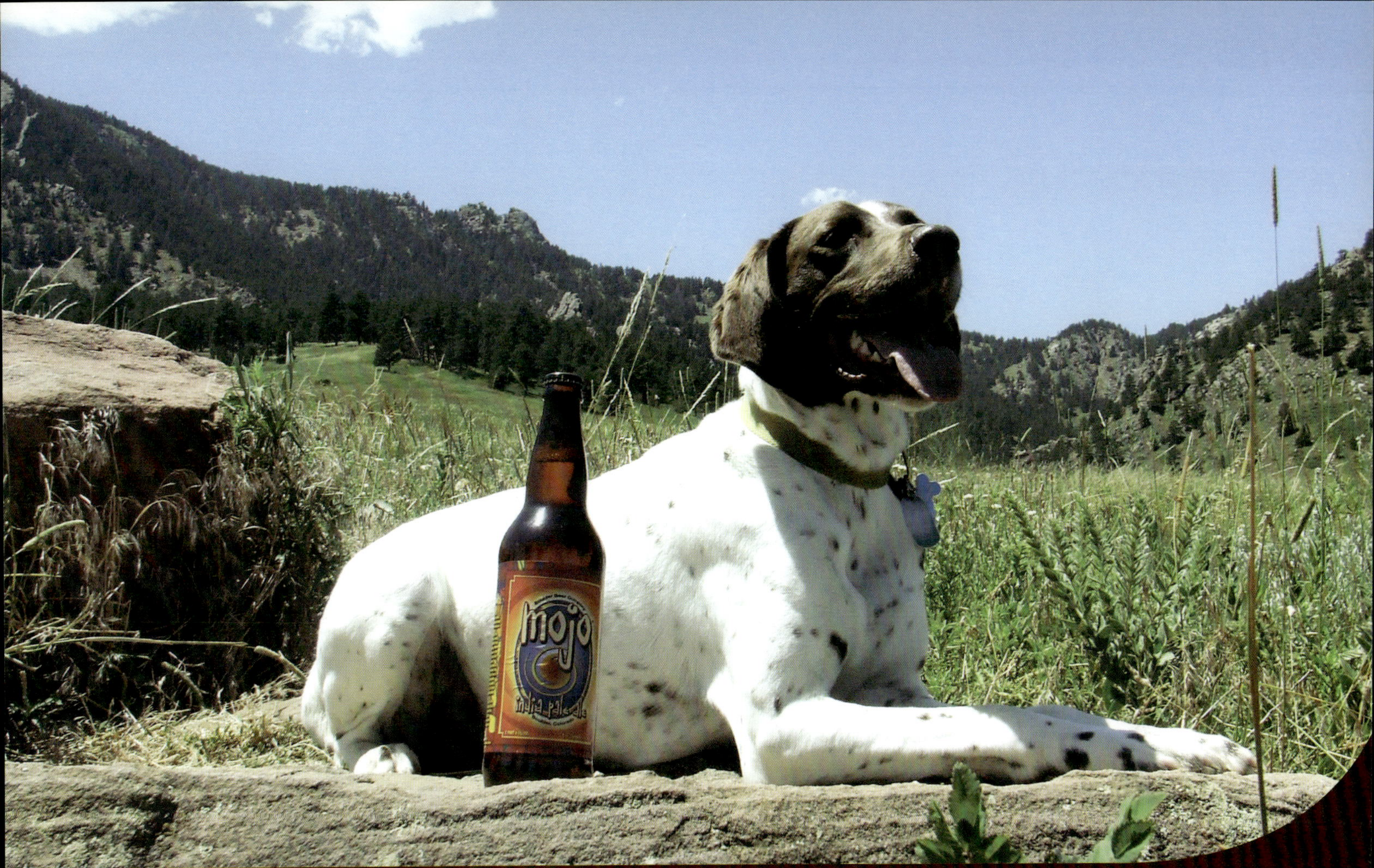

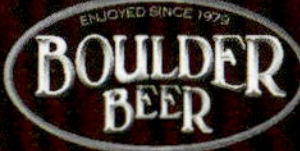

Quincy, 5, German Shorthaired Pointer   Owner: David Zuckerman

Logan

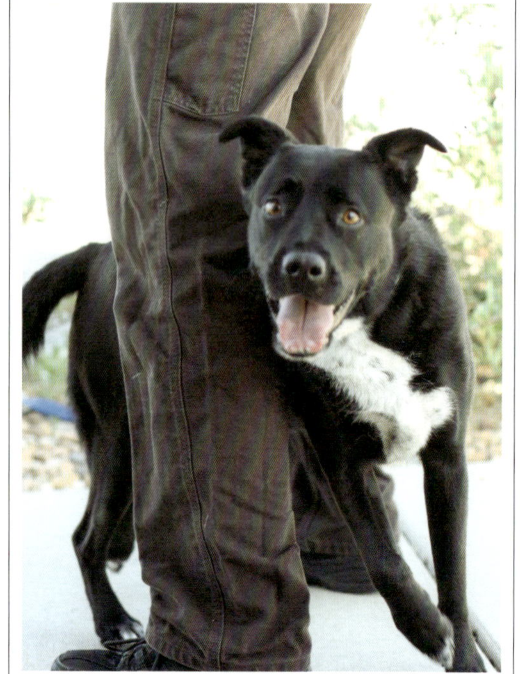

Favorite Toy: Stuffed pink bunny rabbit

Favorite Food: Cheese

Best Trick: Runs a Figure 8 between Jason's legs

Naughtiest Deed: Ate ornament off Christmas tree

Founded 1999

Labels feature animals: Eagle, Redhawk, Lynx, Rattler

Redhawk Ale is signature brew at Redhawk Ridge Golf Course

Mother bears with cubs don't run was a lesson Logan learned while climbing Mt. Columbia. Owner and Rockyard brewer Jason recalls, "When the mama stood up, Logan did an instant one-eighty." Logan has climbed 10 "fourteeners" with Jason, including Pikes Peak at the age of two. It was in Logan's favorite hangout, Colorado Springs' Bear Creek Park, that he experienced a brush with brewdog destiny when attacked by a pack of coyotes. Jason rescued him by whipping the attackers with Logan's leash. 🐾

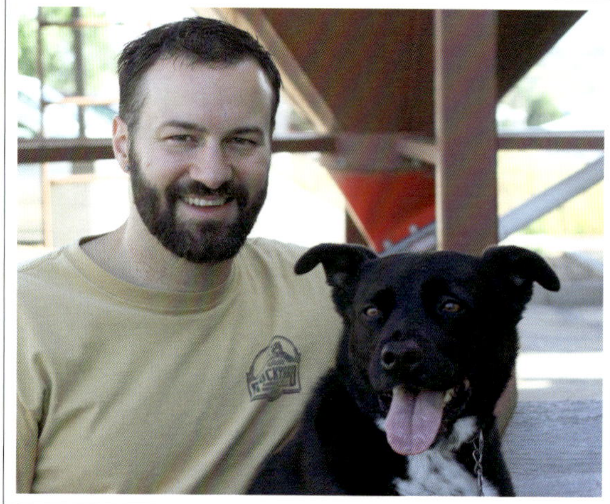

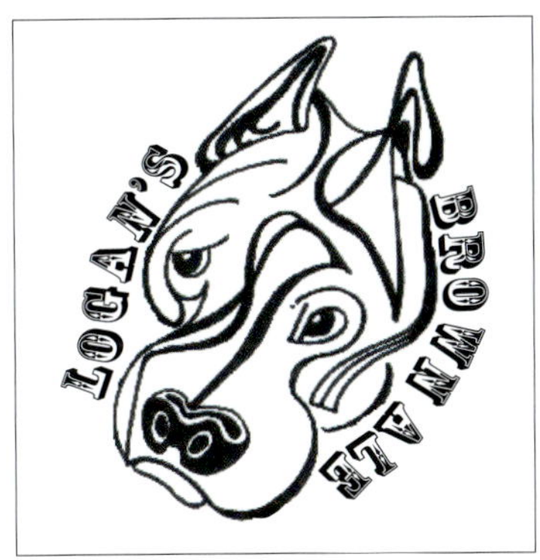

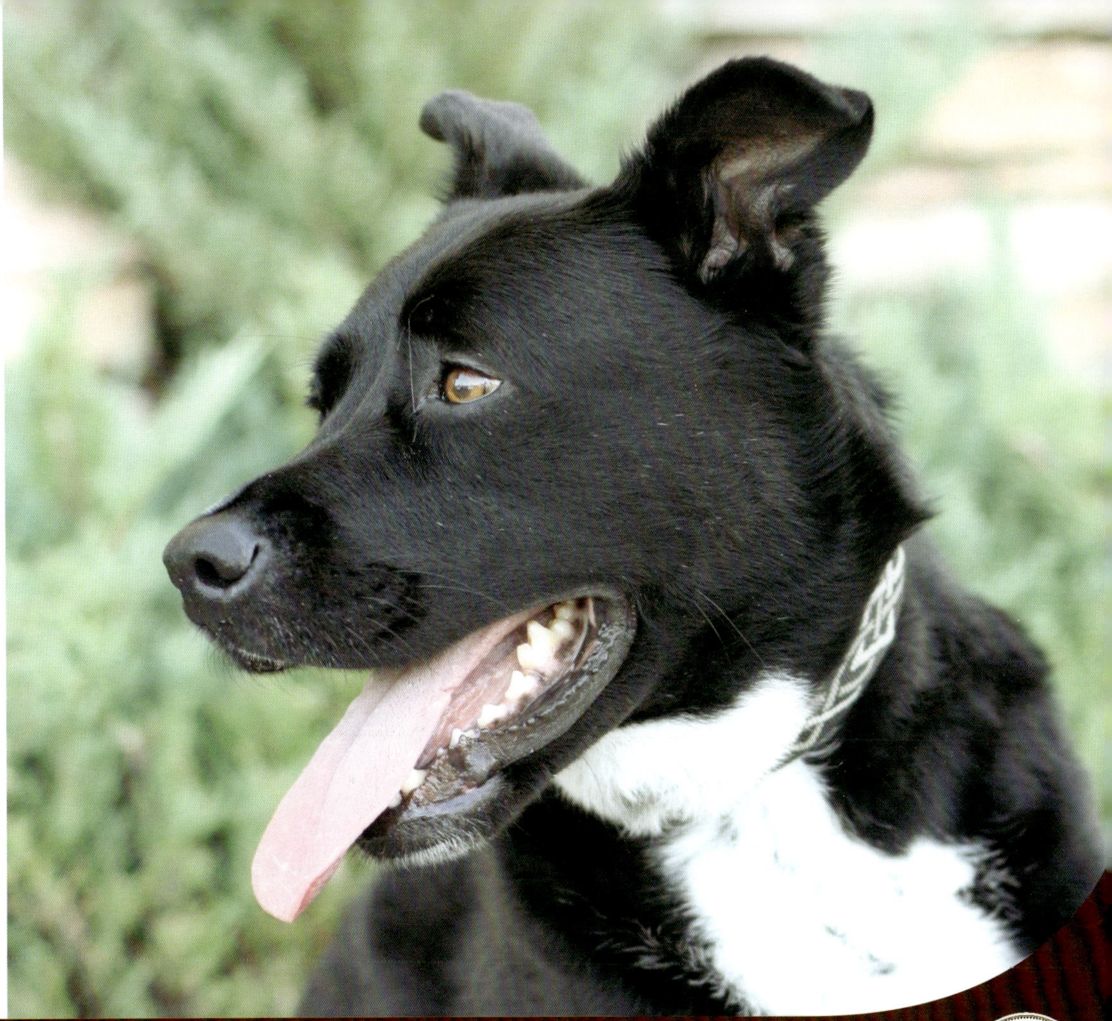

Logan, 5, Lab Mix   Owner: Jason Buehler

Cody Maverick

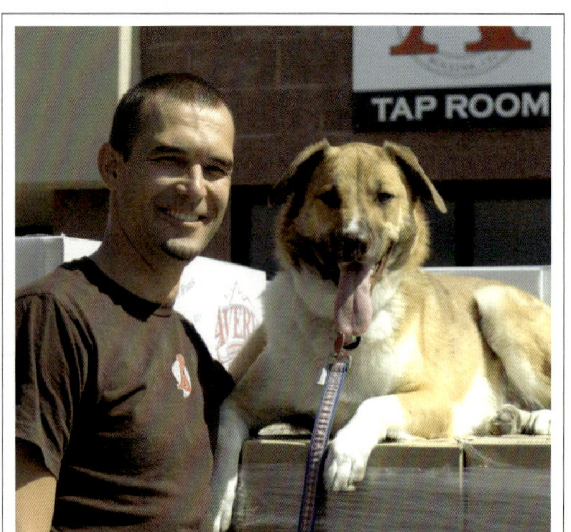

Mischievous Act: Steals balls while on walks

Best Trick: Can open any door

Annoying Habit: Snores loudly

Hobby: Foosball (just kidding)

Founded in 1993

14'er E.S.B., is named for the 54 Colorado peaks that rise above 14,000 feet

Ellie's Brown Ale named for Adam Avery's late (2002) Chocolate Lab, Ellie

Cody Maverick is a "Bitsa," says Australian Peter Archer, marketing specialist at Avery Brewing Company. He's "bitsa" this and "bitsa" that. With his fluffy appearance and playful nature, it's hard not to like Cody. At 18 months old, he fully earned his second name, Maverick, by learning how to open any door to make his escape. When Peter isn't busy at the brewery, he takes every opportunity to snowboard outside of Boulder, and surf when near the ocean.

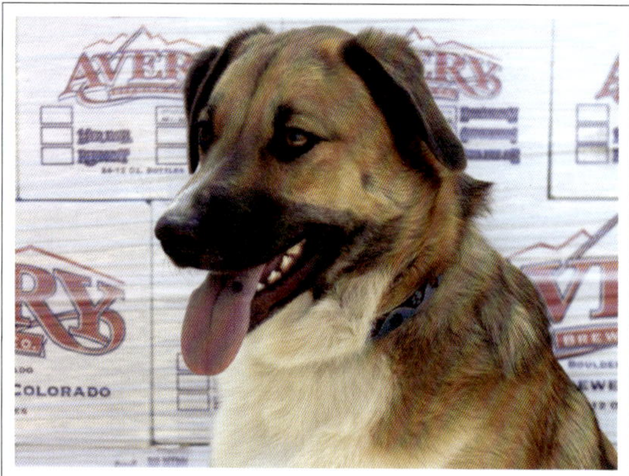

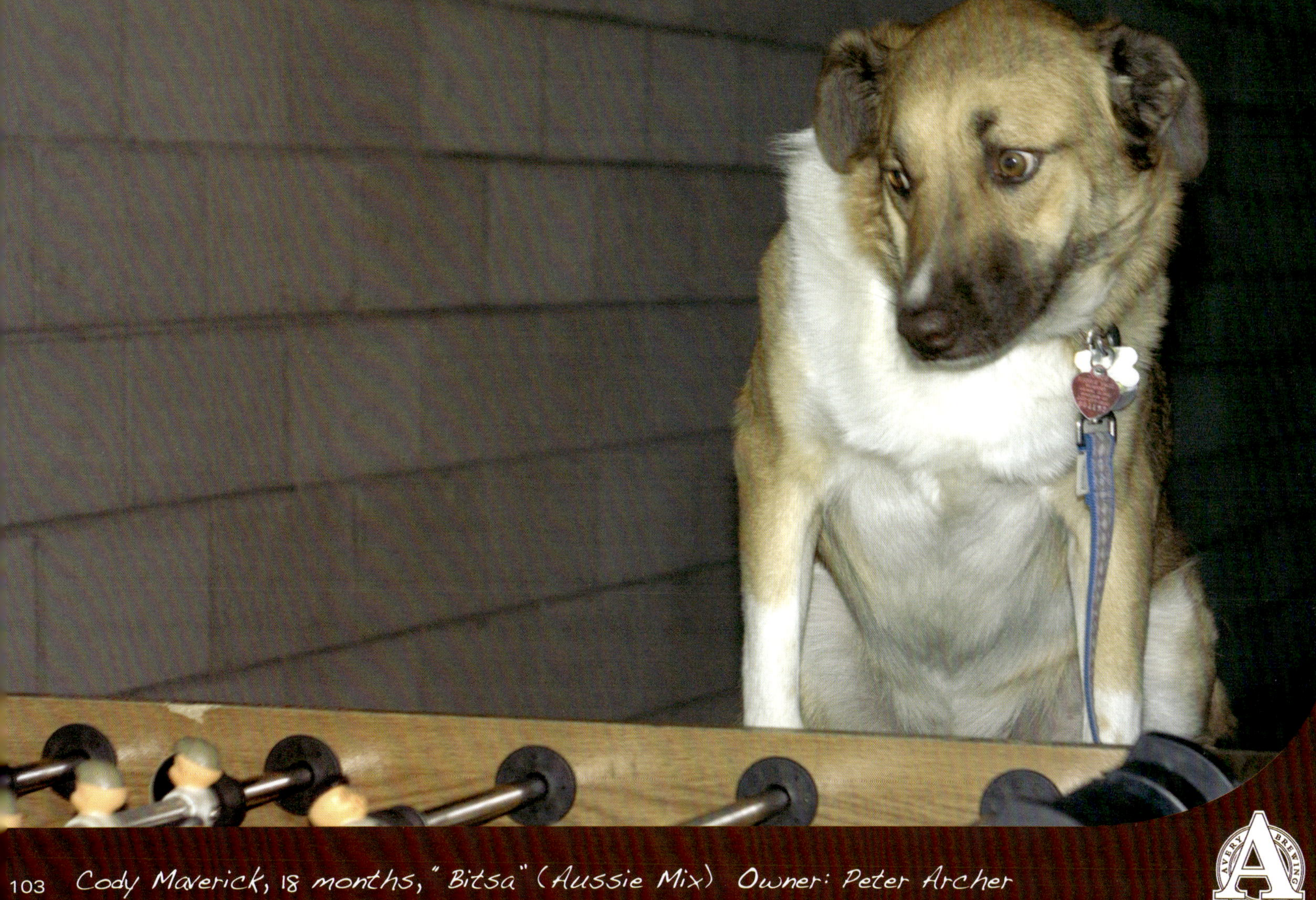

103 Cody Maverick, 18 months, "Bitsa" (Aussie Mix) Owner: Peter Archer

Dart and Duke

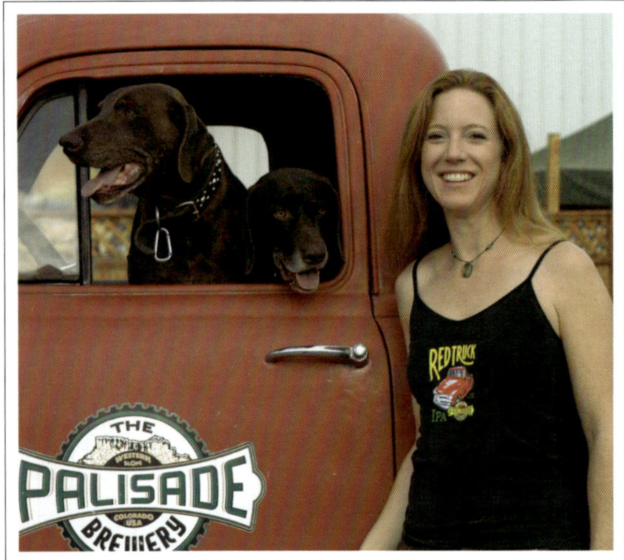

Dart's Best Trick: Can howl, "I love you"

Best Friend: Each other

Favorite Hobby: Hunting varmints

Naughtiest Deed: Stealing shoes and socks before running outside with them

Founded 2004

Teams with Jackson Hole Soda Company, brewing award-winning soft drinks

Annual production: 2,000 barrels

Palisade peaches...yum! Duke picks them right off the tree, plays with them for a while and gulps them down for a snack. Dart has a taste for homegrown grapes, and plops right in the middle of a vineyard to eat. Palisade is famous for both peaches and vineyards, so there are plenty of snacks. When hunting season arrives, these guys are right in their element, says the brewery's VP, Christine. A ride in the red truck, which inspired the name for their IPA, gives Dart a reason to break into song. 🐾

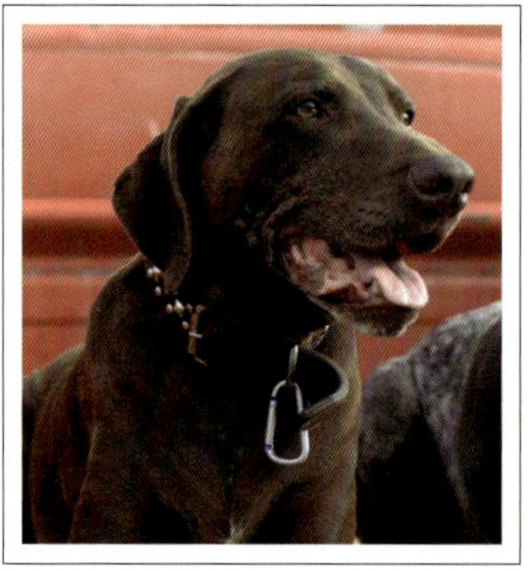

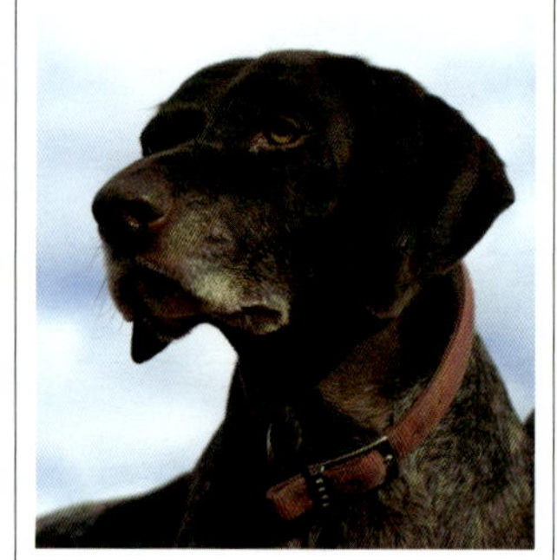

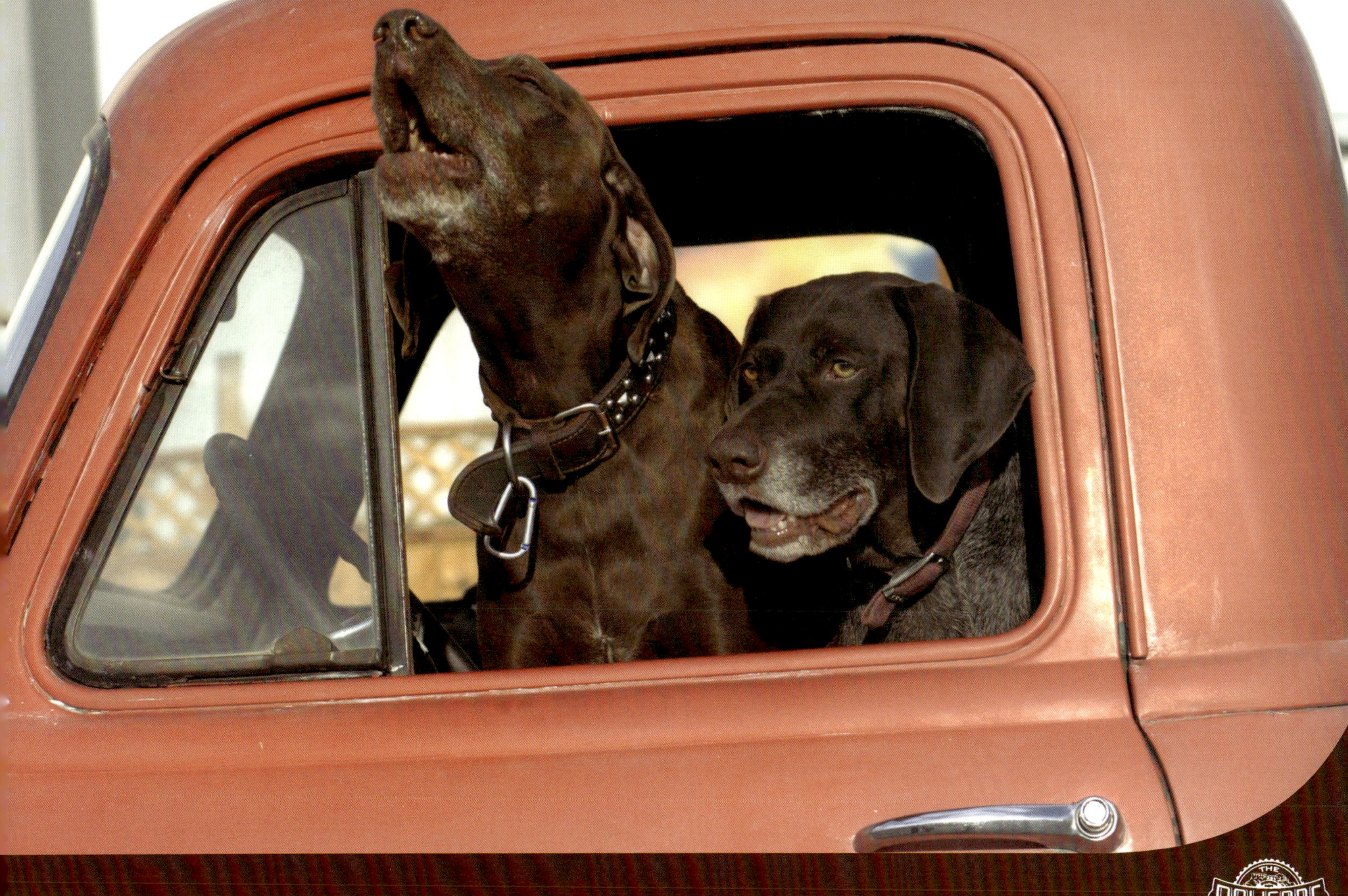

Dart, 10 & Duke, 6, German Shorthaired Pointer & Weimaraner/German Shorthair Owner: Christine Greenwald

Brewer

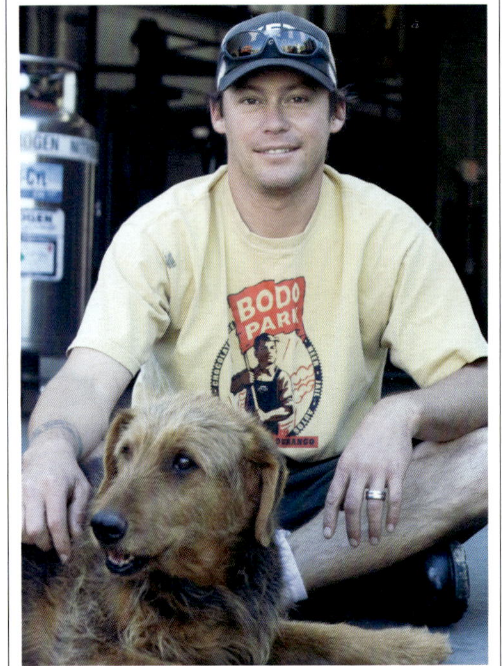

Began commercially in 1995

Bronze Medal 2009 GABF

SKA beers available in five states

True to his name, Brewer comes to work every day with Matt, one of SKA's co-founders. At 13, Brewer should be part of the "staff" since he is senior to most of the employees at SKA. Matt says his "brewdog" pal stays by him pretty much all of the time, "a loyal bad-ass dog." After two hip replacements and knee surgery, Brewer can't high jump for sticks anymore, but his sniffer is still sharp. He can find a tennis ball anywhere: in a neighbor's yard, in a dresser drawer or your pocket. Watch out. Do they have "ball dogs" in tennis? 🐾

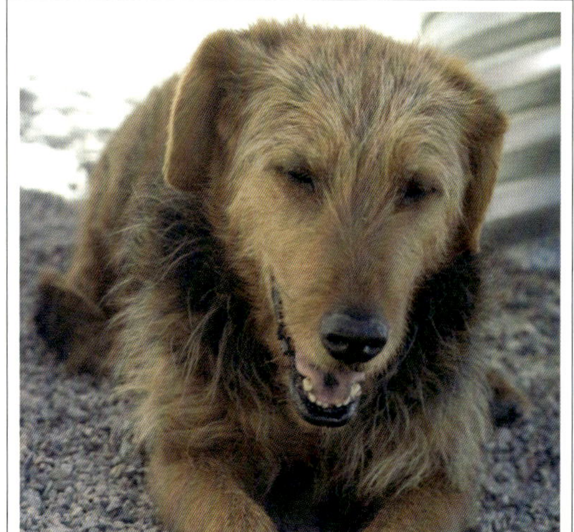

Favorite Hangout: SKA Brewing Company with Matt

Excellent Adventure: Rafting the Arkansas River

Favorite Toy: Tennis ball

Annoying Habit: Barking incessantly at a stick

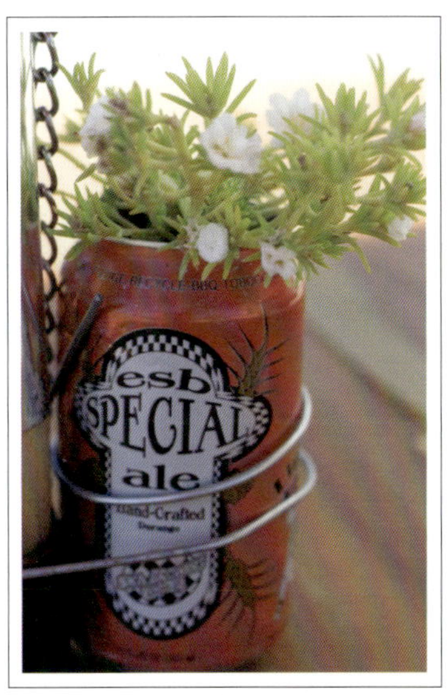

 Brewer, 13, Airedale/Lab   Owner: Matt Vincent

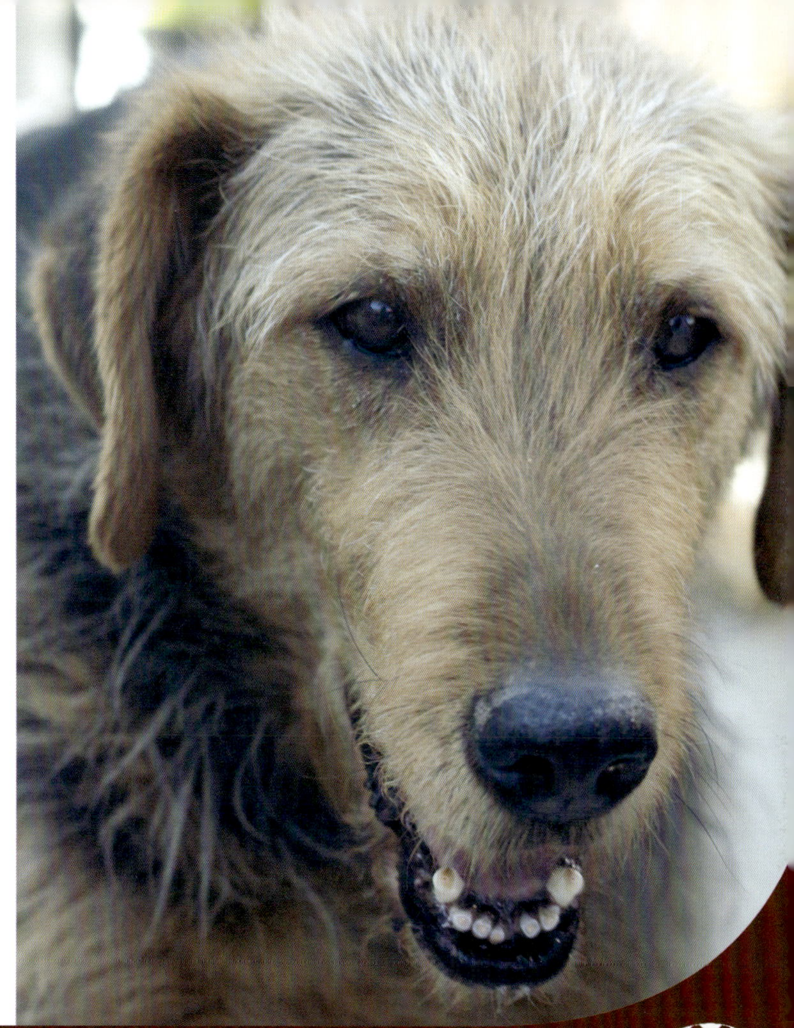

Marlo

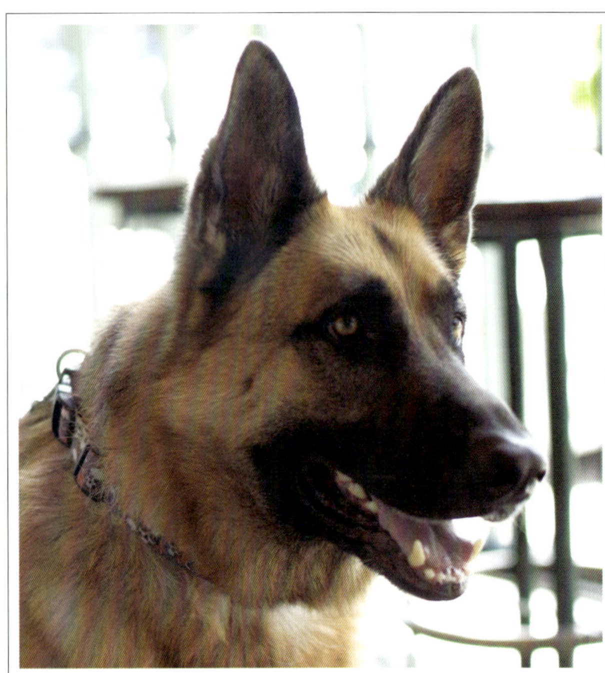

Most Excellent Adventure: Escaped with accomplice Riley, crossing six lanes of traffic

Favorite Toy: Tennis ball

Naughtiest Deed: Tipping over trash can

Favorite Hangout: Cherry Creek State Dog Park

Started 1988

Produces and sells on premises the nation's largest volume of beer

The brewery is named for Edward "Ned" Wynkoop, Colorado's first territorial sheriff, 1858

"**I have never once heard Marlo growl,**" says Martha Williams, co-owner of The Wynkoop Brewing Company, Colorado's first brewpub. Even though he is a large shepherd at about 140 pounds, Martha continues, "He is the nicest dog ever and I love him." Marlo grew up with Martha's 4-year-old grandson, and as a puppy could often be seen riding in the baby's car seat. 🐾

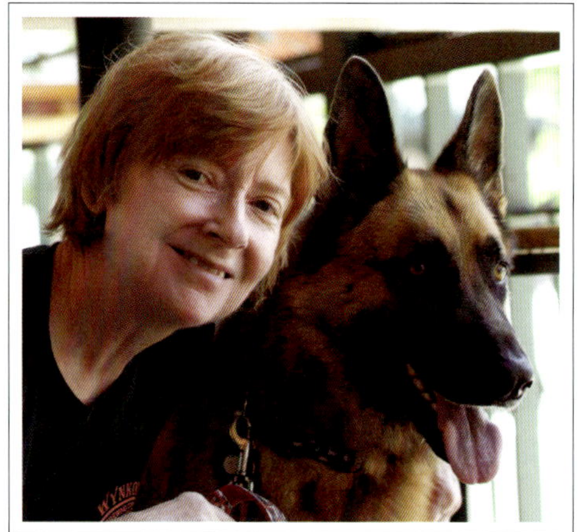

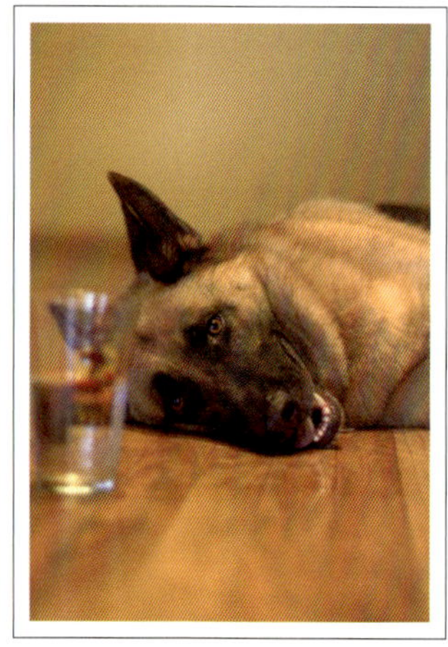

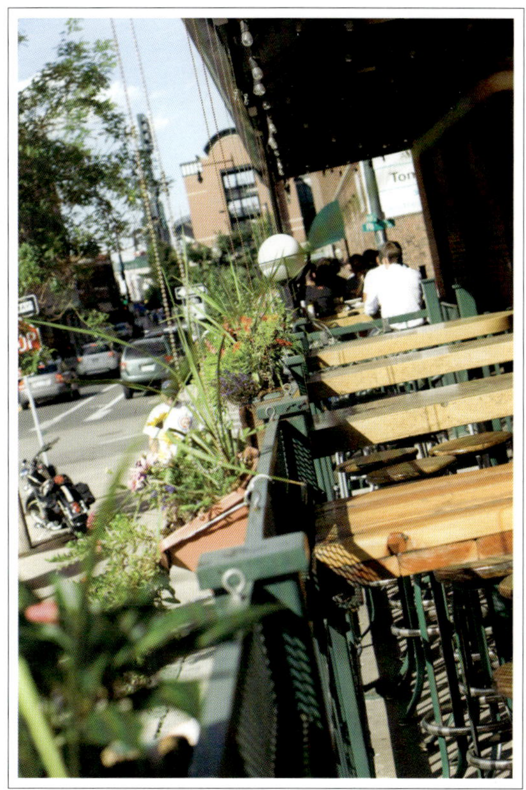

 Marlo, 4, German Shepherd   Owner: Martha Williams

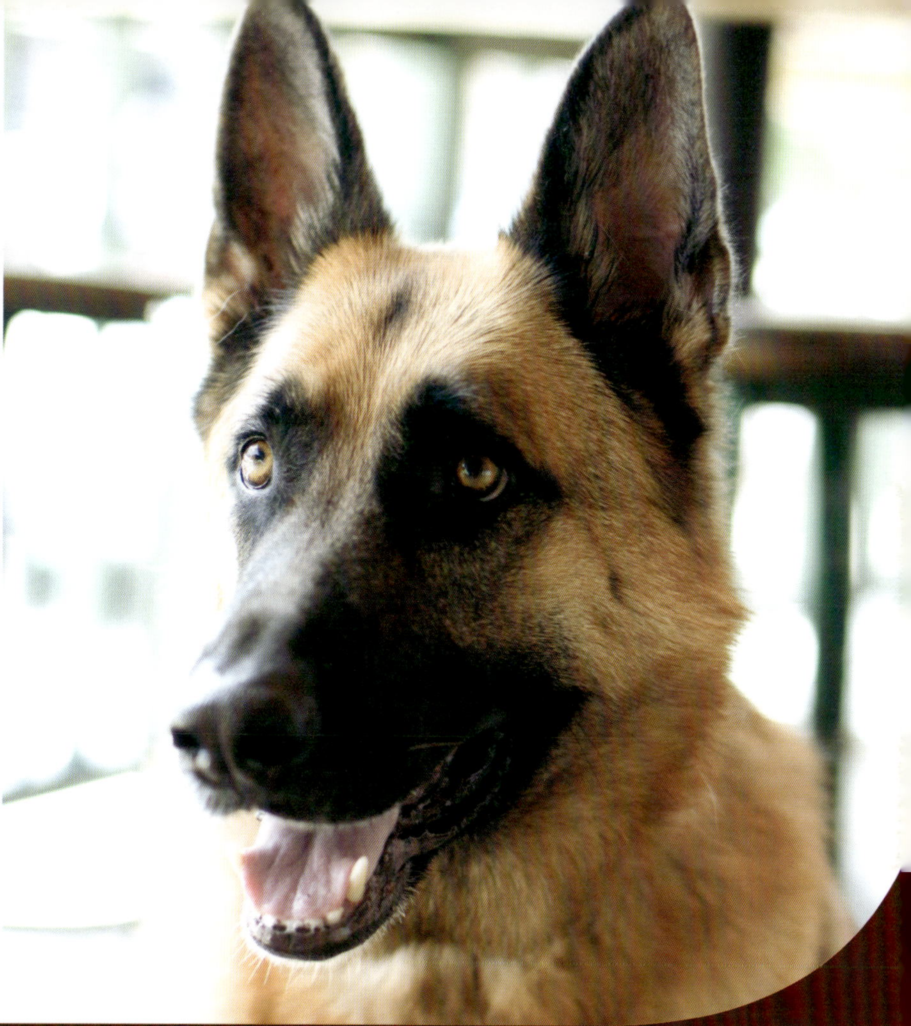

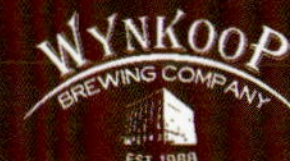

Layla

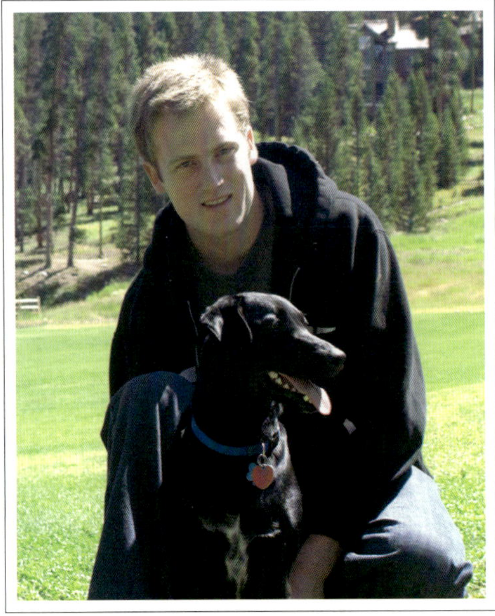

Best Trick: Bounces around like Tigger from Winnie the Pooh

Naughtiest Deed: Brings dead birds into the house

Most Excellent Adventure: Yellowstone!

Best Friend: Drake

Opened in 1990

Three locations in Colorado

Produces 30,000 barrels of beer a year; distributed in 25 states

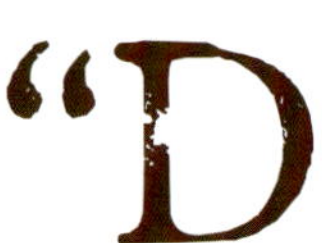

"**D**on't hurry. Don't worry.** You're only here for a short visit. So don't forget to stop…roll around on your back for awhile…and smell the flowers along the way." This is Layla's interpretation of the quote from American golfer Walter Hagen. Adopted from Rocky Mountain Lab Rescue, she appreciates the simple things in life: going for long walks in the mountains around Breckenridge and spending time with her family, brewmaster Drake and his girlfriend. 🐾

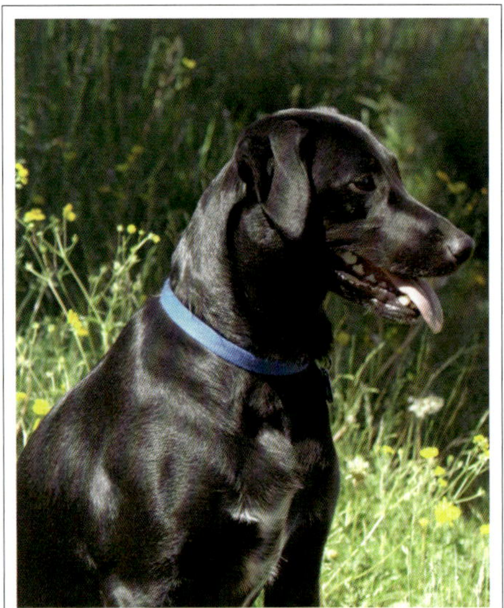

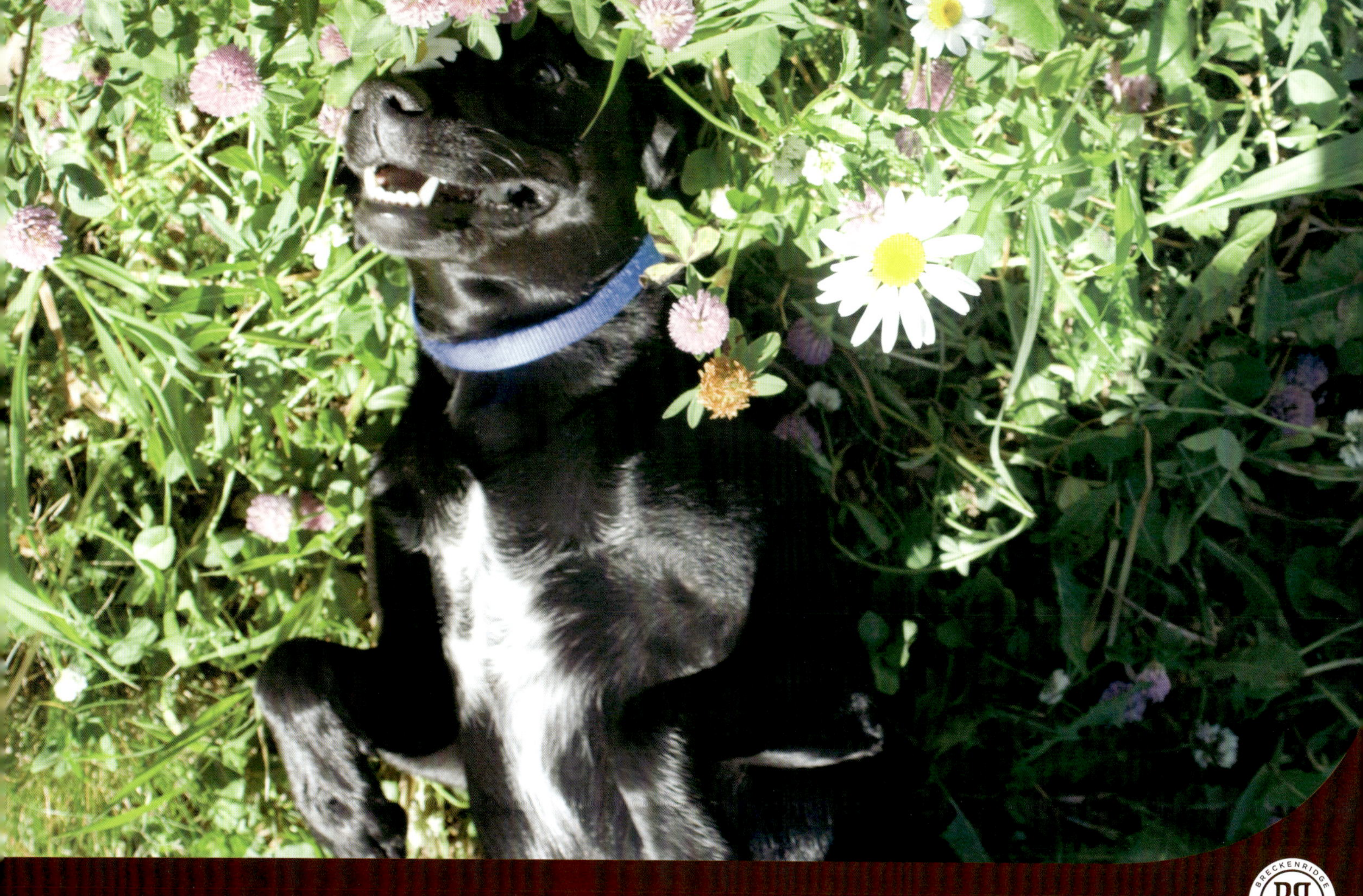

 Layla, 1½, Lab/Whippet Owner: Drake Schmid

Milka, Oscar and Nanaimo

Founded 2005

Restored historic century-old downtown location

Brewmaster Alan Stiles has been brewing over 20 years

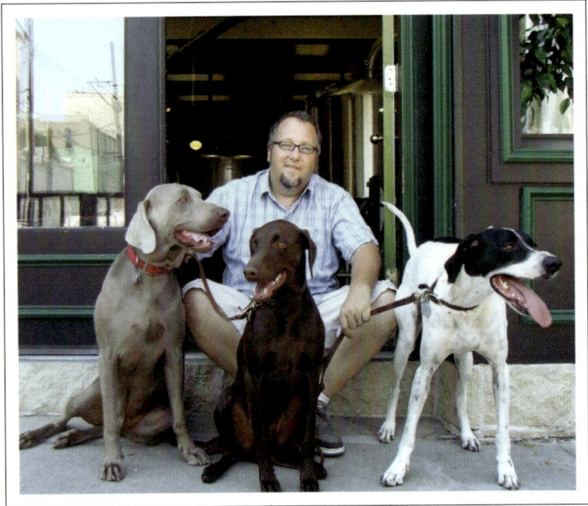

Tree climbing, making an escape and singing in a band are the individual talents of brewer Alan Stiles' brewdogs. Waking up is particularly entertaining as Nanaimo breaks into his morning song, "woo, woo, woo" and dances on his front paws, while Milka "crawls like a frog" and Oscar just sleeps. Who needs an alarm clock? Their most excellent adventure is going to the brewery, where dogs are on all the labels. 🐾

Naughtiest Deed: Oscar has gone through 3 sets of furniture

Annoying Habit: Group howling, which Nanaimo instigates

Best Friends: Each other

Pet Peeve: The dog days of summer

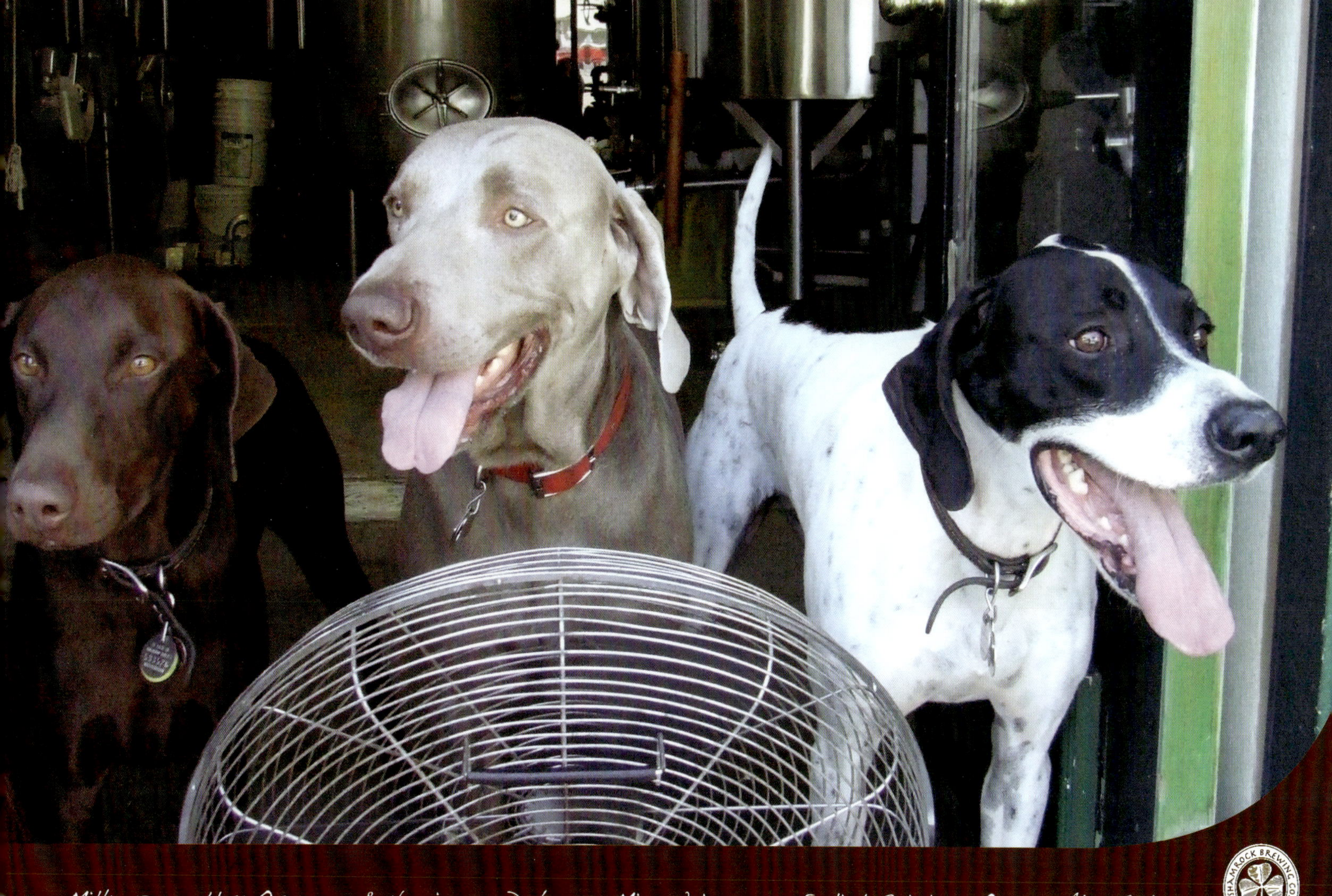

Milka, 18 months; Oscar, 3; & Nanaimo, 5 Doberman Mix, Weimaraner, English Pointer   Owner: Alan Stiles

Zoro and OT

Founded 1995

True Blonde Ale Bronze Medal 2009 GABF

"Open Source" program offers recipes to home brewers

Zoro and OT are goofy, **excitable, whimsical** and sometimes stubborn dogs that spend most of their time underneath Dave's feet, where they watch Dave, one of SKA's co-founders, make some of the finest craft brewed beer in the state. Being true country dogs, they take pride in chasing their neighbor's horses and adventuring into the woods by themselves. OT hates feet and will let you know by giving you a quick nip if you are barefoot.

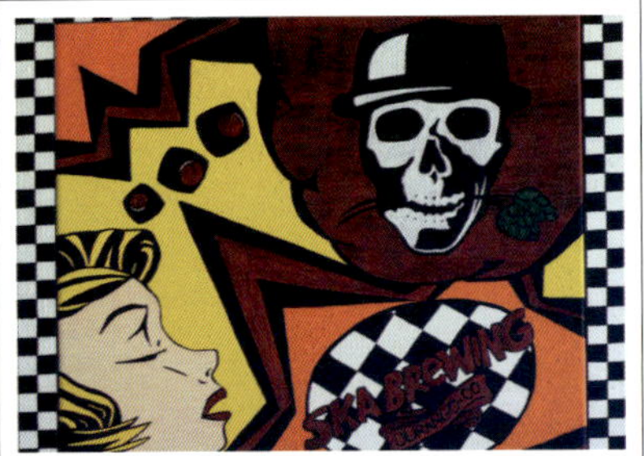

Gets Excited About: Freaks out when truck goes from blacktop to gravel

Best Friend: Each other

Best trick: OT: catching Frisbee

Favorite Toys: Zoro: Small animals OT: Squeaky crab

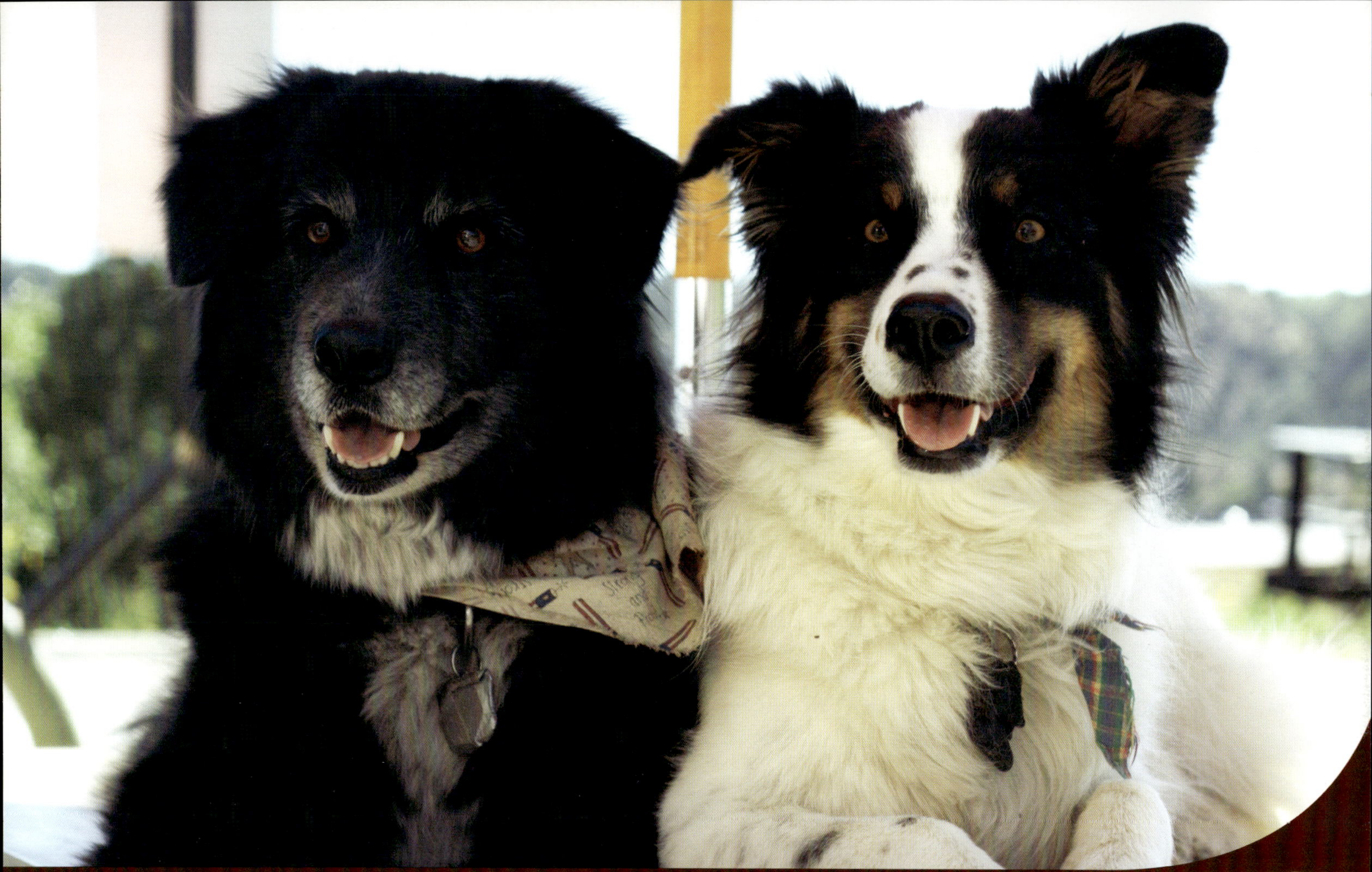

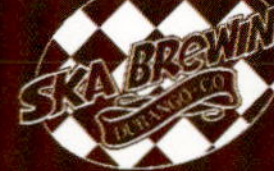

OT, 9 & Zoro, 5 Border Collie Mix Owner: Dave Thibodeau

Angus

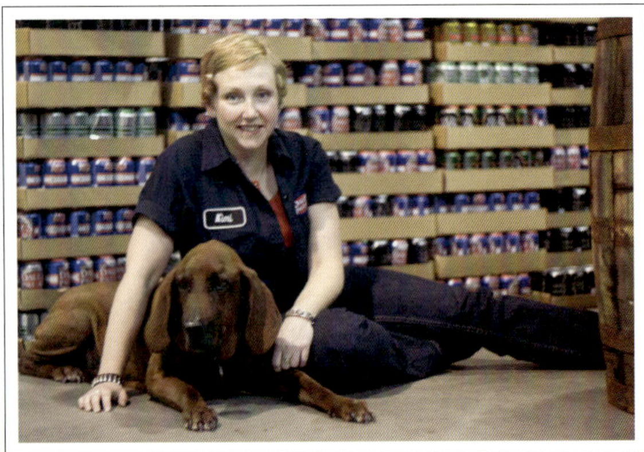

Favorite Pastime: At age 14, sleeping

Annoying Habit: Shakes his head, slinging slobber from ceiling to walls

Gets Excited About: Cookies

Favorite Toy: Rawhide chewies

Brewery opened 1997

Became a brewpub in 1999

Cajun-inspired atmosphere

"**W**ise old soul,**"** is how Kimi Hendrix, merchandising manager, describes Angus. His rescue from a ditch in Tennessee, after apparently being "beaten, starved and left for dead" is a survival story in itself. "He was timid for almost a year," says Kimi. Now, it's eggs on Sunday morning, backyard sunshine and frequent face rubs at his loving home. "He likes to howl and sing along to loud music. He's a real hound dog." 🐾

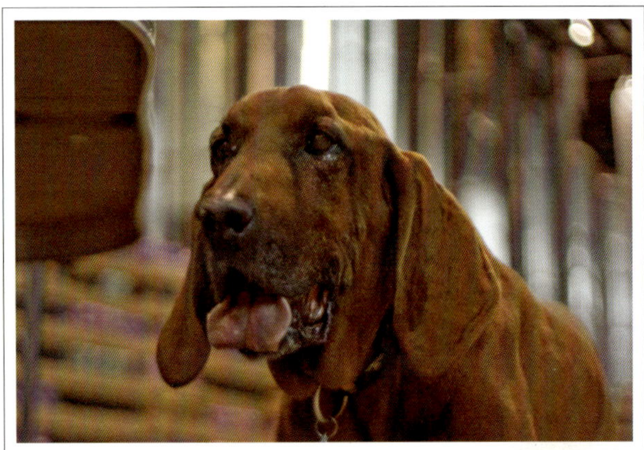

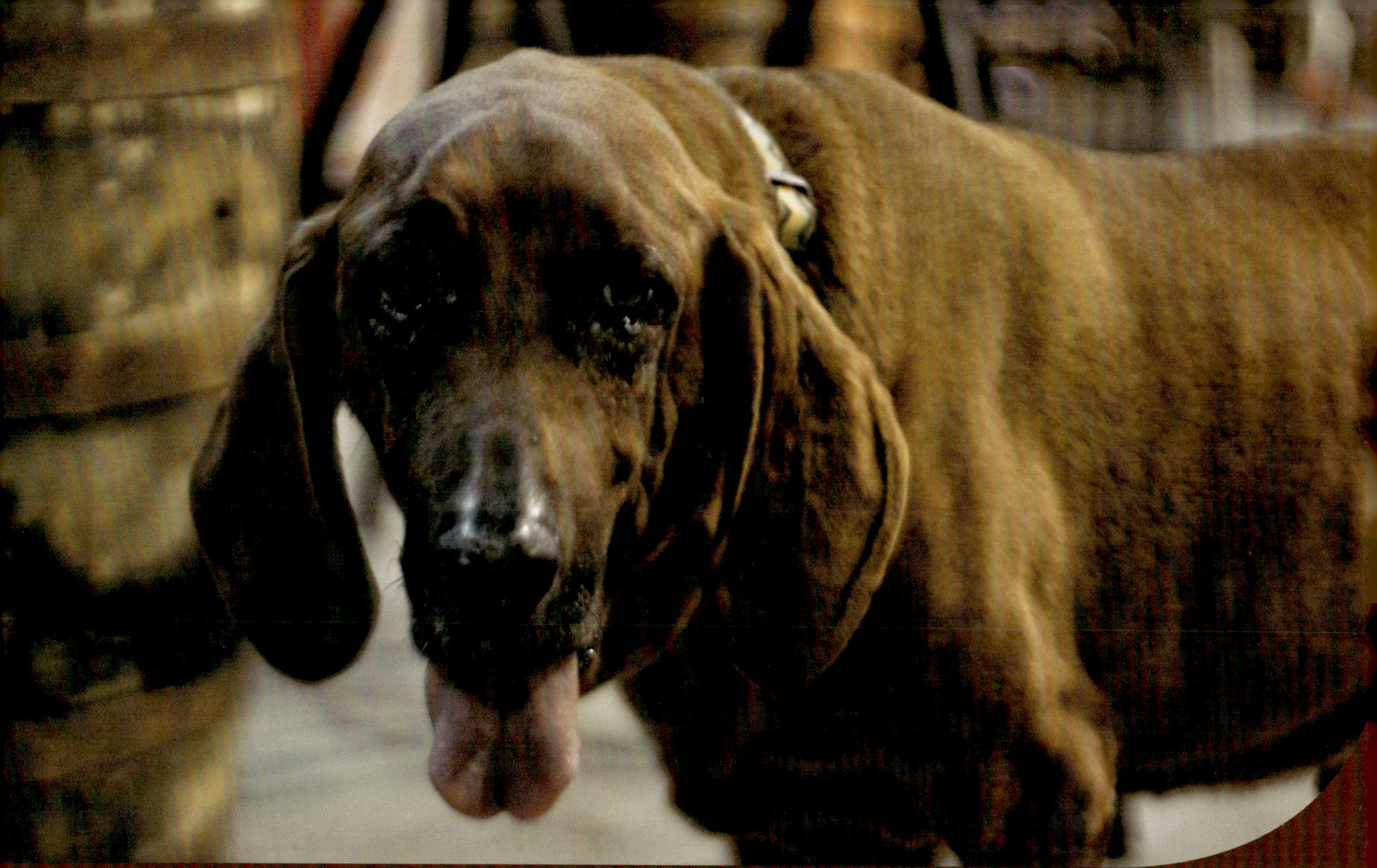

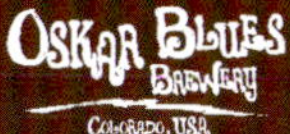

17 Angus, 14, Redbone Coonhound   Owner: Kimi Hendrix

Finnegan

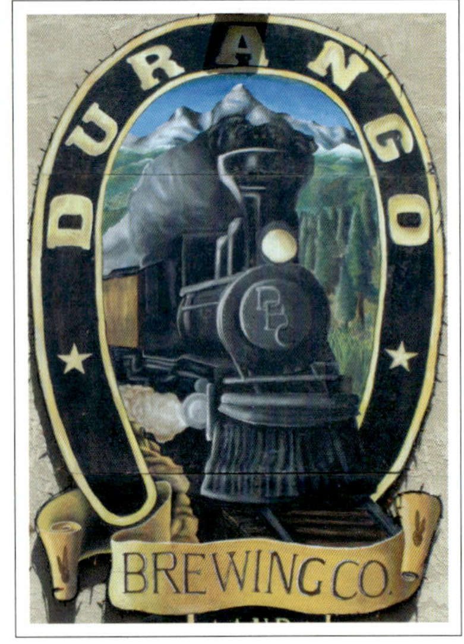

Favorite Toy: Little stuffed toy bird

Best Friend/Accomplice: Mark and Karen's son, Mason

Mischievous Act: Provoking Comet

Best Trick: Stands and twirls on two legs

DURANGO BREWING COMPANY
DURANGO

Founded 1990

Third oldest Colorado craft brewery

Gold Medal Winner GABF 2009

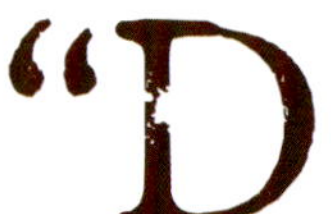

"Dog overboard" is the call when the boat gets close to shore. "Finnegan is usually shy about the water," Durango Brewing Company owner Mark says. "But he hates the boat even more, so he just jumps out and runs around on the rocks." Finnegan is cuddly and likes to climb on the back of the chair to rest his head on your shoulder. Loud noises make him skittish, but so far Mason's stereo hasn't created any incidents. 🐾

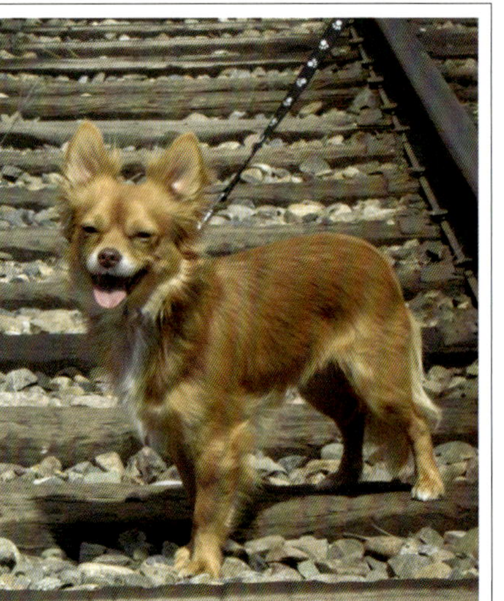

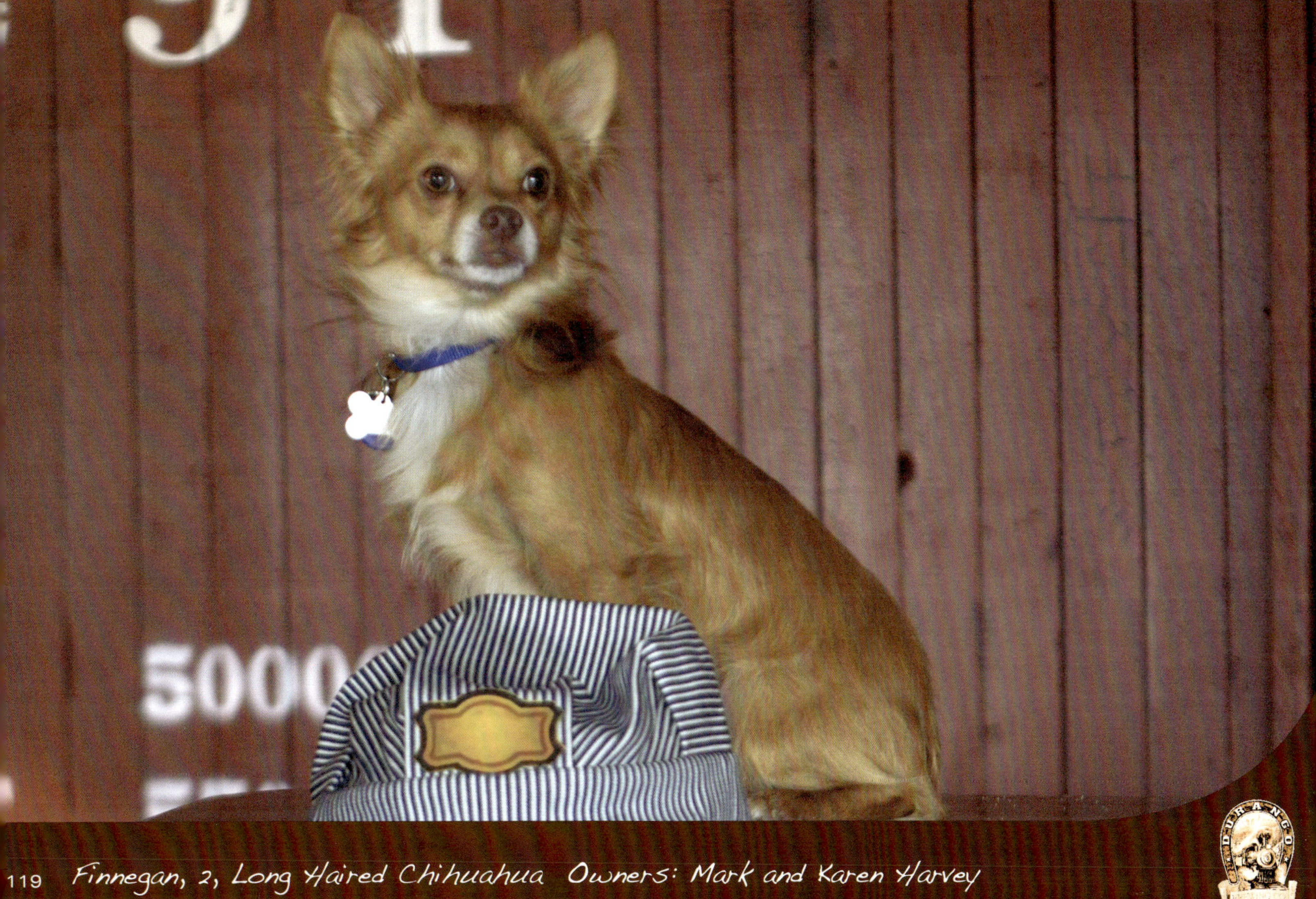

119 *Finnegan, 2, Long Haired Chihuahua Owners: Mark and Karen Harvey*

Logan

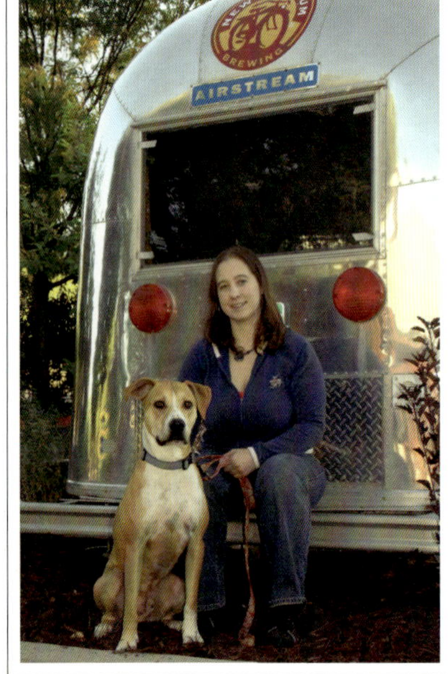

Naughtiest Deed: Dug a hole in the sofa cushion to bury his bone

Favorite Hangout: That spot on the sofa where the hole is, especially when he's in trouble

Funny Habit: Snaps bugs out of the air to eat

Favorite Treat: Cheese

NEW BELGIUM BREWING COMPANY
FORT COLLINS

Home brew roots to commercial production in 1991

Country's first wind-powered brewery

Because of growth, now classified as a "regional craft brewery"

Friendly, friendly and friendly, is how Tamar describes her rescue dog, Logan. He loves everyone, and leans on them to receive pats and scratches. Logan loves to hike and run in the woods, so when Tamar isn't working in the fermentation and filtration cellar, they are often on a trail somewhere. "We have a deal on our hikes," she explains. "He pulls me for a couple of miles, and then I pull him for a couple." 🐾

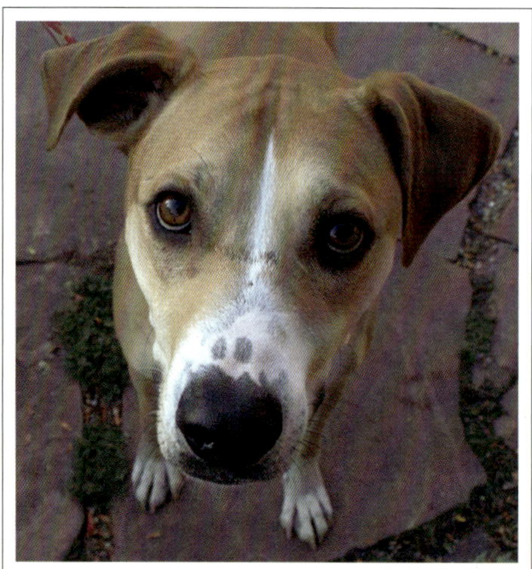

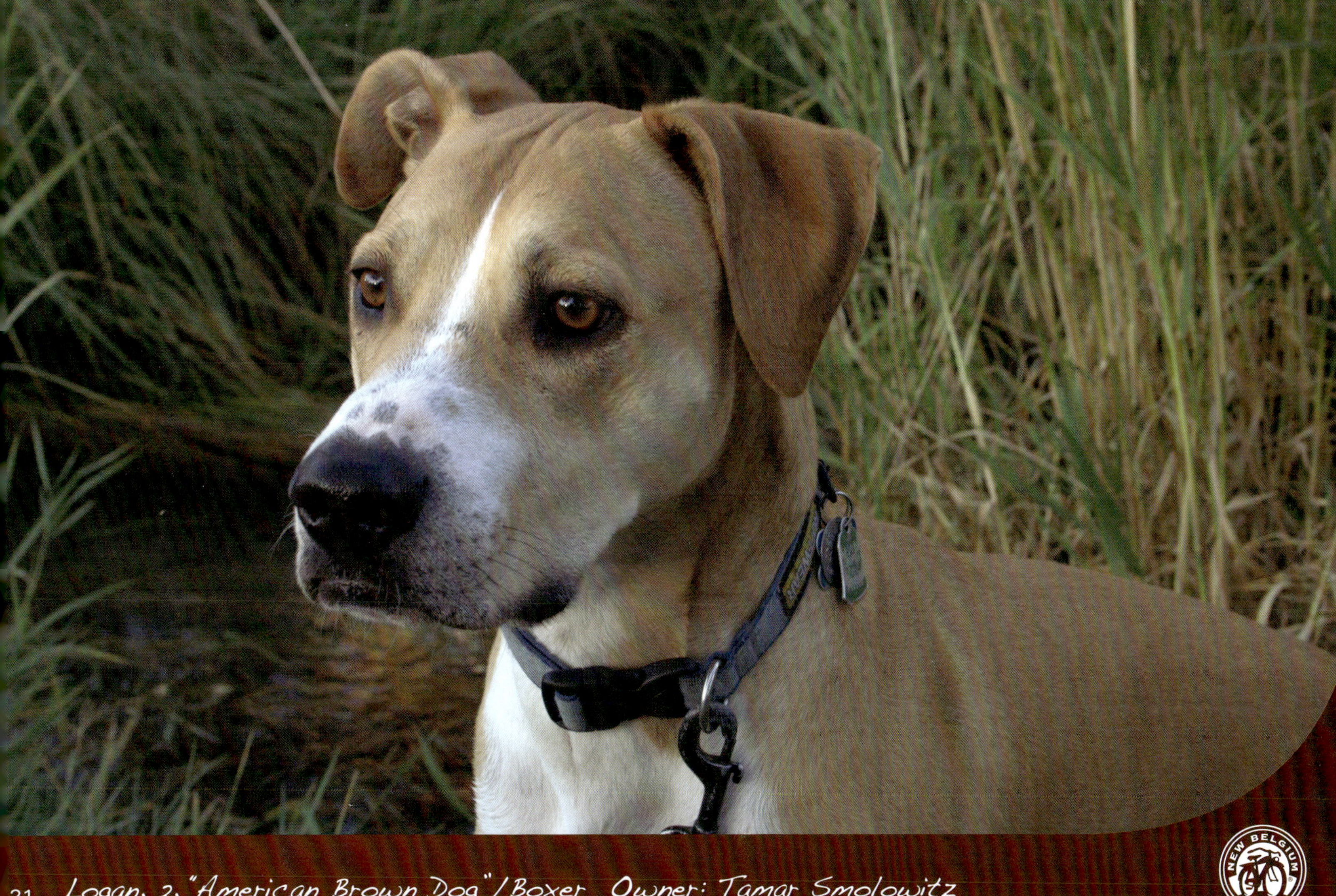

21 Logan, 2, "American Brown Dog"/Boxer Owner: Tamar Smolowitz

Harvey and Rita

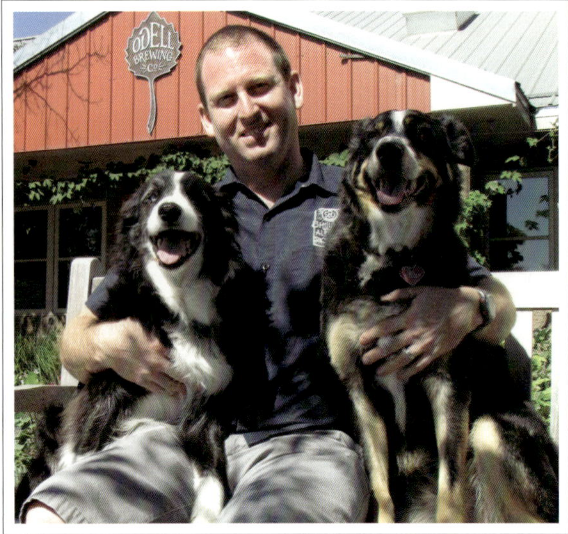

Best Trick: Patrolling the kitchen to keep cats off the counters

Best Adventure: Escaped from the house and crossed six lanes of traffic; were found wandering the snack-food aisle at PETCO

Favorite Snack: "Pupperoni" and chicken strips

Annoying habit: Harvey develops Hulk-like muscles when he's frightened and can un-latch screen doors to escape from anywhere

Opened in 1989

Second microbrewery to open in Colorado

Began bottling in 1996

Thunder and lightning, oh no! Rita and Harvey became brewery dogs out of pure necessity. Their fear of electrical storms has sent them breaking out of the second story window of Odell's packaging manager John's house. After Harvey panicked during another storm, chewed through the drywall in the kitchen and bit down on the main electrical line, blowing off half a tooth, John decided they would be happier closer to people during the day! They now spend most of their time greeting employees at the back entrance of the brewery. 🐾

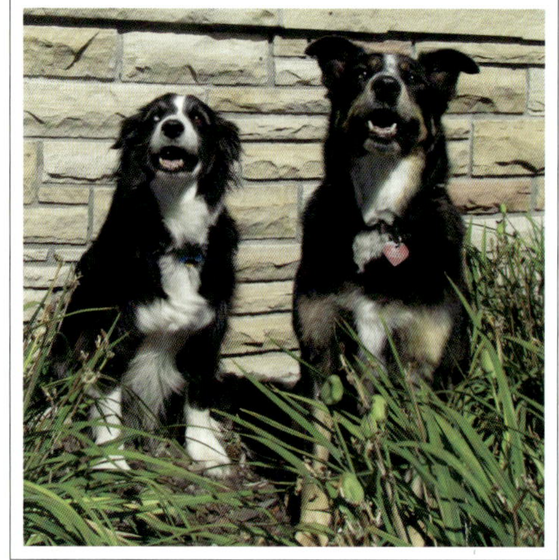

"

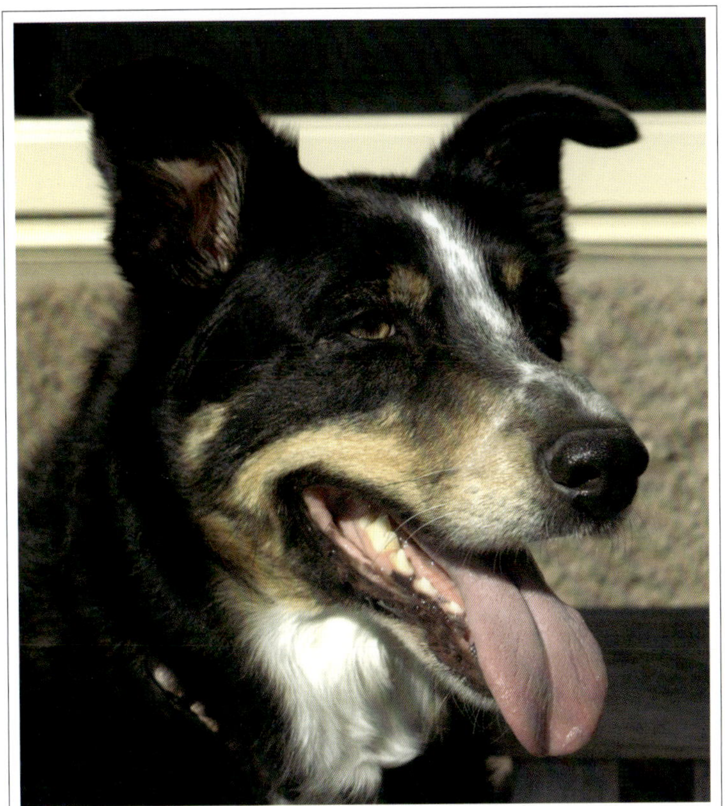
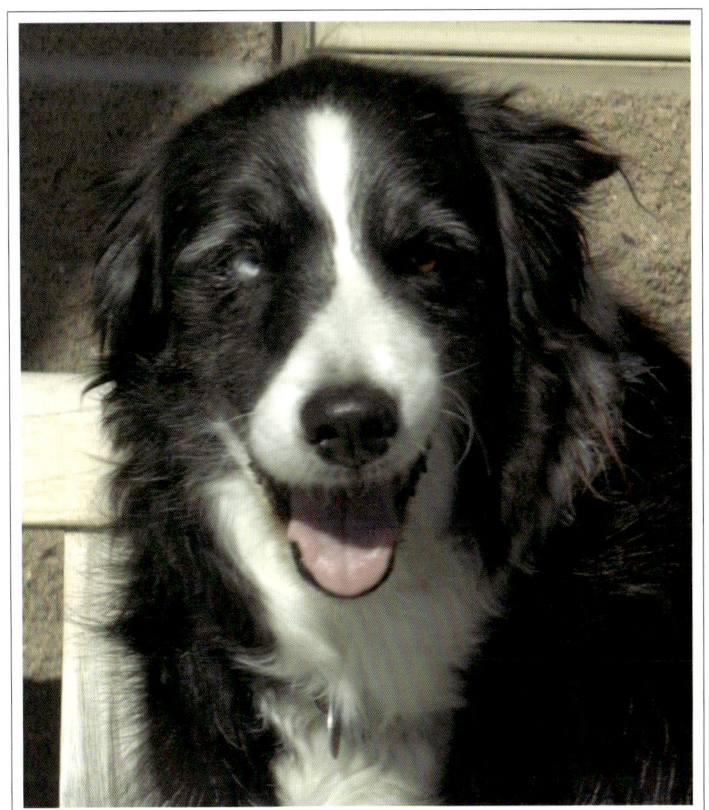

 Rita, 5 & Harvey, 8 Border Collie and Border Collie Mix Owner: John Baise

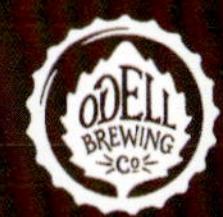

Fezzik

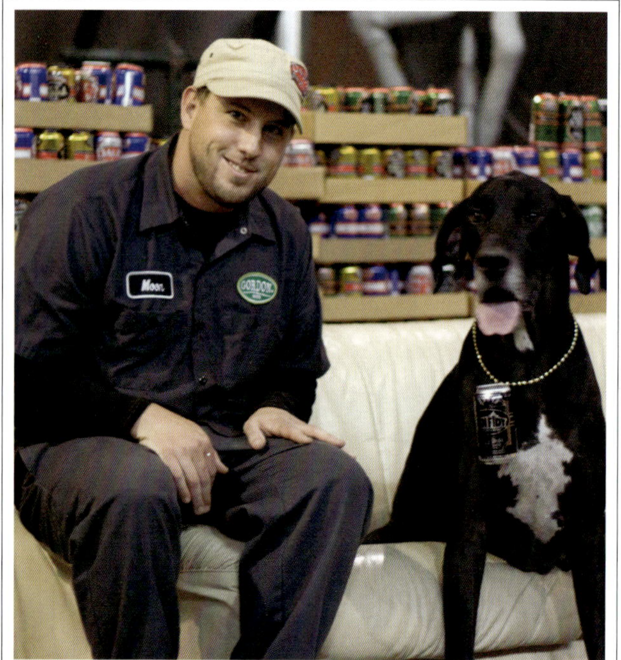

Funny Habit: Regularly scratches face by crossing paws over nose

Excellent Adventure: Six-hour snowshoe hike in three feet of snow

Best Trick: Blending into the sofa

Favorite Toy: Paper towel roll

Founded 1997

First microbrewery to brew and can (2002)

Largest brewpub producer of canned beer

Colossal cutie is how people describe the loveable character of Fezzik. Tall enough to help himself to anything off the counter, Geoff, from Oskar Blues' canning department, says that Fezzik will also go for the roll of paper towels, leaving torn pieces across the house. That's about as mischievous Fezzik gets, however, as he prefers playing with kids and other dogs at the park. If he only knew the cartoon character Marmaduke, they would be best friends. 🐾

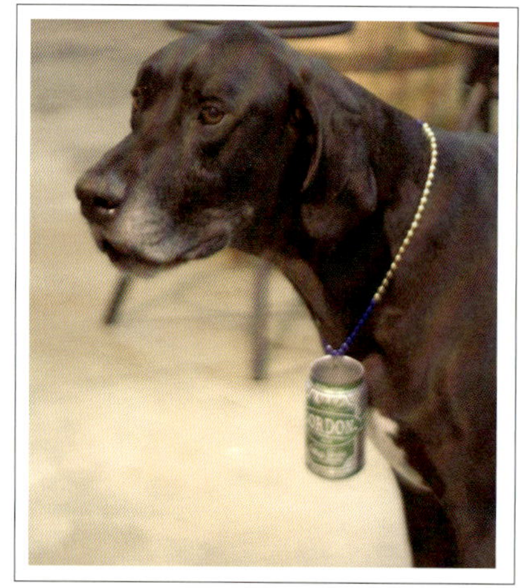

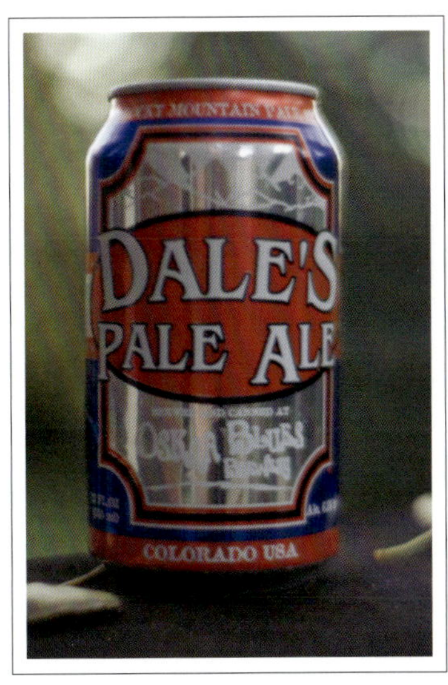

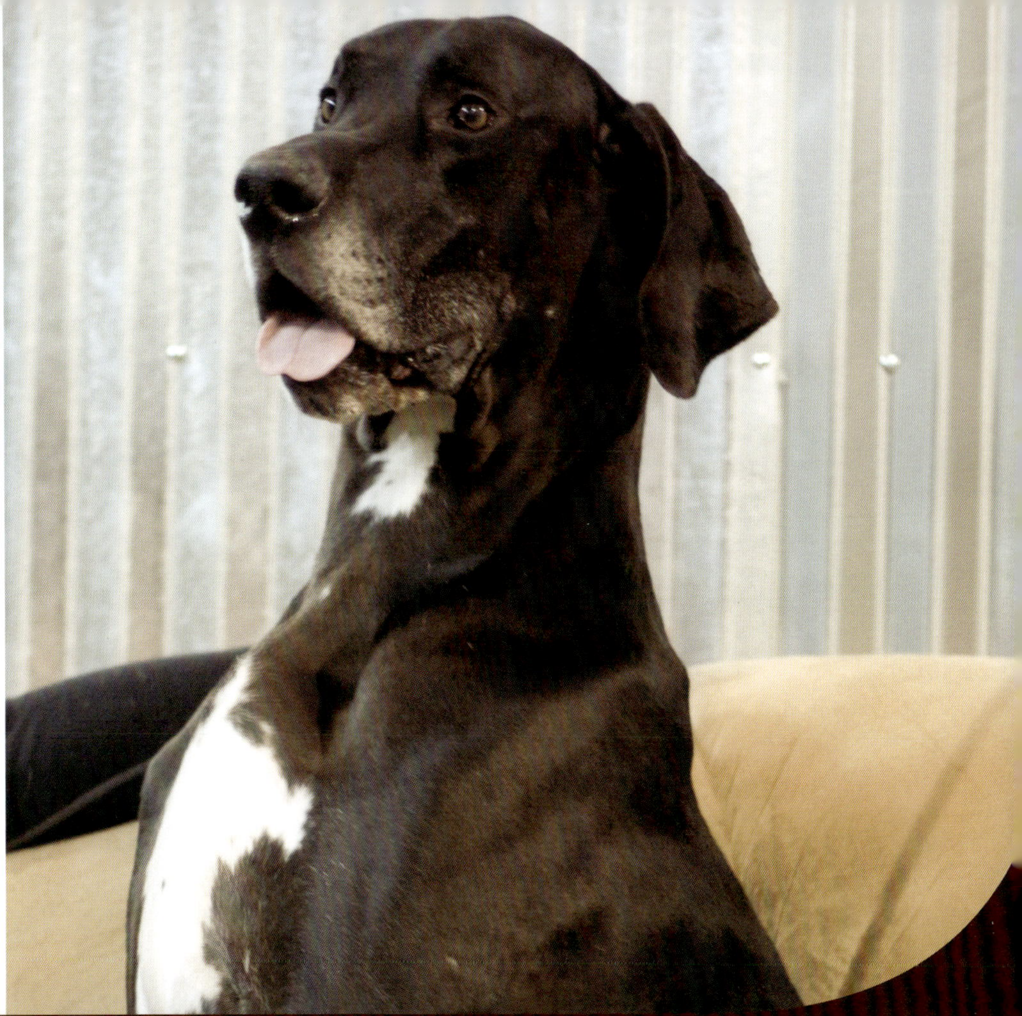

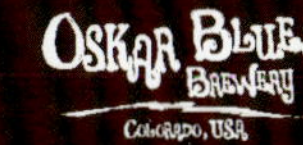

125 *Fezzik, 5, Great Dane/Lab   Owner: Geoff Mooney*

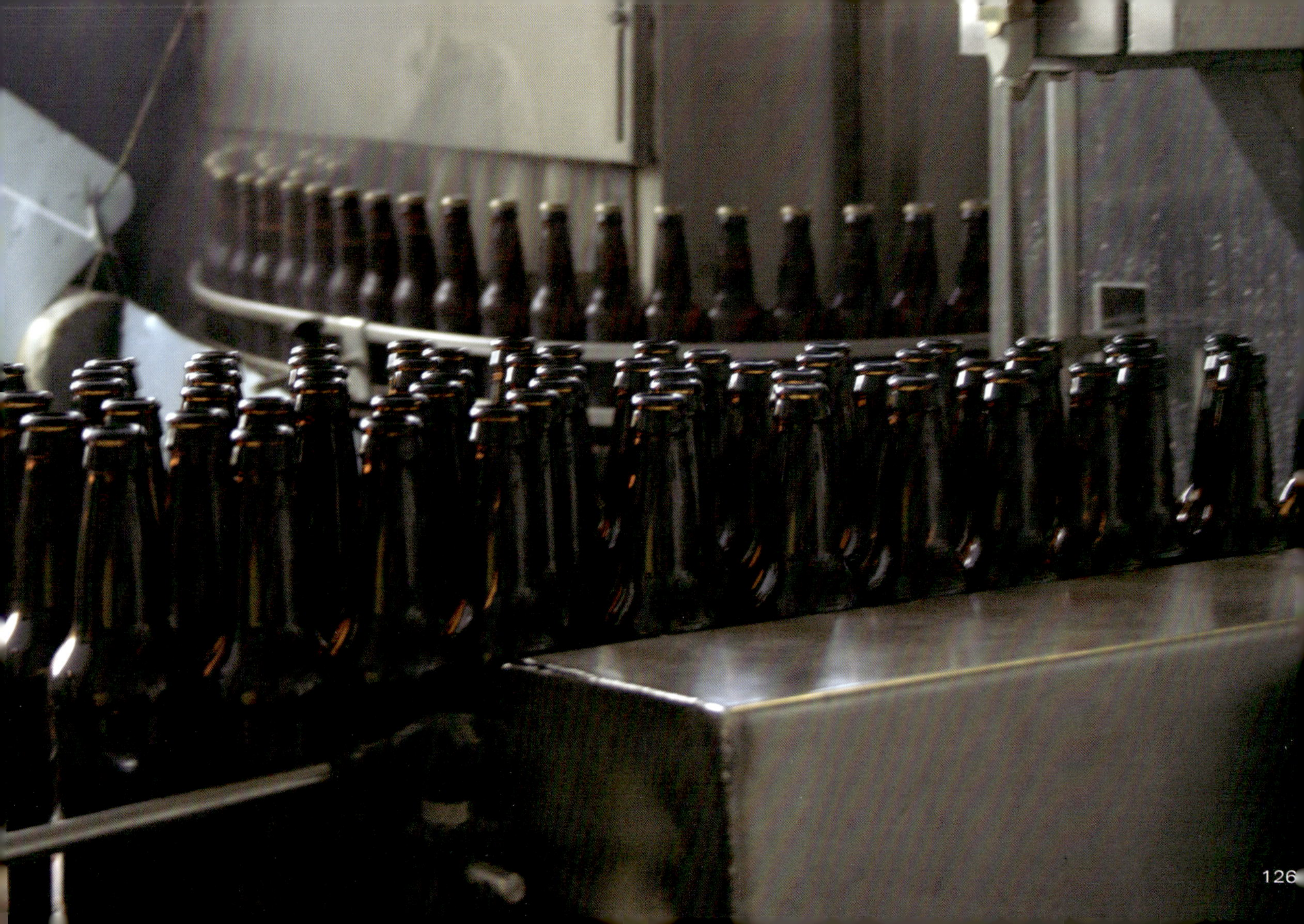

Appendix

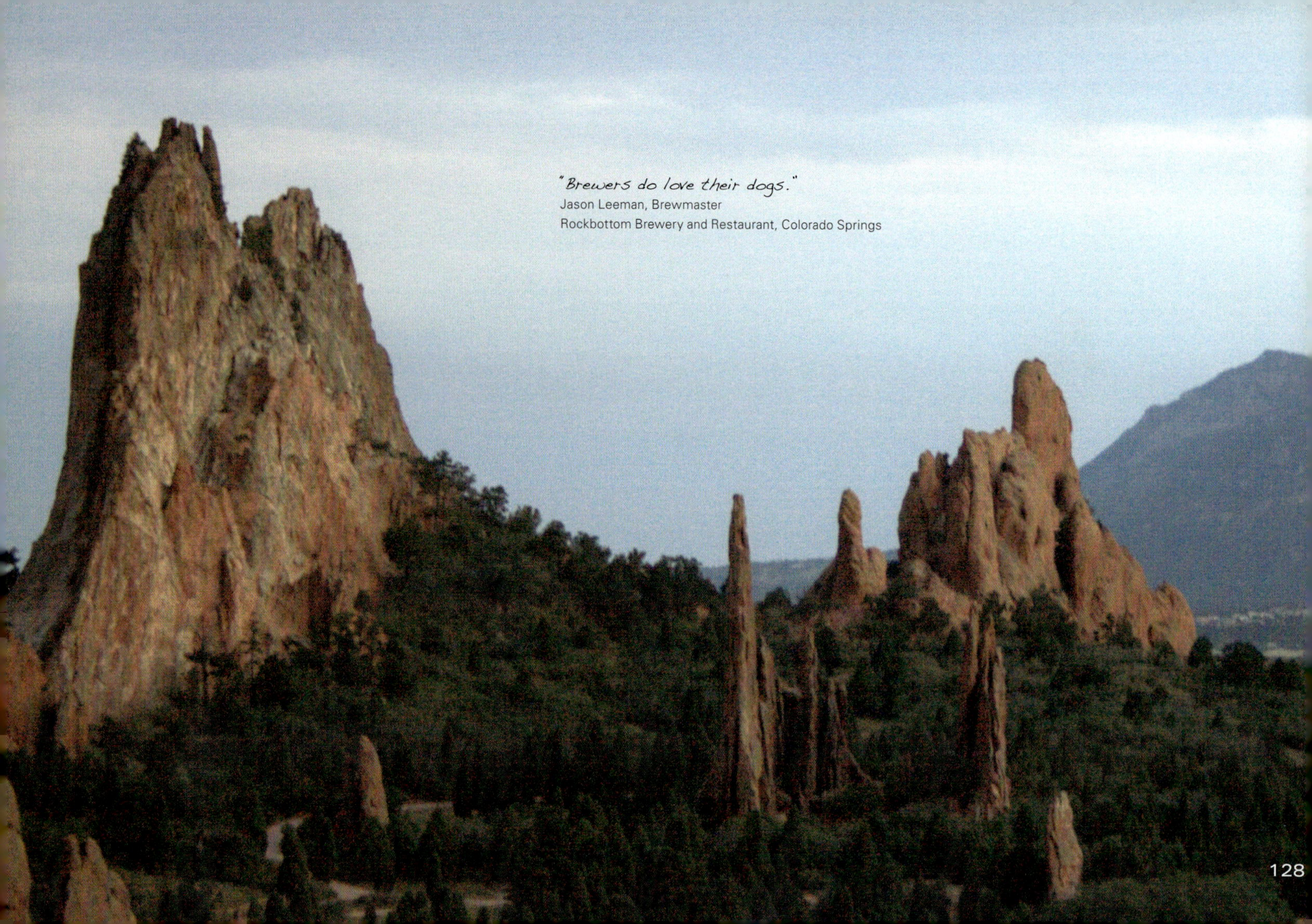

"Brewers do love their dogs."
Jason Leeman, Brewmaster
Rockbottom Brewery and Restaurant, Colorado Springs

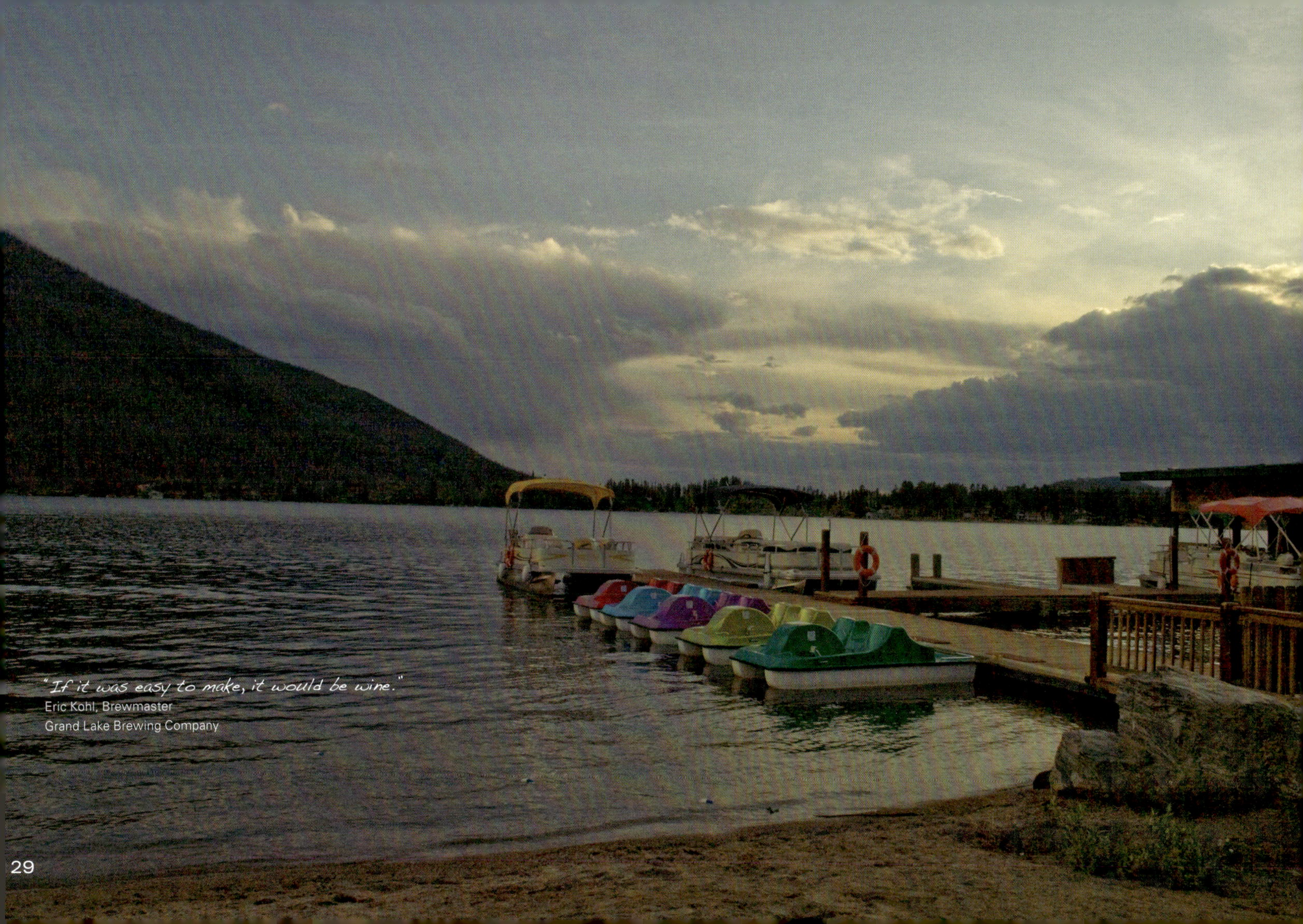

"If it was easy to make, it would be wine."
Eric Kohl, Brewmaster
Grand Lake Brewing Company

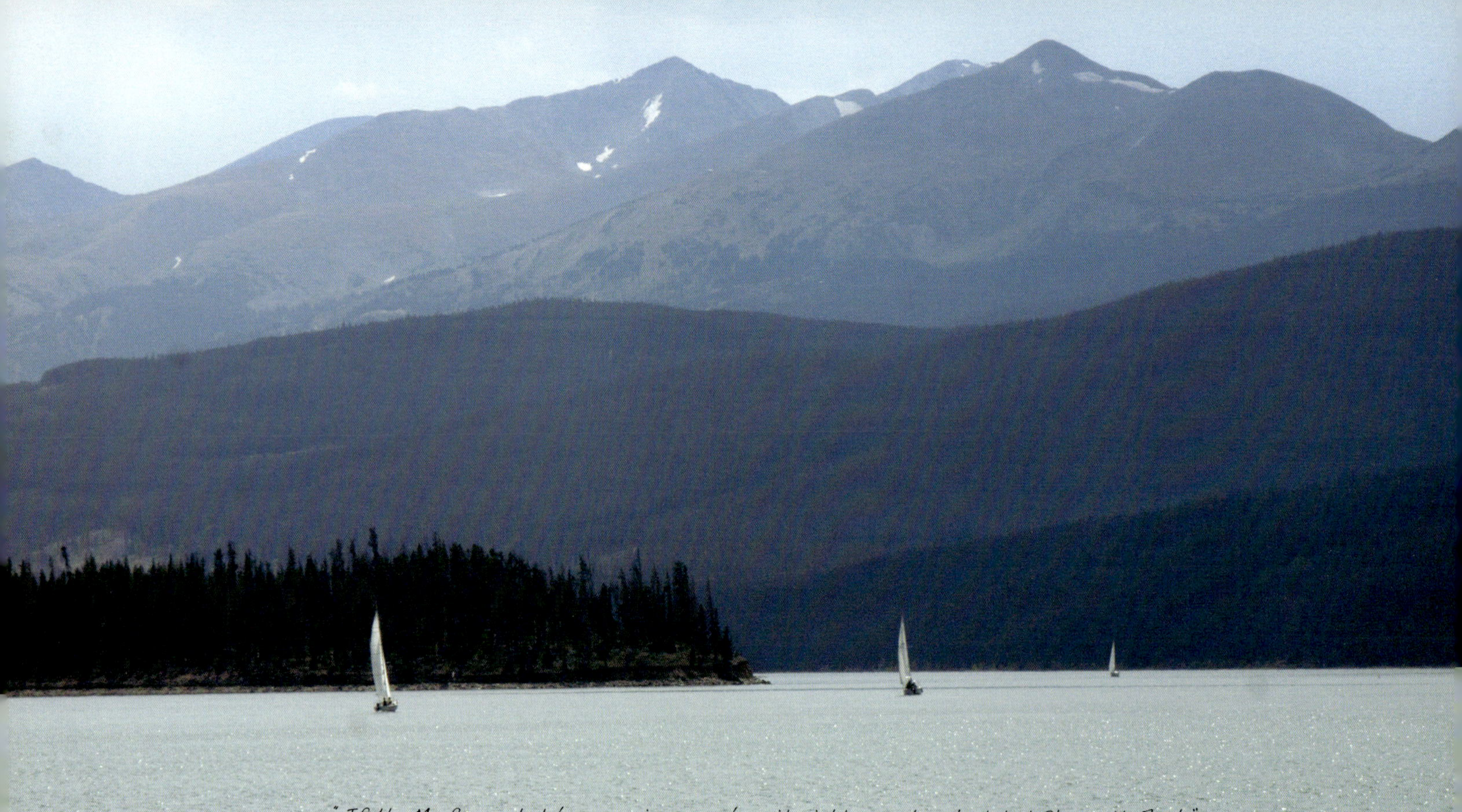
" If the Mayflower had been carrying more beer, it might never have landed at Plymouth Rock."
The Beer Institute, citing the diary entry of a passenger: " We could not now take time for
further search. . .our victuals being much spent, especially our beer."

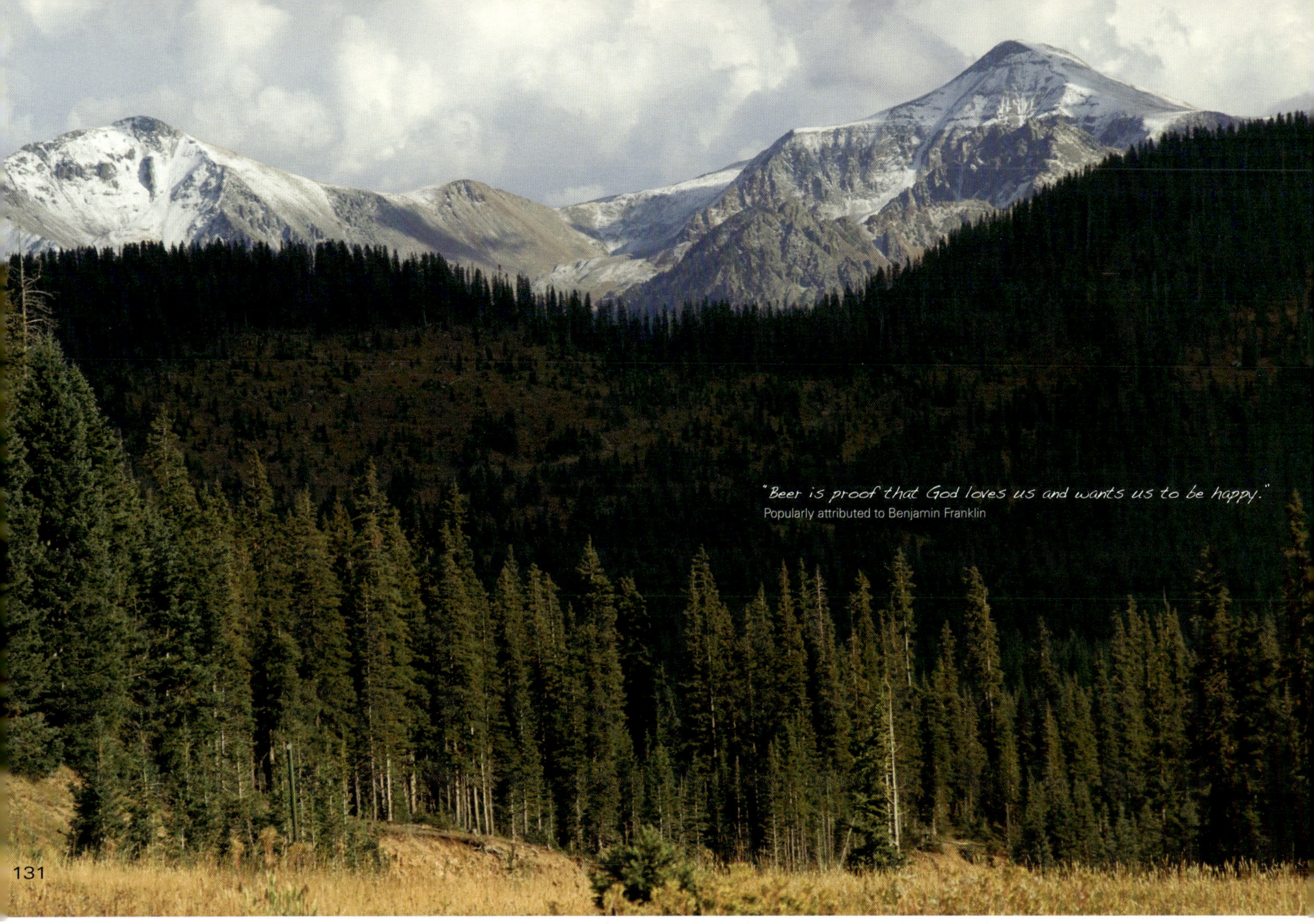
"Beer is proof that God loves us and wants us to be happy."
Popularly attributed to Benjamin Franklin

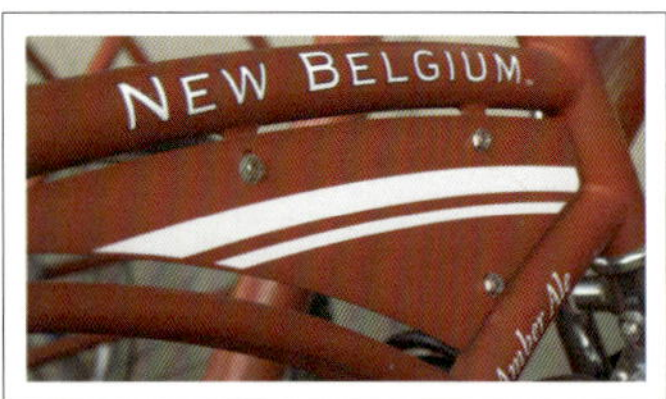

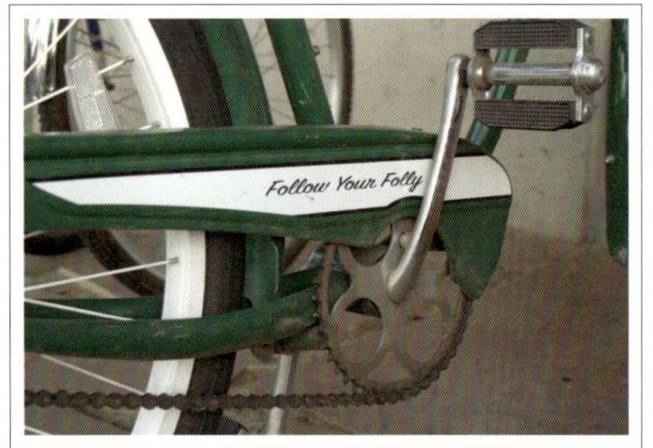

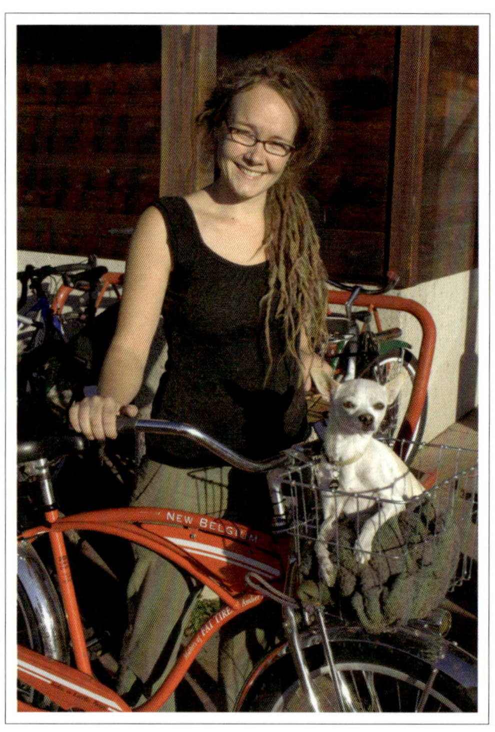

New Belgium Brewing brewdogs: (left to right) Sienna, B.J. Rutledge, Ken Petroski, Hellis, Soren Daugaard, Gomez, Andrew Sturm, Riley, Jenny Duer, Cheech, Tamar Smolowitz, Logan, Jager, V.J. Hartman, and Mala.

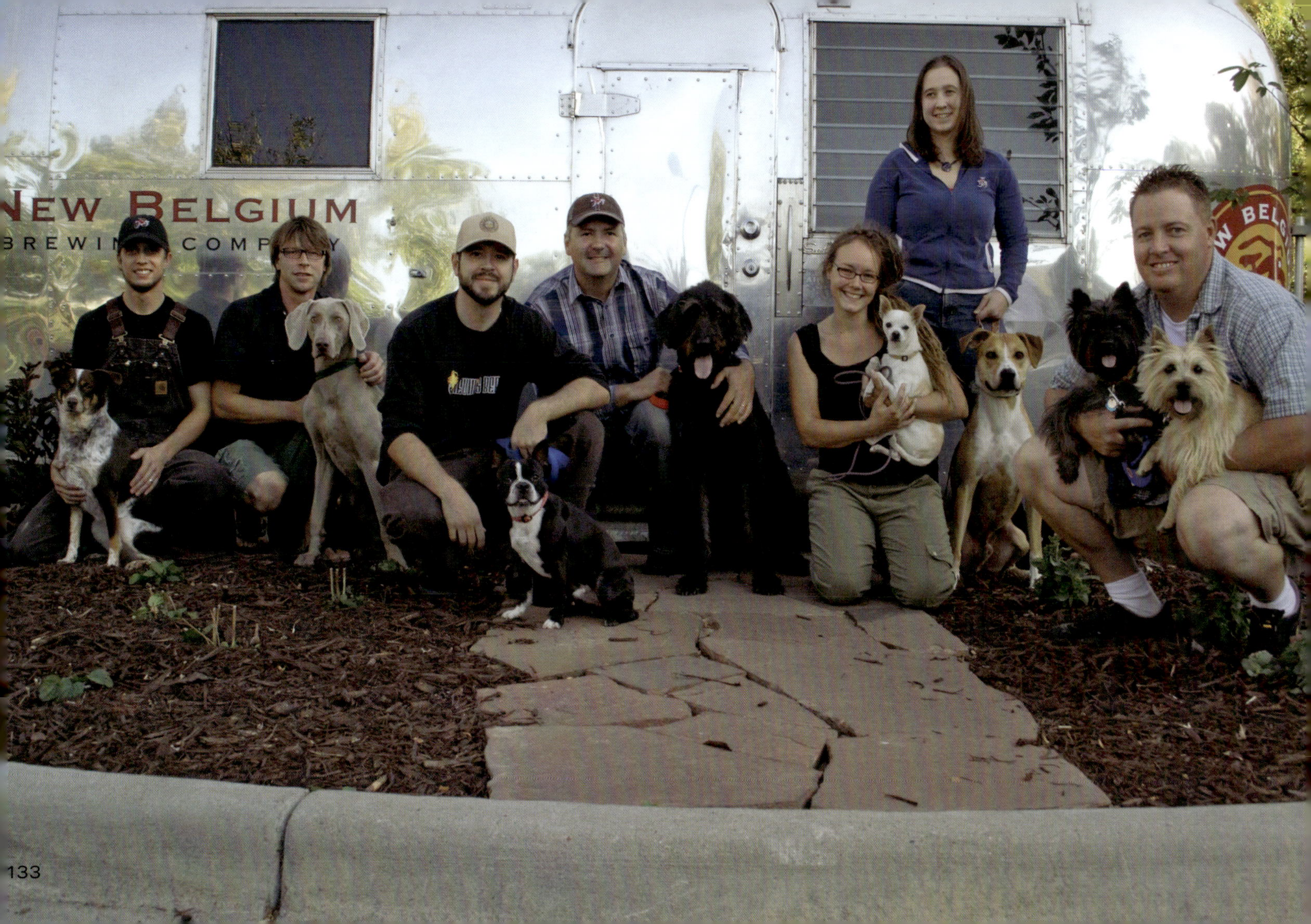

New Belgium
Brewing Company

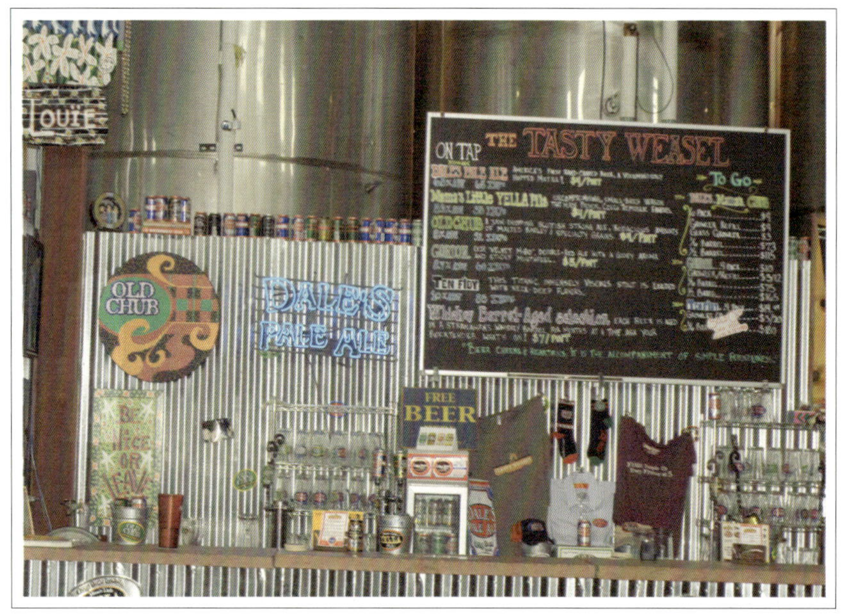

Oskar Blues brewdogs: (left to right) Geoff Mooney, Fezzik, Kimi Hendrix, Bruno (front), Angus, Jeremy Rudolf.

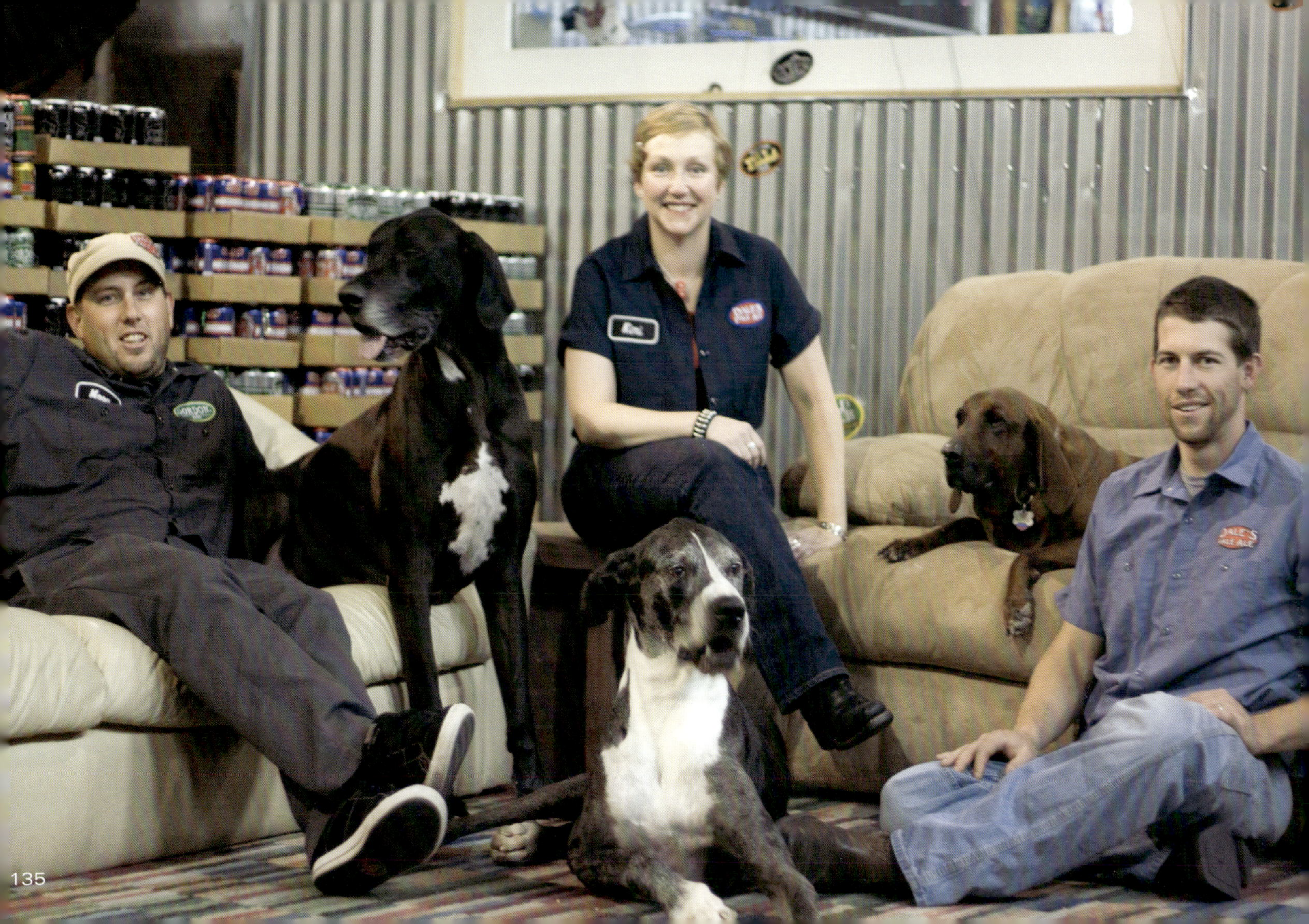

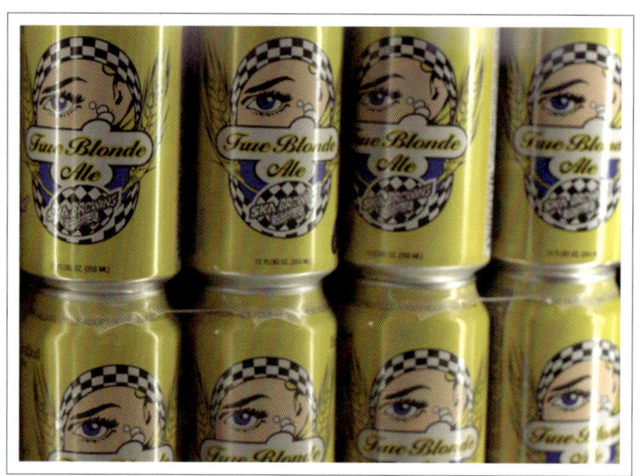

SKA brewdogs: (left to right) Matt Vincent, Brewer, OT, Bill Thibodeau, Zoro, Bill Graham, Blue and Bailey.

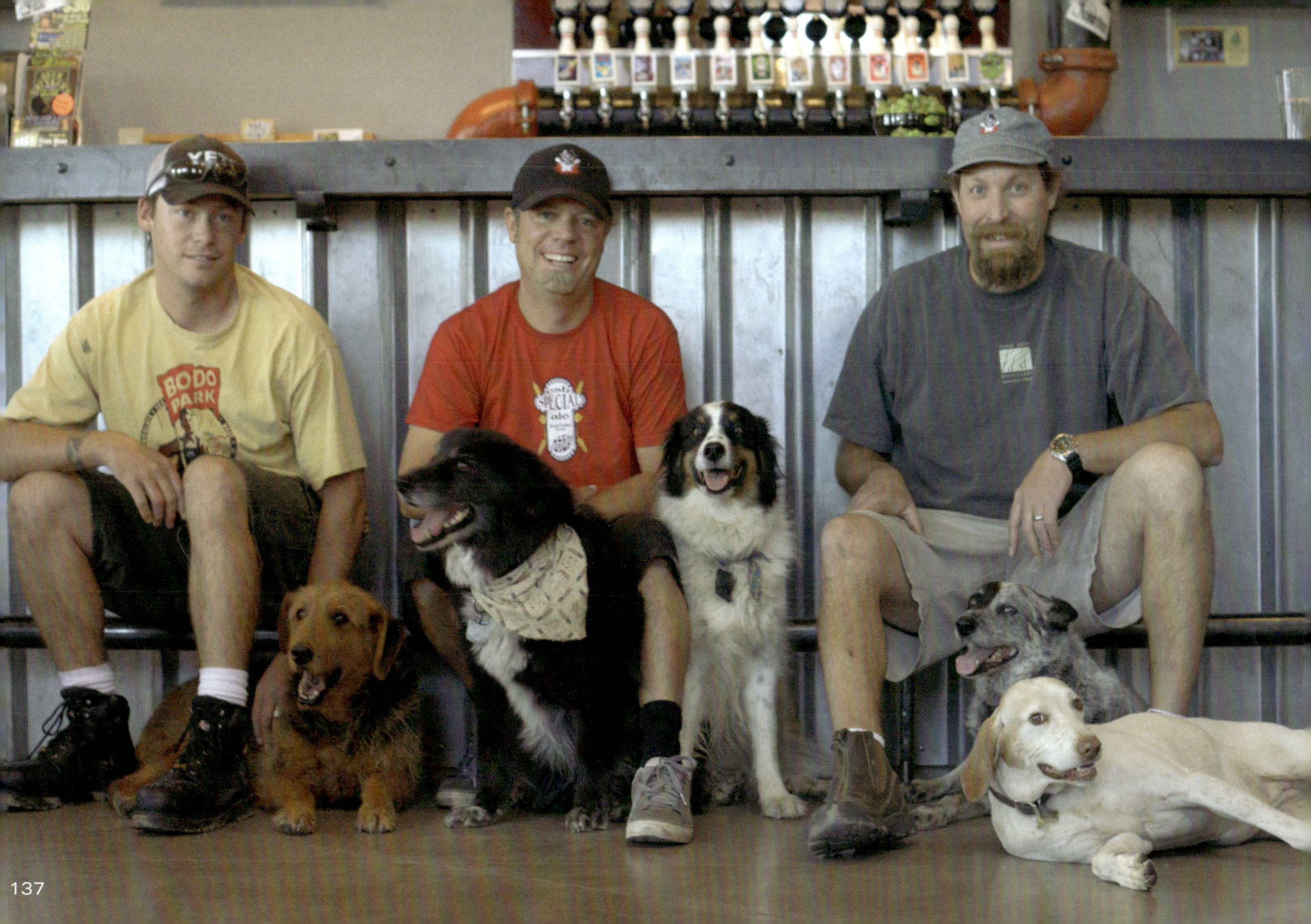

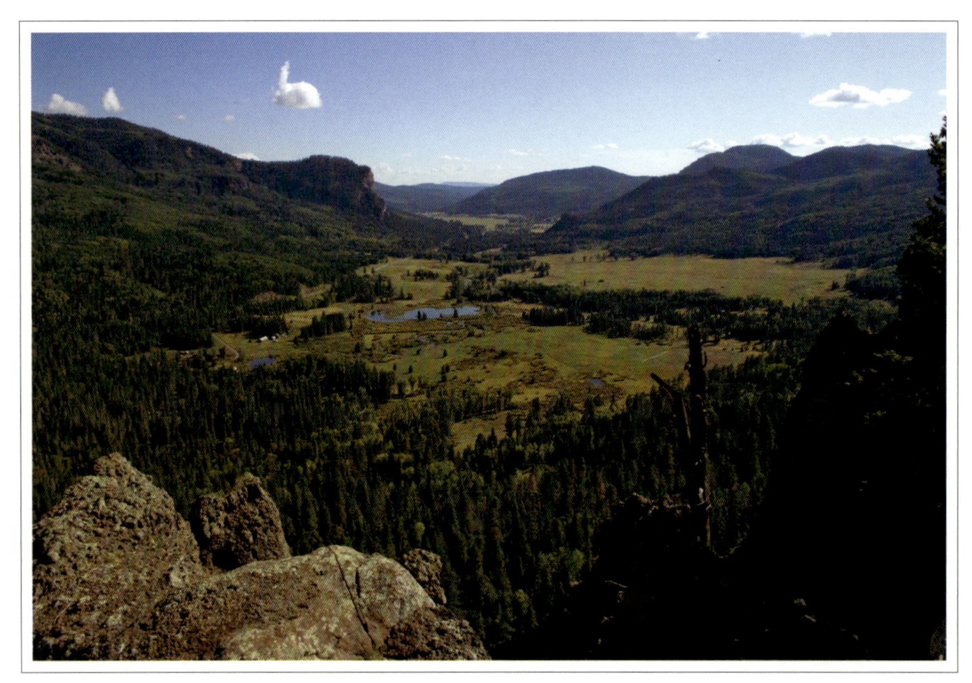

Steamworks brewdogs: (left to right) Ember, Patrick Jose, Ruca, Teddy Bear, Spencer Roper

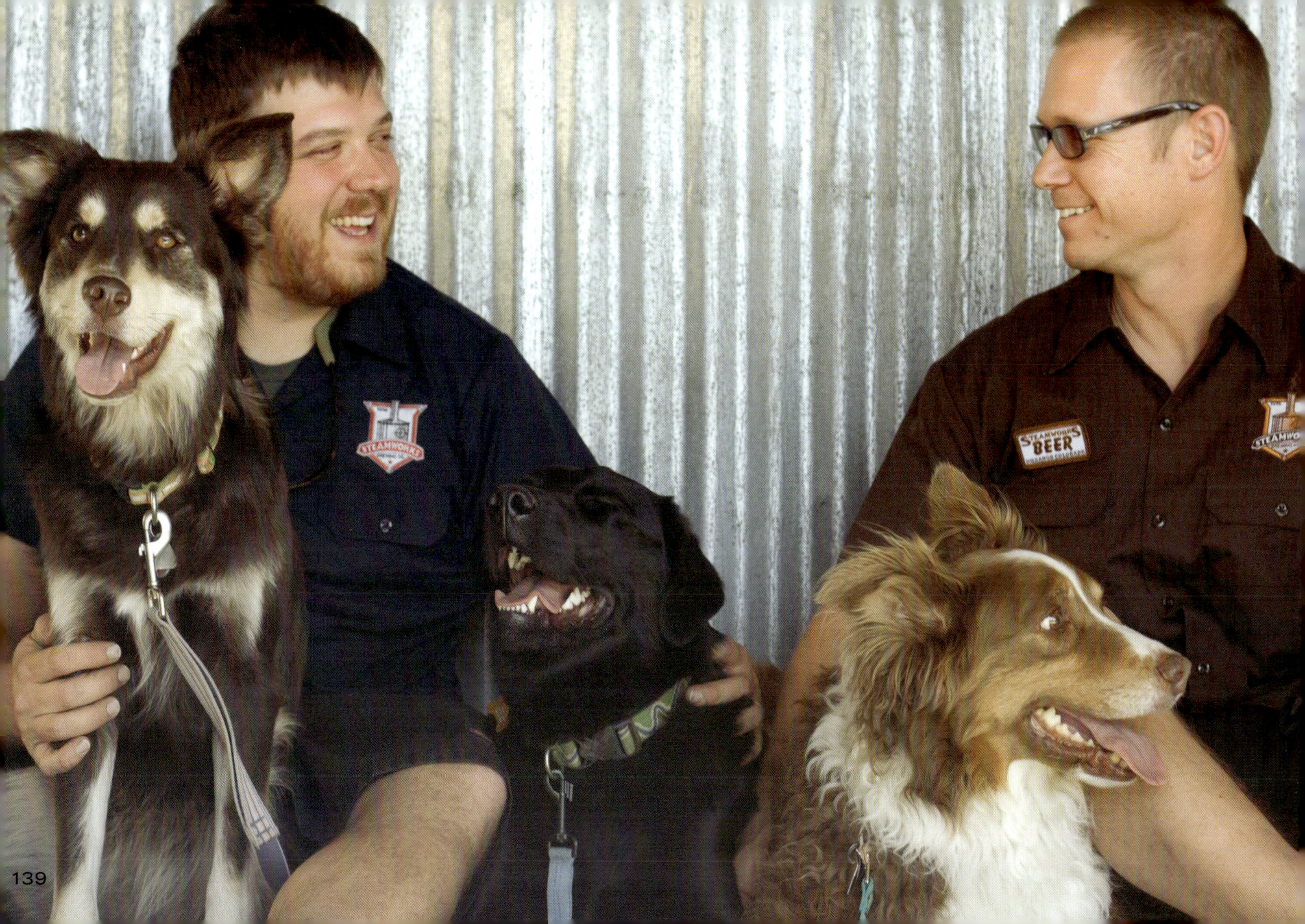

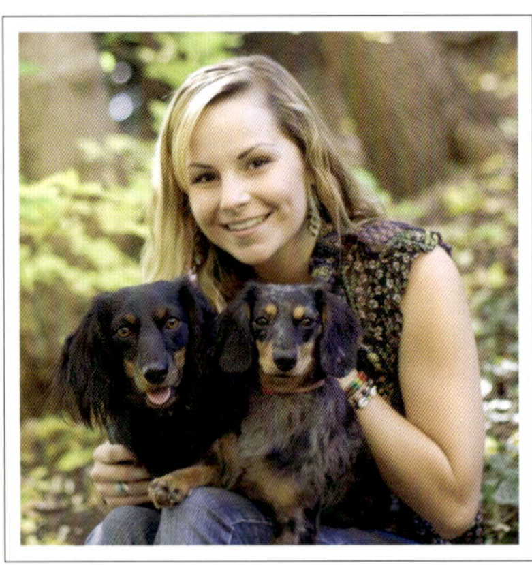

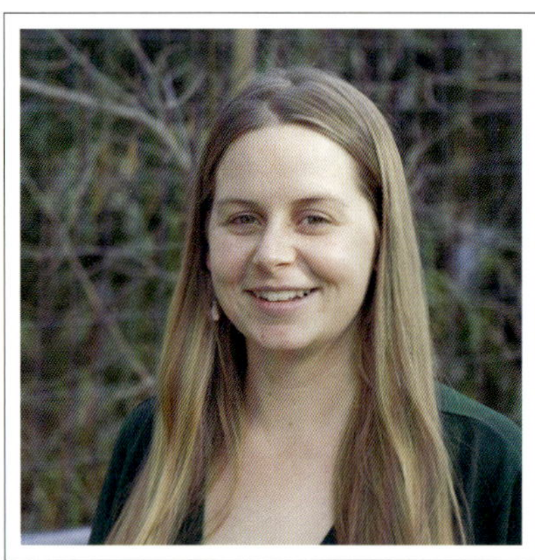

Lauren Olson, the youngest member of the team, on summer break before her senior year in college, was the initial project manager. In the summer of 2009, job opportunities (internships) were scarce so she created her own, and learned the skills of starting a new business. Networking in the Colorado brew festival scene led to relationships and opportunities.

Her organizational and time management skills became highly developed as she set appointments, photographed dogs and interviewed "brewdog" owners across Colorado. By the end of the summer, she had become a part of the Colorado craft brewing landscape.

Kristen Olson, of Fort Collins, Colorado, developed relationships and produced photographic content and storylines (dog tales) for the breweries at the northern end of the state, and in the south from the San Luis Valley to Durango. She has a background in Cultural Anthropology, a passion for creative expression, and a palate for fine beer that is on hold since she is expecting her first child in February 2010.

Brian and Becky Bennett

Mother and Stepfather, Becky and Brian Bennett came up with the idea for the book in the early spring of 2009. With positive feedback from their closest friends, they decided to make the book a reality. Becky and Brian participated in photography, writing, business organization and management. They organized a library of over 15,000 photo files that were created for the project.

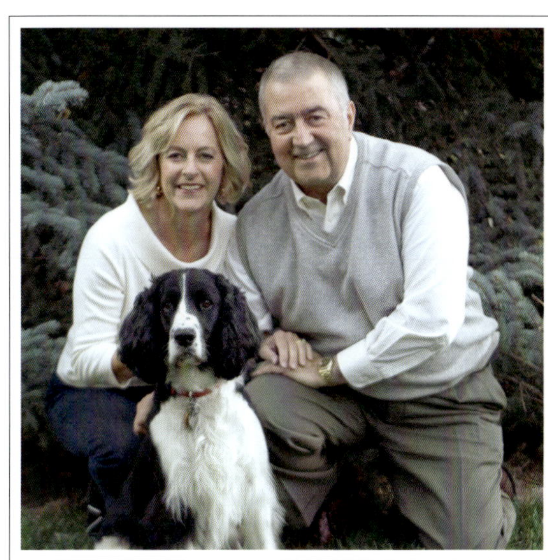

Ozzie says, "Please remember to support your local animal rescue organizations."

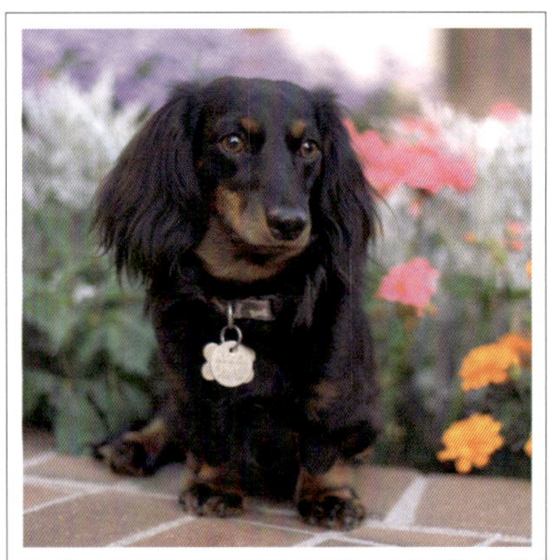